The Government We Deserve

"Democracy is a device that insures we shall be governed no better than we deserve."

—George Bernard Shaw

"Democracy is based upon the conviction that there are extraordinary possibilities in ordinary people."

—Harry Emerson Fosdick, D.D.

C. EUGENE STEUERLE,
EDWARD M. GRAMLICH,
HUGH HECLO, AND
DEMETRA SMITH NIGHTINGALE

THE GOVERNMENT WE DESERVE

Responsive Democracy and Changing Expectations

THE URBAN INSTITUTE PRESS
Washington, D.C.

Library of Congress Cataloging in Publication Data

The Government We Deserve: Responsive Democracy and Changing Expectations/ [C. Eugene Steuerle . . . et al.].

Includes bibliographical references and index.

1. United States—Politics and Government—1993–2. Democracy—United States. I. Steuerle, C. Eugene, 1946–.

JK271.G723   1998   98-6761
320.973'09'049—DC21   CIP

ISBN 0-87766-676-8 (paper, alk. paper)
ISBN 0-87766-675-X (cloth, alk. paper)

Printed in the United States of America.

Distributed in North America by:
University Press of America
4720 Boston Way
Lanham, MD 20706

THE URBAN INSTITUTE is a nonprofit policy research and educational organization established in Washington, D.C., in 1968. Its staff investigates the social and economic problems confronting the nation and public and private means to alleviate them. The Institute disseminates significant findings of its research through the publications program of its Press. The goals of the Institute are to sharpen thinking about societal problems and efforts to solve them, improve government decisions and performance, and increase citizen awareness of important policy choices.

Through work that ranges from broad conceptual studies to administrative and technical assistance, Institute researchers contribute to the stock of knowledge available to guide decision-making in the public interest.

Conclusions or opinions expressed in Institute publications are those of the authors and do not necessarily reflect the views of staff members, officers or trustees of the Institute, advisory groups, or any organizations that provide financial support to the Institute.

*To our children—Ashley, Gregory, Kristin, Lynne, Robert, and Sarah—
and to their children, in hope that they come to own and share fully in
the government we bequeath them.*

ACKNOWLEDGMENTS

This book has benefited from comments, advice, and support from so many individuals that it is impossible to pay them all their due. It began as a project under the Ford Foundation to examine the future of the public sector. The foundation's support and patience, as well as the advice of June Zeitlin, Robert Curvin, Lance Lindblom, Michael Lipsky, and Ronald Mincy, are what made this book possible. Two individuals contributed mightily and unselfishly to the writing itself. Over the past year, Andrea Barnett rode herd over the project, analyzed data, helped edit the manuscript, and contributed significantly to our understanding, especially of family issues. Felicity Skidmore, our editor, often made us appear literate where we were not and suggested innovative ways to summarize vast amounts of research that could be highly technical.

Several other individuals also made major contributions to the book. Gordon Mermin carried out large amounts of research, data development, and graph preparation in the book's early stages; he proved to be a teacher as well as an assistant. An often-unsung hero, Scott Forrey marshalled the manuscript through two galley copies to final printing and spent countless hours checking every detail for accuracy, consistency, and readability. Krista Olson provided early guidance, coordination, and wisdom, while Pamela Loprest was a constant source of direction on the project and on a related series of briefs on "The Future of the Public Sector." Joseph Pickard and Ann Guillot provided administrative assistance beyond what we either deserved or expected.

Drafts of the manuscript were reviewed by Gail Fosler, Howard Gleckman, Jane Hannaway, Robert Lerman, Dan McMurrer, Nancy Primus, Jeffrey Roth, Thomas Skidmore, and two anonymous reviewers. Their invaluable comments and good sense forced us to redraft more than we had hoped, but always helped us to clarify our thinking and avoid making unjustifiable assertions.

An early conference and other review of background papers helped us test our concepts and their integration against the wisdom of Henry Aaron, Rodolfo de la Garza, Martha Derthick, E. J. Dionne, Christopher Edley, Michael Fix, Mary Furner, James Gibson, Howard Gleckman, William Gorham, Robert Greenstein, Jane Hannaway, Heidi Hartman, Tom Joe, Robert Lerman, Pamela Loprest, Ronald Mincy, Lawrence Mishel, Marilyn Moon, Milton Morris, William Niskanen, Hillard Pouncy, Stanford Ross, Isabel Sawhill, Max Sawicki, Margaret Simms, Herbert Stein, James Sundquist, Susan Tanaka, Ronald Walters, and Margaret Weir. Josh Distler and Mark Long also provided valuable research assistance. Finally, extremely helpful comments were provided at the New York University Colloquium on Tax Policy and Public Finance, organized by David Bradford and Daniel Shaviro; the Virginia Tax Study Forum, organized by Ed Cohen; and numerous sessions at the Urban Institute involving colleagues and friends too numerous to list and too insightful to merit so little recognition.

CONTENTS

FOREWORD

The book in your hands differs from most of the work of the Urban Institute but could never have been written without it.

The Urban Institute's reputation rests on reliable research on American society and evaluations of government's domestic programs. Our approach is highly analytical and often quantitative, even though our aim is down-to-earth—bringing to the attention of the public and public officials useful objective information on how the public sector is working. Over the decades, we have evaluated hundreds of federal, state, and local policies and programs; built models now used to weigh the impacts of proposed policy changes; tracked complex social and economic trends; and identified and quantified such worrisome conditions as homelessness, the growing underclass, and the numbers of the medically uninsured.

The Government We Deserve is more speculative and visionary than most of these tightly wrought technical studies. It belongs with a handful of "big picture" books that spring from our discovery that all the careful monitoring and dispassionate analysis we do occasionally opens a new window on the future and from our conviction that we owe it to the public to describe what we see. The first time we spread our wings in this way was in the 1980s, when we carried out a 10-year appraisal of what impacts the "Reagan revolution" had on American politics, society, and economic prospects—a series of books we called Changing Domestic Priorities. The most recent, another multi-year project, tracks how the shift in responsibility for America's social safety net from the federal government to counties and states affects the size and shape of the net and those allowed in or forced out.

The Government We Deserve is even more ambitious. It starts with a "weather report" on where our society finds itself at the close of the twentieth century, when public trust has eroded at the same time that satisfaction with the country's economy can almost be cut with a knife. The book then moves on to what it will take to create a constructive national dialog on the political choices that the next decade will bring no matter how robust or well-behaved the economy.

Exploring a sweeping range of concerns—from those about the economy to those about the family—the authors (two from inside the Urban Institute and two from outside) turn up other American paradoxes, too. Consider, for example, that domestic government has grown more under Republican presidents, such as Richard Nixon and Dwight Eisenhower, than under Democratic presidents, such as Franklin Roosevelt. Or that today's government decisionmakers are so straitjacketed by obligations set in motion by yesterday's that the percentage of discretionary funds that they can earmark for anything new or different is shrinking even as the total amount of federal spending continues on its traditional upward course. Or that in this age of 24-hour-a-day news broadcasts and political open books American citizens are harder pressed than ever to get the information they need to both watch and participate in government.

Wrestling these paradoxes to the ground prompted the authors to make eight proposals that would, as they put it, "return ownership" of the government to the American majority and restore the political dynamism lost if most of the decisions about the future were foreclosed by long-term commitments made with only the short term in mind or obscured in the poisonous fog of hate radio and in endless reporting on political horse races. Whether readers agree with all or any of the eight is not my concern. They all open vitally important questions that citizens and leaders must answer sooner rather than later. They all take root in the careful nonpartisan analysis that has been the Urban Institute's stock in trade for 30 years. And they all make the kind of practical but principled sense that Americans seem particularly hungry for right now.

William Gorham
President

Chapter One

INTRODUCTION

"We are surrounded with insurmountable opportunities."
—Charlie Brown

Americans have always been ambivalent about government—distrusting its powers but eager for its services. But something is indeed different today—not the argument but the context in which it is taking place. Citizen distrust of government has been unusually high while voter turnout has been low. Even the rising optimism and satisfaction that accompanied the long economic expansions of the 1980s and the 1990s raised levels of trust only modestly and voter participation not at all.

What underlies this current period of political alienation? Our conclusion is that more Americans than ever do not feel that they own their own government. It is there. They identify with its symbols and believe passionately in its constitutional character. They constantly interact with it as taxpayers and program beneficiaries. But it is not theirs, and this feeling goes far beyond allegiance to political party or candidate.

Three interrelated developments have fueled this loss of ownership.[1] First, Americans feel that government is not responding to their current needs. They find it busy, even meddlesome, but at the same time removed from their current condition and concerns. Second, Americans no longer consider the information they receive from either the media or elected officials reliable. Although they ostensibly live in a society more openly and inclusively democratic than ever before, they sense they are being manipulated, pandered to, and seldom presented with the facts needed to come to their own informed conclusions. Third, for the tenure of most federal legislators and the voting life of most people under 35, it must look as though the federal government's main function is managing the deficit. In fact, the deficit, or surplus, is just what is left after public expenditures are subtracted from public revenues. Making and implementing these spending and tax policies is the main business of government.

Imagine for the sake of argument that there is some new purpose toward which government should turn its attention. The first step must be to ensure that proposed action is realistically tied to the actual economic and family circumstances of Americans. Otherwise there is little chance that resources will be matched to needs even if the resources are available for government to respond. Whether resources are available for the chosen purpose will depend to a large extent upon the level of commitments we have already made. It turns out that our government has made so many commitments—to programs with literally eternal growth rates—that it can do very little that is new without reneging on promises it has already made. This restraint holds even if no deficit is projected for the future based on current law. In other words, we will never be able to rethink our opportunities unless we rethink our commitments at the same time. None of this rethinking, however, gets us very far unless we have a political process that accommodates legitimate expectations for change and reform— some way to build goodwill and trust, to distinguish fact from fiction, need from want, priority from possibility.

Restoring citizen-owned government, therefore, is like rebuilding a three-legged stool. No single leg or pair of legs is enough. The carpentry work will take years, if not decades, requiring much private initiative as well as legislation. Because our current dilemmas of self-government are interdependent, we must develop simultaneously (1) ways to compare relative needs and opportunities, (2) budget flexibility through reasonable limits on growth in prior commitments, and (3) a political process for making informed decisions. Only then will the government we deserve be one we own.

FINDING COMMON GROUND

Before buying into anyone's vision of where public policy should be going, it makes sense for Americans to think seriously about where we are now and about the important conditions that underlie the current debate over the nation's domestic policy choices. The public debate is often unconstructive precisely because people are pushed into debating what paths the country should take without first understanding the common ground that is inevitably our starting point.

Thinking clearly about government's role requires that we understand four major dimensions of our current situation and how we got here. The first two dimensions are very closely related: our economic and family lives. We must consider how well off we are overall, where (and for whom) things are better or worse, and why these particular changes occurred. The third dimension, our government finances, requires that we know what kinds of public promises our government is now bound to keep and how they have evolved. And finally we must determine what kinds of political processes we have as a society for reaching policy choices on what should be done—and how.

The next four chapters address these four dimensions. The patterns we find shape not just the opportunities for public policy action but, equally important, the constraints. Without a sense of history and context, we cannot distinguish unavoidable controversy over realistic alternatives from wasteful fighting over journeys from someplace we have never been to places we can never go.

OUT OF THE SHADOWS

Plato's metaphor for learning about the world is making sense of shadows. Though cast by reality, the shadows are all we can see. To learn and truly understand is to realize the distinction and correct for the distortions. In today's political debate, it is important to gain a realistic picture of the opportunities in our economic and family lives, the policy commitments we have made, and the ability of political processes to help or hinder citizens' choices about what kind of nation this is going to be.

A century ago, Americans were engaged in an analogous debate about difficult choices facing society and government's role in making these choices. Social commentators fell roughly into two camps. Some saw an America whose best days were past now that the frontier had closed. Others saw a triumphal country on the cutting edge of progress.[2] Truth, it turned out, lay somewhere in between, and describing the middle ground of constraints and opportunities within today's debate is the aim of this book.

At the turn of the twenty-first century, we have immensely greater knowledge about what is happening to ourselves as a people—our economic well-being, our families, our way of life. In 1790, all the Bureau of the Census did was count the population. Today, it provides detailed information on everything from family structure and income levels to how local governments finance infrastructure investment, how companies ship and store their inventories, even how much fertilizer farmers use. The national income and product accounts, which provide continual updates on the quantity of goods and services we produce, date back only to 1929. One prominent measure of the condition of our society, the percentage of people in poverty, was not invented until 1963. Furthermore, this knowledge, once restricted to a small group of government specialists, is now available to anyone with access to the Internet.

While more knowledge can help us understand our world, this incalculable new benefit comes with strings attached. As knowledge accumulates, the synthesis and analysis required to make sense of it become more complex and controversial. Knowing more stimulates more questions and highlights new areas of what we do not yet know. As the easy questions are settled, the unresolved issues come into sharper focus. These often concern not what is happening but why. And "why" questions have a way of becoming contentious and value-charged.

Even with today's much better information about social conditions, so much of our increasing knowledge is prepackaged by the media, politicians, and policy advocates that distortion is inevitable. All selectively filter information. Even ostensibly nonpartisan journalists and analysts can be enticed into playing the recognition game—enjoying greater exposure when they highlight data that support or denigrate some highly publicized claim. It is only human nature, when facing an audience, to "talk to win." But in today's public forum the result of talking to win is growing public suspicion of all claims to inform. It is no wonder opinion polls indicate that nearly half of all Americans think the government manipulates statistics to mislead people.[3] In this book we take a different approach. We delineate Americans' common ground before pointing to paths forward, and we provide facts and historic trends in sufficient detail to enhance each reader's ability to choose alternative paths.

Our discussion builds and expands upon several recent analyses. Others have convincingly argued that the early postwar period—with its recent victories over economic depression and fascism, along with unparalleled and unexpected economic growth—engendered unrealistic expectations about what society could do. We take the next step by recognizing how legitimate concerns about economic and family life remain even after we adopt more realistic expectations. Second, a range of studies has demonstrated that the nation's past and projected future deficits reduce national saving and weaken long-term growth. We again take the next step, enlarging the narrow deficit debate into one concerning the extraordinary level of prior government commitments even if the budget is balanced. Finally, by pointing out four key characteristics that mark the landscape of our present-day democracy—inclusiveness, openness, distortion, and manipulation—we build upon research showing how our political processes and media communications can distort decisionmaking. Our aim? To demonstrate that the government citizens deserve requires dealing simultaneously with the economic, family, fiscal, and political changes of our times.

TWO TRAPS

Our approach skirts two traps. One is excessive attention to whether government is too big or too small. In our opinion, a true grasp of specifics always leads to the conclusion that government needs to do more of some things, less of others. And even if we could determine the optimal size of government today, we certainly can't know the optimal size for dealing with the uncertain conditions that future generations will face.

Obsessing about government size can even be a sign of lazy thinking. Working out the details of government programs and making choices require more complex reasoning. Defending government action simply as a means of redistributing more or attacking it simply as a means of taxing less does not get the job done. To be productive, civil discourse requires some depth.

In one sense, government will inevitably grow. Public revenues will grow significantly as long as the economy grows, so that government is likely to do substantially more in the future—regardless of whether it ends up as a smaller or larger *share* of the overall economy. With good luck, the size of the economy will double in 30 years. With bad luck, the doubling could take 50 years. If government represents a comparatively smaller share in that doubly large economy, its real expenditures will still probably grow by 75 percent or more in real terms; if it occupies a larger share, real expenditures could grow by up to 125 percent. Americans need to be just as concerned about how to allocate that growth—be it 75 percent or 125 percent—as about how large it will be.

The second trap is projecting cultural worries onto government—a national pastime. Society seems especially unsure of its social landscape right now, and many arguments about government are projections of broader worries about life and culture—of who we think we are as a people and what we think we owe others and are owed by them. According to many measures of well-being—life span, income, consumption, years of schooling, foreign threats, and the like—Americans have never had it so good. But not all groups in our society are sharing in these good times. And opinion researchers of all political stripes describe a public deeply concerned that much of life seems on the wrong track and out of control. The worries apply not only to such conventional political issues as taxing and spending but also to values and family life, the culture to which children are exposed, work, and the future itself.

With such "policy problems" as welfare, education, budgets, health care, and many others frequently used as metaphors to cover deeper cultural worries, it's tempting to think that culture and government are the same thing. But they aren't, and there are some problems that no government official or public policy can fix.

Once liberated from the idea that everything preying on the public mind requires government to do or stop doing something, Americans can get a better sense of the lay of the land for domestic policymaking and see some practical steps for moving forward.

OUR PROPOSALS FOR ACTION

The economic, family, fiscal, and political dimensions laid out in *The Government We Deserve* demand a set of responses that add up to a major agenda for changing the face of American policy and politics in the twenty-first century. The eight pathways that fall out of our analysis, while certainly not defining the entire public agenda, would take domestic policy in a direction decidedly different from where it has been heading for the past several decades. This choice of paths abandons prior practices that were neither dynamic nor adaptable to continually emerging circumstances and needs. While few readers will agree with every detail and many may disagree with the major components, we hope most people will concur that only a comprehensive approach unblocks paths for restoring government ownership to its citizens.

1. *Free our fiscal future.* We must create some fiscal slack in our budgets, so current and future generations have the requisite flexibility to decide what the most important needs of their time are. We must also free our elected representatives from a position in which nothing new can be done without essentially reneging on past promises to the public or constantly raising tax rates on future generations. At its core, this goal requires constraining the automatic growth in programs and reducing the competitive disadvan-

tage that new programs and discretionary programs now face in the legislative process.

2. *Give social insurance a modern face.* Much of the growth in government expenditures derives from a historical and partially outmoded design of social insurance. Retirement and health policies, in particular, have large built-in growth due to insurance models that are decades old. A modern face means going beyond a simple budget focus to a comprehensive assessment of the relative priority of different programs for Americans collectively. It also requires paying more attention to the responsibilities of those who reap the benefits of social insurance.

3. *Make a government for all ages.* Our retirement and health programs are scheduled to increase lifetime benefits in constant terms by several hundred thousand dollars for the typical baby boom couple—and even more for later generations. That's on top of the half a million dollars promised to an average-income couple retiring today. A government for all ages would put this policy into the context of our other social needs, including education and opportunities for accumulating wealth, especially for those who have little net financial worth. It would also redirect retirement policy toward the elderly with the greatest needs—such as the very old, who are typically much poorer than the near-elderly and young elderly. It would ask each of us to look less myopically at benefits for people of our own current age and more at how public programs might best serve each citizen over a lifetime.

4. *Increase everyone's chances to build financial security.* Opportunity is crucial to creating the government we deserve. Americans believe that all individuals deserve a chance to improve themselves, support their families, and partake in society's gains. This book does not tackle issues of class, race, or gender directly— though it does identify those who are falling behind. It suggests several means of moving through and beyond those issues. One is by creating opportunities to accumulate assets for financial security, especially among those facing the greatest disadvantages. In this way society can give everyone a greater stake in the future and the common good. Much of twentieth century social policy, ranging from welfare to social security, created a safety net by redistributing income. Without abandoning those redistributive aims, we must recognize the limits to this approach and how it can reduce incentives to create wealth. We should look to the twenty first century as a time to move beyond simple redistributive policy

toward "cumulative" policy. The aim is to strike a new kind of balance between security and opportunity.

5. *Stress learning over a lifetime.* Even more important than creating financial wealth is creating human capital through education. Lifetime learning is a key to developing and maintaining the human capital vital in a technological and service-oriented economy that so richly rewards both knowledge and education. We argue not just for extending educational opportunities but for improving education at all stages of life, from early childhood through our elderly years.

6. *Occupy our children more fully in settings with adult or parental supervision, guidance, and mentoring.* Because of many changes in family life, including large growth in single-parent families and two-earner couples, children are increasingly left on their own during after-school hours and summer breaks. Statistics tell us our children are most likely to get in trouble or simply to direct their activities poorly during these times. Research also shows that children's relationships with adults are essential for their healthy development. Yet, government programs—geared to provide between one-half and one million dollars in retirement and health benefits to today's couples when they retire—continue to neglect the fundamental need of each child for adult stimulus and supervision.

7. *Support the modern family.* Many government tax and expenditure policies are built around stereotypes that do not fit modern families. The policies born of these stereotypes are neither equitable nor efficient, and they often contradict important values in society. Government now punishes low-income individuals by reducing their combined incomes by as much as 30 percent simply because they marry, for example. It also heavily penalizes secondary workers, usually women, so that a married couple with two earners receives substantially fewer social security benefits than a one-earner couple who contributes no more taxes to the system.

8. *Foster a new democratic citizenship.* As agonizing politically as it might be to move down any of the paths we have outlined, most are at least amenable to legislative action. Capping automatic growth rates in programs, for instance, may be difficult in the context of special interest lobbying, but many of the steps required are fairly obvious. Revitalizing citizenship, in contrast, depends more than anything else upon each of us as citizens trying to do the right thing to build trust in our civic life. Doing so requires improving media communication, nourishing deliberative and thoughtful public opinion (including polling), and supporting institutions that encourage responsible journalism and civic educa-

tion. Resources from private individuals and nonprofit organizations are crucial to building and maintaining momentum. And the path will be long. The erosion of public trust took many years, and the process of rebuilding it will, too.

* * *

While writing this book, we talked with many concerned citizens, policy analysts, and foundation officials deeply concerned about the poor, children, education, welfare, urban problems, crime, health care, or high tax rates. Many came to agree that government cannot do much on any of these counts—or a host of other pressing issues—if each is considered in isolation. Instead, real headway can come only from understanding how needs and demands are changing in the economy and family life, how prior public commitments now tie up most new government resources, and how political processes can be manipulated to deter citizens from making realistic trade-offs among competing needs. We hope to persuade you to reach the same conclusion.

Notes

1. In his own, parallel, analysis of public distrust, Bill Galston argues that the level of public discontent in this country is higher than in the past because, "in the eyes of the American people, the federal government wastes money. It tries to do too much, including things that it has no business doing. And, as a result, it has a diminished capacity to solve problems. At crucial junctures it doesn't tell the truth. It doesn't care enough about average citizens." Based on a presentation by Bill Galston at a conference at the University of Virginia called "Democracy on Trial," September 26–28, 1996.

2. H.W. Brands, 1995, *The Reckless Decade: America in the 1890s.*

3. *The Washington Post*, October 13, 1996, p. A.38. One recent example highlights the potential threats to true understanding posed by new data and selective data use. In late 1996, news stories picked up on U.S. government data that the number of cases of child abuse and neglect had nearly doubled between 1986 and 1993. (Data from the 2nd and 3rd National Incidence Study of Child Abuse and Neglect, Department of Health and Human Services, National Center on Child Abuse and Neglect, 1986 and 1993 respectively; the total increase was from 931,000 to 1,553,800.) However, it was never clear what people should take from the size of the change because experts disagreed on whether more children were actually being abused or more cases of abuse were being reported or both. Some used the information to build public support for additional child abuse programs and social services. Others argued that the data exaggerated social ills in a way that distorted policy choices. Whether the public was as enlightened about the problem of child abuse as it could have been is doubtful, although the media coverage probably did serve to raise public consciousness of the issue.

Chapter Two

ECONOMIC TRANSFORMATIONS

It is the first step in wisdom to recognize that the major advances in civilization are processes which all but wreck the society in which they occur. . . . The art of a free society consists, first, in the maintenance of the symbolic code, and secondly, in fearlessness of revision. Those societies which cannot combine reverence for their symbols with freedom of revision must ultimately decay from anarchy or from slow atrophy.
—Alfred North Whitehead, *Symbolism, Its Meaning and Effect*, 1927

Thinking realistically about the role of government depends first on understanding the kind of society we have become. In a democracy such as ours, people expect to use government to help address needs not well met by the private markets. And this in turn presumes some broadly reliable understanding of actual economic and social conditions. Current domestic policies in many cases have been set by legislation adopted years or decades ago. When based on no-longer-reliable perceptions of our economic and social conditions, these policies sometimes result in unintended and unwanted consequences for current or future generations.

Although most of us can give a fairly accurate report of our own personal circumstances, democracy also calls on people to make judgments about their collective circumstances and needs—not just what's happening to "me" but what's happening to "us." The next two chapters give an account of what is happening to us in the context of the larger economy and changing family patterns.

The debate about the role of government is typically cast at one of two levels: either grand philosophical generalizations or micro-analyses of a particular problem. We take another tack, illuminating the government issue in terms of what might be called a middle landscape—neither forest nor trees but the revelant bits of both. In particular, we highlight interrelations among a number of trends that must be taken into account to develop effective domestic policies. Any policy to tackle the problems facing the younger generation, for example, needs to be developed in light of the changing demands of the workforce, well-being of children, consumption levels of the elderly, and so on.

The picture that emerges from our examination is of an extraordinarily dynamic society—a society that requires a similarly dynamic public sector if we are to achieve the government we deserve.

THE ECONOMY AS A WHOLE

One need not be a trained economist to appreciate that remarkable changes have been taking place in the U.S. economy. The following account, based on the last five government censuses, captures experiences millions of Americans can verify from their lives or the lives of people they know:

> A generation ago a young white man with a high school education, a dedication to work, and a strong back could likely find a good blue collar job... He could afford to marry while in his early twenties, and he and his wife could buy a starter home in the suburbs before they reached thirty. . . . Divorces were rare, and wives expected that their husbands would support them while they stayed at home taking care of the two, three, or even four children. . . .
>
> It is a very different country now. A young man graduating from high school with a strong back and a dedication to work may find a good job, but, the job will pay much less. . . . A young [married] woman knows her chances for middle class prosperity are slim unless both of them work full-time and one of them gets specialized training. Since more than half of all recent marriages end in divorce, a realistic young woman must also recognize, that by her late thirties, she may well be raising a couple of children on her own (Farley 1995).

Like all generalizations, this one is overdrawn. Not all young high school graduates of the 1950s got good jobs, not all marriages were stable, and not all children were raised in two-parent families. By the same token, many high school graduates today get good jobs, most marriages are stable, and a minority of children are raised in one-parent families.[1] Nonetheless, this account does a fair job of capturing the source of many complaints about major economic changes since the 1950s.

A place to start is with the economy as a whole. We turn later to how different members of society have fared in that economy, and then to how opportunity is spread among us. In the past half century, a tight connection between national policy decisions and the economy has become virtually automatic in people's minds, with presidents and Congresses claiming credit and laying blame for even modest economic changes. Political assertions and claims aside, what can people realistically expect to understand about the contemporary transformation of our economy?

The economy has been growing almost continually throughout our history. An economy's performance is typically captured by its economic growth.[2] To grow is to have more; to keep growing is to get richer. America is an extraordinarily rich nation and it is getting richer every year. Although this fact is often overlooked in today's debate, experts generally agree that the United States has long had and still retains one of the most vibrant and healthy economies in the world. In every decade of this century the average income and consumption of Americans has increased by a minimum of 20 percent, even in the Depression era of the 1930s.[3] In the last 100 years, after taking account of inflation, the average real income of Americans has increased five-fold.[4] Such continual growth means ever higher living standards. By today's poverty standards, for example, almost all Americans living in 1900 were poor; by the standards of 1900, virtually any American living today is rich.

Economic growth is now deeply embedded in the American view of life. Next year, in the nature of things, people expect more. As long ago as 1958, a highly popular book urged Americans to recognize that they had left behind the world of mass poverty and should rethink their situation as an "affluent society."[5] Since then the income and consumption of Americans has more than doubled.[6] If nothing else, this basic information about economic growth should make us circumspect in talking about what Americans or the economy as a whole can or cannot afford. It should also make us hopeful about the vast array of options and opportunities that lie ahead of us.

Economic growth entails disruption. That the U.S. economy is vibrantly healthy is not to say that everything about economic life is attractive. Economic growth inevitably brings with it economic change, some of it pleasant (more choices about what to do with one's money) and some unpleasant (jobs and investments lost, familiar ways of doing things abandoned). As these disruptions accumulate and interact, patterns of economic growth become evident. Unfortunately for our peace of mind as we go through these disruptions, such patterns become clear only in the rearview mirror of history.

It is useful to look in that mirror briefly for perspective on our present situation. The big picture shows a nineteenth century America reaping the gains of plentiful land and commercialization of agriculture that propelled the economy forward. This strong resource base of agriculture and raw materials overlapped increasingly with an expanding industrial revolution as that century ended. With a continental-scale customer base, industrial mass production and marketing to American consumers drove economic growth in the twentieth century. One estimate puts annual economic growth between 1820 and 1972 at 3.8 percent (which included substantial population growth).[7] There were many ups and downs in this long time span, but the economy recovered so vigorously from each downturn that any decline in production was soon wiped out by a new growth surge.

The more drastic economic cycles of our history are outside the experience of most Americans today. Observers of the current economic scene often forget the erratic swings in growth that characterized all American economic history up to the mid-twentieth century. These cycles have been brought under considerably more stable management for the past 50 years. The "good old days" of sharp booms and busts in the economy are unknown to Americans born after the Depression. Like growth, this kind of fundamental stability—which helps undergird the continuing prosperity of the U.S. economy— tends to be taken for granted. The success of the federal government in helping to engineer this feat is also often ignored.

The years between 1947 and 1973 now appear as the crowning jewel in this economic growth story. With America the major military and economic power emerging from World War II, and with its industries uniquely geared up for mass production, the economic times after that war were very good indeed. Between 1947 and 1973 annual economic growth was more than one-third higher (at 3.8 percent) than it had been for the years between 1900 and 1947 (at 3.0 percent)—a period covering booms and recessions around World War I, the Great Depression of the 1930s, World War II, and the recession immediately after that war. When one adjusts for the much slower population growth rate in the period between 1947 and 1973 relative to earlier periods, those 26 years represented perhaps the best sustained economic performance in U.S. history (see figure 2.1).

The United States had a competitive edge in world trade, of course. Many of the countries that later became our main trading partners had suffered great destruction during the war. But even after the economies in Europe and Japan were rebuilt, the U.S. economy still performed extraordinarily well, with rapid growth, low unemployment, and low inflation. In terms of productivity per worker, real GDP rose from a growth rate of 1.3 percent in 1900–1947 to 2.2 percent in 1947– 1973 (see figure 2.2). While a jump of almost one percentage point in annual growth rates might not seem large, the magic of annual compounding meant that by 1973 the overall economic output for each American worker was about one-fourth higher than it would have been had the pre-1947 growth trend continued.

Figure 2.1 GNP GROWTH: SELECTED PERIODS

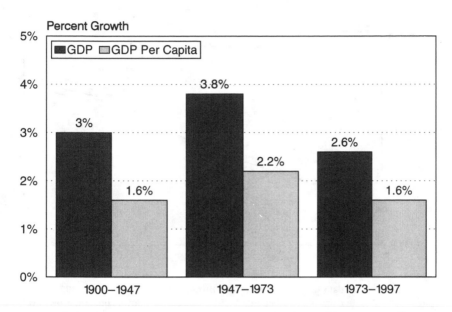

Source: The 1900 to 1947 comparison uses GNP, which typically grows at the same rate as GDP. GDP and GNP data from the Department of Commerce, Bureau of Economic Analysis, and population data from the Bureau of the Census.

But just as individuals were adjusting expectations to more rapid growth, it slowed down abruptly. Over the 1973–1997 period, output per worker after inflation rose at about 40 percent of the rate of the early years after World War II and about 70 percent of the rate experienced in the first half of the twentieth century.[8] Again, we should not be misled. A drop of one percentage point or more in a growth rate over a period of years is a big deal, except this time the magic of compounding worked against us. The slower growth rate from 1973 onward yielded by 1997 an economy about 2.5 trillion dollars smaller in terms of gross domestic product—about $25,000 less per household—than if the 1947–1973 growth rate in GDP per worker had continued.[9]

Even with the economic slowdown of the last quarter century, it is still economic growth we are talking about. Any discontent today occurs in a general context of still mounting material riches. Televisions, stereos, automobiles, and telephones are available in hereto-

Figure 2.2 REAL GDP PER WORKER 1900–1997

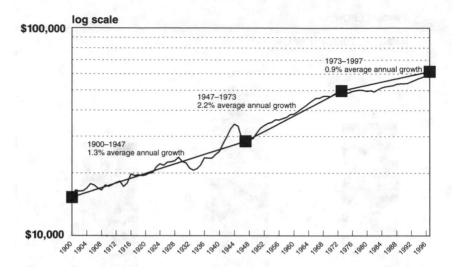

Source: Post-1947 data on workers from the Bureau of Labor Statistics, 1997, Internet site; pre-1947 data from Stanley Lebergott (1964). Log scale allows constant growth rate to be shown as straight lines. Workers are defined as the employed portion of the civilian labor force and total armed forces.

fore unknown quantities. Housing space per person is higher than for past generations. Food and clothing are generally in greater abundance, even among the poor. And items that over one-quarter of Americans at the end of the twentieth century considered necessities (microwaves, telephone answering machines, home computers) did not even exist for 1973 consumers.[10] Even though seven out of ten Americans think family incomes have fallen behind inflation over the last two decades, this is simply not true at an overall level.[11] A significant share of the decline in output per worker was offset by increased work effort (as can be seen by contrasting figure 2.1 with figure 2.2). The misconception is also partly explained by the continually increasing value of services such as health care, which people rarely remember when they think about whether they are richer or not. For example, workers seldom count as part of their pay the increased value of the health insurance they get for themselves or the Medicare they are buying for the elderly generally and their parents or grandparents, in particular. Yet growth in health care spending per capita rose from about one-eighth of real per capita income growth in the 1960s, to about one-third today.[12]

Americans middle-aged and older will remember that the economic problems in the 1970s were at first attributed to oil embargoes and the rapid rise in energy prices. But the slowdown continued long after that rise in energy prices had been digested. Real energy prices are now lower than they were before their 1973 rise. So there are now other presumed causes of the slowdown—a natural return to more historically typical growth rates, completion of the conversion of productive wartime technologies, and growth in government regulation. Some even see an ending to the gains from mass production that for so long favored American economic growth. They wonder whether the new "revolution"—having to do less with industry and more with the massive technological changes of an information-based society—will yield the same rate of future gain. The fact is that experts disagree about what happened to slow the growth rate over the past quarter century and about the magnitude of future economic growth.

Most agree, however, that the growth rate is probably not as slow as the measured statistics indicate. The major reason is that, despite spectacular improvements in statistical information, we have probably overestimated inflation and, as a consequence, underestimated real economic growth.[13] In measuring the economy's output it is difficult to distinguish quality improvements from price increases. Economy-wide measures of inflation reflect not only increases in the prices of the same goods and services but also changes in the quality of what is produced, including new items not previously available at any price. Sorting this out is technically complex and often subjective. Computers are examples of items that have almost certainly improved the quality of consumption, but what value do we put on this quality increase? Compared to increases in quantity (e.g., more of the same automobiles), increases in quality (better health care, financial services, and the like) are both harder to measure and more dominant in the service economy of today. As time proceeds, it becomes harder and harder to interpret comparisons in growth rates over time since they are measuring very different types of improvements.

When we're talking about families, economic growth sends signals that are even more mixed. Demographic changes complicate the story of economic growth. These changes in the American household are examined in more detail later. But it helps the story here to highlight the relationship between growth in family income and changes in family structure. Slow growth in household or worker income (as well as negative growth for some groups) is not inconsistent with stories of more significant growth for the economy as a whole. Thus, national income accountants tell us that per capita personal income rose by 48 percent between 1976 and 1996, while the census indicates that average household income rose by only 5.9 percent and wages of full-time workers by only 14 percent for women. They actually fell for men by 8.4 percent.[14] (A variety of sources of error affect these statistics, but the general relationship is not open to dispute.)

It should not be surprising that household and worker incomes have grown at slower rates than income per person for some time now. Two causes are worthy of note here. First, adults delayed marriage and had fewer children.[15] Second, increasing proportions of the adult population worked outside the home—as more women went out to work and the large baby boom cohort entered its working years. The decline in family size meant that income per person could (and did) rise faster than family income. More paychecks, in turn, meant that material consumption per American could continue to increase significantly even as the income per *working* American grew more slowly.[16] These differing trends make it easy for those who wish to tell a particular story to find a measure that suits their purpose.

THE CHANGING SHAPE OF AFFLUENCE

If the continued growth of America's remarkable prosperity is often overlooked, the same cannot be said for its distribution. Most Americans correctly believe they have been living in an era of growing economic inequality. The concern voiced in public conversation is usually not with economic inequality in the abstract but with the kinds of inequality that violate American ideas about fairness. To discern better where we stand, it is worth working through the changing shape of U.S. affluence.

Americans have stopped sharing equally in the benefits of growth. In the last quarter century or so, a rising tide did not lift all the boats. Unlike many earlier epochs in American history, when families in different economic circumstances either rose or fell together, the post-1973 period has been one of a significantly increased income inequality.[17] In the three decades following World War II, people at different income levels saw their economic situations improve together. Since then sharp differences have emerged. The varied fortunes of five different income groups (figure 2.3) tell the story. The real incomes of all five groups moved together until 1979—increasing

Figure 2.3 RATE OF REAL ANNUAL FAMILY INCOME GROWTH BY QUINTILE

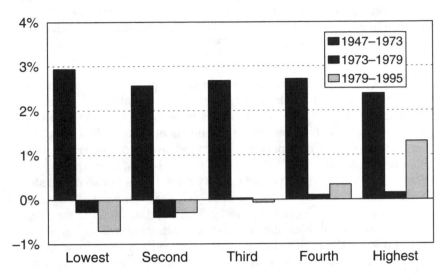

Source: Data from the Bureau of the Census, 1997, Internet site. Changes to the Current Population Survey increased the reported income of the highest quintile in 1993, 1994, and 1995. However, the increases in income from 1993 to 1995 should only have a modest effect on the growth rate from 1979 to 1995.

on average up to 1973, and stagnating between 1973 and 1979. After 1979, those in the higher-income groups returned to doing better, but the lower-income groups continued to see their incomes stagnate and the very lowest group saw them actually decline.[18]

That income is increasingly concentrated at the very top is even more clearcut. In 1979, the top 0.5 percent reported 6.0 percent of total adjusted gross income from all tax returns. By 1993, their share had increased to 10.3 percent of the total.[19] Dramatic growth in the incomes of the super-rich—executives, professional specialists, athletes, and the like—heightens the feeling of increased inequality.[20] Though the super-rich are too few to have a very large effect on aggregate income distribution statistics, for many they epitomize the dramatic inequality of the recent era. Moreover, many parts of the American marketplace now offer economic rewards to those at the top that seem vastly out of line with any differences in their performance compared with the performance of those further down the income scale.[21] They are also conspicuously out of line with the rewards of persons in similar positions in other major democracies.

Among families, changing patterns of employment and pay are also important. Thus some of the growing disparity is explained by the increase in employment, wages, and hours of work for women married to more highly compensated men.[22]

Perhaps most disturbing are the income figures for single parents with children, an increasing segment of the population. In recent decades, larger proportions of families have fallen into the economically vulnerable categories where the heads of household are unmarried and divorced single parents. The trend away from marriage alone accounts for about half of the increase in child-income inequality and more than the total rise in child poverty rates.[23] It is not so much slow income growth among single mothers, but their increasing numbers, that drives this rise in child poverty. The popular focus is on single mothers because of their numbers, but similar economic vulnerability afflicts the smaller group of single fathers as well. In 1995, for example, the median incomes of married dual-earner couples averaged $55,800—which is $23,400 more than for single-earner couples, $25,400 more than for single men, and $35,000 more than for single women.[24] Even after a divorce in which the sole breadwinner maintains custody of the children, the family's income often declines, because raising children takes time, which can put significant constraints on employment. It is also not surprising that children in families headed by a never-married mother have the highest rates of poverty.[25] Never-married mothers tend to be younger and less educated, making their families more economically vulnerable than other single parents.[26]

Recent changes in government taxing and spending policy have been only bit players in the changing distribution of income. Much has been said about the significance of government actions in changing the income distribution. It has been charged, in particular, that tax policy under the Reagan administration contributed to rising inequality in the 1980s. These claims are less prevalent now that the nation has followed the terms of two Republican presidents with two terms of a Democratic president, and the growth in inequality has continued. All along, however, analysis has shown that growing inequality began before President Reagan took office and that changes in private sources of income dominate changes in government taxes and transfers (transfers that are largely Social Security and Medicare, not traditional welfare). This suggests that the forces at work go much deeper than the various policy changes made by shifting teams of politicians through the years.[27]

If one compares 1973 with 1997, for instance, taxes and transfers reduce inequality in both years. Taxes exceed transfers for the rich; the reverse is true for the poor. Thus, throughout the period, as designed, the U.S. tax/transfer system has provided, and still provides, a base level of support to those in the lower part of the income distribution.[28] Moreover, except at the very top of the income distribution, average tax rates for each income group changed little when all the tax reforms of that period are considered together.[29] But even after taking account of taxes and transfers, income still became more unequal following the 1970s. In other words, the changes in taxes and transfers in recent years did not offset the *additional* income inequality arising elsewhere, particularly in earnings.

This does not mean that taxes and transfers have no effect on incentives to work and to save. They certainly do, which in turn, further affects the income distribution. But among most of the nonelderly, the changes in tax and transfer rates have been minimal while family incomes have become much more unequal. Thus, government programs cannot explain the large changes that have taken place in the distribution of income—in particular, the very low rates of growth in wages for many middle-income, full-time, workers who have had little change over recent years in either the tax rates they pay or the transfers they receive.

Growing demand for educated workers is usually associated with increased economic differences among Americans, but it could become a source of increased opportunity for all. For the past 20 years, the more highly educated groups have fared considerably better than those with less education, at least when it comes to employment and income growth. In fact, while earnings have continuously increased since World War II, not all workers have experienced gains. For example, from 1979 to 1989, average real weekly earnings increased by about 6 percent annually for all men but by over 10 percent for men with at least some college education. For men without a high school diploma real earnings declined by over 12 percent.[30] Most statistics show that the gains from education have increased dramatically in recent years as we have moved toward a technological and knowledge-based society.

One of the nation's leading experts on productivity finds that the relationship between individual income and education has a parallel in the relationship between a firm's productivity and the education of its workers. "Explanations of industry productivity change that emphasize physical capital," argues Murray Foss, have given way to explanations focusing on "changes in human capital." Until recently firm productivity increased by expanding such factors as hours of plant operation—productivity gains that can be readily shared as wage gains among all workers in the plant, regardless of education. In recent years, this source of gain seems to have disappeared. But productivity still increases with the percentage of workers who are college-educated.[31] The Conference Board recently found a consistent trend—that industries with the greatest gains in productivity were those with the most intensive new use of computers.[32]

This does *not* mean that increasing returns to education are automatic. Even among people with the same levels of education, earnings differentials have increased—as can be seen from the increasing numbers of university-educated workers who are taking high-school level jobs with commensurately lower pay. This apparent inconsistency is at least partially explained by the varying levels of actual skills that people acquire regardless of their education.[33] Some of the disparity might also reflect the growing demand for workers with technological skills rather than other education. The overall message here is that success is achieved not simply by receiving a particular degree. What one takes away from education also matters.

There is cause for optimism about the prospects offered by the new technology if handled the right way. Demand for higher skills by employers creates a greater incentive for investment in education by all of us, and as technology improves we will continue to demand even more. Robert Lerman argues that rapid job growth in recent years has directly corresponded to the technological advances. "Technology demands more workers with knowledge and the ability for lifelong learning." The overall argument is that the process reinforces itself: expectations about the qualifications of the workforce influence a company's technology decisions, which affect the skills the company demands, which affect the incentives created for workers as suppliers of labor. Thus, the potential is for more workers to find fulfilling occupations from this increased demand for higher skills.[34]

Deregulation and expanding international trade are not responsible for inequality; they primarily reflect a response to the same market conditions that are increasingly rewarding knowledge and adaptability. An explosion in information technology certainly is a bellwether of the greater premium on education and its by-products—adaptability and flexibility.[35] A long list of studies, examining separately wages and hours of work for primary and secondary workers in a family, support this view.[36] This is not to say that there are not complementary and reinforcing mechanisms—increasing competition, the decline of unions, the growth of high tech industries—that make it harder to join the middle class without more education. But if knowledge is power, then deregulation and expanding markets are less causes than responses that allow Americans to compete in these new markets.

A rigorous assessment of American markets also shows that most shifts in demand come from within-country, rather than international, sources. In addition, among international trading partners, most American trade is with countries like Canada and Germany, not developing countries with much lower-cost labor. While the United States does have a higher level of income inequality than much of Western Europe, it has also witnessed an employment increase of over 30 million jobs in the last two decades.[37] Over the same period, in contrast, most of Europe has experienced almost zero private job growth and very high unemployment.[38]

OPPORTUNITIES FOR EMPLOYMENT AND WEALTH OWNERSHIP[39]

Income inequality *per se* is not the primary focus of the political conversation in the United States. But inequality of opportunity is something about which Americans care deeply. In fact, Americans tolerate substantial inequalities in the income distribution, in contrast to most Europeans, because they believe America is an open, meritocratic society where individuals have the opportunity to do and become what they want. "Anyone can become president and often does" is a joke, but not one that is to be dismissed lightly as a description of what Americans believe.

Opportunity, in the sense of being able to move to a different income class from that of one's parents, has remained generally constant, but its sources have changed. There is substantial economic and social mobility in the United States, as measured by the movement of Americans from one part of the income distribution to another. A helpful analogy used by Daniel P. McMurrer and Isabel V. Sawhill is to think of the income distribution as a ladder with five steps (quintiles). In a given year they found that more than one of every five Americans move from one step to another on this ladder. In a single decade, more than three out of five make such a move. The United States is not unusual in this regard. However, despite all the moves around the ladder, the chances for the average American to move up the ladder have changed little.

Two major, offsetting factors have influenced recent economic mobility. The first is economic growth. The downward trend in overall economic growth in the United States in the past three decades or so has reduced the chances for an average American to move up the ladder because fewer new opportunities are created. As we have discussed, this makes realizing the American dream—that is, ending up higher on the real income ladder than one's parents—more difficult. Over the same period, however, the influence of one's social position at birth has weakened.[40] While class still plays a considerable role in determining the lifetime chances of Americans, younger generations have more equal chances than their parents of moving up (and, therefore, down) the economic ladder based on their own individual effort and skill. But the economy provides less of an upward push for everybody than it did 30 to 50 years ago.

The overall risk of job loss has changed little, but it is being spread more widely. An important part of many people's dreams of a good life is the promise of economic security—the confidence that next week, next month, or next year they will still be able to feed and clothe their families, put a roof over their heads, and keep them free from want. Since most Americans get the majority of their income from work, job security is a good part of economic security.

The traditional measure of job insecurity is the unemployment rate. Here the news was generally negative in the 1970s and early 1980s, but has been increasingly positive since then.[41] Although much depends upon proximity to and frequency of recessions, recoveries from the two most recent recessions (1981–82, 1990–91) both extended for very long periods by historic standards, while the unemployment rate in the 1990s recovery fell below 5 percent for the first time since 1973.[42]

Is there more job insecurity in the sense that people are changing jobs more than they used to or being permanently laid off more frequently? The research indicates that if there is any trend it is certainly small. However, the increased *feeling* that jobs are less secure has at least one straightforward explanation. The distribution of job loss among those who have held the same job for a relatively long period (three years or more) is changing. Among these "long-tenure" job holders, white-collar workers and workers in the service industries form a higher *proportion* of job losses than in the past, when blue-collar and manufacturing workers tended to dominate the jobless statistics. Between the early 1980s and the early 1990s, for example, the proportion of all long-tenure job losses accounted for by the service industries grew from one-third to over one-half, and the proportion accounted for by white-collar workers from two-fifths to over one-half.[43] There is nothing like extending a risk to groups that used to feel immune to raise the feeling that things are getting worse.

The lower unemployment rates of recent years provide potentially increased job opportunities for lower-skilled workers. Throughout much of the 1970s and early 1980s (and the 1990s in Western Europe), industrial nations became accustomed to higher and higher unemployment rates even in nonrecessionary periods. While economists hotly debate the cause, this unemployment trend in the United States has reversed since the mid-1980s.[44] If and when more recessions hit, the hope is that we may still be able to maintain a lower average unemployment rate over entire economic cycles than in previous periods. Many Western European countries, in contrast, maintained much larger deficits and social welfare programs on average in the mid-1990s, while tolerating unemployment rates roughly double those of the United States. The question is still open as to whether the United States, or any developed nation, can maintain tighter labor markets and lower unemployment rates without eventually re-igniting inflation. One reason for new hope in the modern period is that the United States now has among the oldest workforces in its history. Older workers are typically more concerned about job security than younger ones—and less likely, therefore, to make inflationary pay raise demands.

Many view the lowering of unemployment and inflation rates in the last two recoveries as a sign of real opportunity. Even a modest increase in the employment rate among those at the bottom of the income distribution will put more money in their hands than any politically conceivable increase in means-tested public benefits. Greater job opportunities also serve to reduce demand for traditional welfare, as higher wages and more secure employment make the choice of work increasingly attractive. If low unemployment also reflects a relatively greater increase in demand for labor, especially for those nearer the bottom of the income distribution, it might well serve to reduce income inequality. Of course, the real trick will be to maintain higher demand not just at the peak of a recovery but on average over the course of new economic cycles—which will include new recessions.

Taking advantage of this potential opportunity may require a reversal of recent trends in labor force participation rates. While women's labor force participation has increased steadily since World War II, men's participation rates have been dropping.[45] Some of the decline almost certainly reflects individual preferences of specific earners to retire at earlier ages, given the greater ability to rely upon the earnings of a spouse in families where there had been two earners. But the decline in labor force participation has been especially sharp for less educated men, even those not near retirement. Among young black males aged 20–29, incomes have fallen significantly, in no small part because a disproportionate number have not worked at all.[46] These types of statistics have prompted some analysts to suggest that the falling real wages available to them over the past 20 years have reinforced income inequality by decreasing their work effort.[47]

Inequality in wealth is still very high, and past equalizing trends in the areas of housing and pension wealth have almost stagnated. Analyzing wealth is always more uncertain than analyzing income because wealth measurement is subject to considerably more error. Even so, it is quite clear that wealth—the financial assets and other possessions a person or family owns at any given moment—has always been distributed much more unequally than income or earnings. Most analysts agree that, for the six decades following World War I, U.S. wealth inequality fell. What is happening more recently to the distribution of wealth among Americans is less clear. One set of estimates puts the wealth share of those at the very top at about the same in 1992 as in 1983, with the top 1 percent of the wealth distribution owning about 31 percent of the nation's total wealth in 1983, 36 percent in 1989, and 30 percent in 1992.[48] Many other estimates indicate that wealth inequality has grown significantly during the period, partly because of growth in the value of stocks, which are typically distributed more unevenly than other assets such as homes.[49]

Regardless of recent trends, no one thinks the nation is making much progress in helping lower-income Americans increase their wealth. Next to finding a stable source of earnings, the most crucial items in expanding wealth ownership among the low- and middle-income classes are increasing ownership of homes and pensions. Pensions and homes are the crucial assets here because together they constitute over half of total household wealth of all families, and they dominate the assets held by families in the bottom half of the income distribution.[50]

From the founding of this country, the government has encouraged home ownership. First, it offered opportunities for landholding on the frontier. Then, with the development of the income tax and rising tax rates in the twentieth century, it offered tax breaks for those who owned homes as opposed to holding assets in taxable instruments such as savings accounts. Home ownership rates have increased slightly in recent years,[51] at least partly because homeownership is more prevalent among older individuals, and the population is aging. Nonetheless, government policy actually deters the achievement of further asset gains in two ways. First, with the growth in the welfare state—in particular, the rise in the percentage of households receiving housing assistance—came a shift in policy away from home owner-ship toward rental subsidies for those with low incomes. Public hous-ing and other rental subsidies actually discourage home ownership, since wealth accumulated to buy a house can remove eligibility for assistance, and subsidies are not generally available for home pur-chase.[52] Second, income tax incentives are inadequate or perverse in some cases. For instance, the tax advantage from owning a home is worthless to someone who is too poor to pay taxes in the first place. In addition, even for homeowners, very generous allowances for de-ductibility of mortgage interest have given incentives to many middle-class families to reduce their equity ownership. Thus, new financial instruments (such as secondary and reverse mortgages) allow individ-uals to spend down any home equity they have built up—threatening to reduce rather than increase the share of society's wealth owned by the middle class.

The government has also used tax incentives to encourage the own-ership of wealth through private pensions. These incentives grew significantly with the rise in tax rates, especially on middle-income families, from the beginning of World War II through the late 1970s. Through deferred taxation and similar breaks for employer contribu-tions to pension plans, government policy has continued to encourage the provision of employee benefits as a form of compensation. But since the late 1970s, it has become clearer and clearer that the current system will not achieve the hoped-for expansion of pension coverage to provide significant benefits for the vast bulk of future retirees. Accrued pension benefits have been leveling out, leaving a significant gap between the pension subsidization of highly compensated em-ployees and other employees. Many workers at the low end are ex-cluded altogether.[53] Between 1962 and 1993, after these tax breaks had been on the books for three decades, for example, private pension wealth among the elderly had only grown from 3 to 10 percent of their aggregate income.[54]

Most people still have very modest savings to support themselves in retirement. In fact, the majority of people will never be able to generate anything approaching significant pensions by the time of retirement if Social Security is excluded from the calculation. Even though many individuals are accruing modest amounts of saving in individual retirement accounts (IRAs), pension saving accounts known as 401 (k) plans, and similar instruments, the accruals for most employees remain quite modest. For individuals between the ages of 51 and 61, fewer than 30 percent have private assets greater in value than the combined insurance value of Social Security and Medicare they can expect to receive (figure 2.4).[55]

For baby boomers (roughly those aged 33–50 in 1997), the saving picture is at least as dismal. Even when asked to count anything and

Figure 2.4 PERCENT OF ASSETS FROM SPECIFIED SOURCES FOR THE
NEAR-ELDERLY (AGES 51–61) BY INCOME DECILE

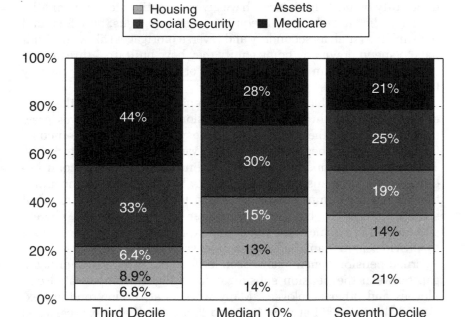

Source: Asset data other than Medicare are based on data from James Moore and Olivia Mitchell, and the Health and Retirement Survey (1992). The HRS survey sample includes people ages 51 to 61. The data on Medicare are estimated from data in C. Eugene Steuerle and Jon Bakija, *Retooling Social Security for the 21st Century: Right and Wrong Approaches to Reform*, 1994.

everything they have as savings, two-thirds report less than $50,000 in retirement savings (with 38 percent having less than $10,000).[56]

Finally, inequality in wealth, housing, and pension ownership is much greater for minorities. Median money income of African Americans, for instance, is about 71 percent of the median money income for all persons, but their median net worth is only about 12 percent.[57] The corresponding figures for Hispanic Americans are 66 percent for money income and 12 percent for median net worth. Similarly, African and Hispanic Americans are less likely to own homes (46.0 percent and 43.1 percent, respectively, versus an overall rate of 71.1 percent).[58] And these figures do not take into account the lower value of homes for those who do own homes. The average total wealth for African and Hispanic Americans near to retirement is only $27,869 and $30,464, respectively, relative to $138,786 for whites.[59]

*   *   *

To summarize, no one should believe anyone who claims to fully understand the economic transformation modern-day Americans have been living through. The post-1973 period repeated neither the growth of the earlier post-war period nor the historically familiar cycle of boom and bust. Despite slowing down since the mid-1970s, the American economic growth machine has continued to churn out substantial increases in material riches. It has done so by transforming itself into an information-, service-, and knowledge-based economy beyond anything imagined in the immediate post–World War II decades. A different way of viewing the same period is that Americans' economic lives have become disrupted, with growing income inequality, shifting patterns of opportunity, and job insecurity more widespread across occupations; at the same time, huge differences in wealth ownership continue to exist. Prosperity has come joined with new stresses and strains in working life—and new meanings for the traditional concept of an American work ethic.

Notes

1. Based on data from the U.S. National Center for Health Statistics, *Vital Statistics of the United States*, 1995, we find that the divorce rate in 1995 was 19.8 per 1,000 married women 15 years old or older. Based on data from the U.S. Bureau of the Census, Current

Population Reports, P20-488, in 1996, 68 percent of families had two parents while only 27 percent were mother-only families and 5 percent were father-only families. Both cited in 1997 *Statistical Abstracts of the United States.*

2. Economic growth is measured by the rate of increase in the products and services that people produce and have at their disposal.

3. Real GDP per capita increased by 12.6 percent from 1930 to 1940 and by 18.3 percent from 1970 to 1980. Authors' calculations based on GDP data from the Bureau of Economic Analysis, 1992 and 1993. *National Income and Product Accounts of the U.S.,* volumes I and II, the Bureau of Economic Analysis, *The Survey of Current Business,* various years, and Robert J. Gordon, 1993, *Macroeconomics,* 6th edition, New York: HarperCollins. Population data are from U.S. Bureau of the Census, *Historical Statistics of the United States from Colonial Times to 1970* and *Current Population Reports,* P25-1045, P25-1126, and P25-1104 appearing in the *Statistical Abstract of the United States 1995,* Washington, DC: U.S. Government Printing Office, 1995.

4. Derived from growth rates in figure 2.1. Robert Fogel argues that the income of the poor actually increased 13-fold. Robert W. Fogel, "Bradley Lecture," American Enterprise Institute, September 11, 1995; should be in a subsequent book tentatively titled *The Fourth Great Awakening: The Political Realignment of the 1990s and the Fate of Egalitarianism.*

5. John Kenneth Galbraith, *The Affluent Society,* New York: Mentor Books, 1958.

6. Based on data from the Bureau of Economic Analysis, we know that real GDP per capita increased from $12,429 in 1959 to $26,019 in 1996.

7. Jeffrey Madrick, *The End of Affluence,* New York: Random House, 1995. Drawing on Angus Maddison, *Dynamic Forces in Capitalist Development,* Oxford University Press, 1991, pp. 50–53.

8. Based on data from the Bureau of Labor Statistics.

9. Estimate is based on data from the U.S. Department of Commerce, Bureau of Economic Analysis.

10. 1973 data from the Roper Organization; 1996 from Henry J. Kaiser Family Foundation/Harvard University national survey. Reported in *The Washington* Post, September 1996.

11. *The Washington Post,* October 15, 1995, p. A1.

12. Data are based on an update of Eugene Steuerle, "Health and Nothing Else," *Urban Institute Policy Bites* (#20), December 1993.

13. This finding was presented by a panel, chaired by Michael Boskin, in "The Final Report of the Congressional Advisory Commission on the Consumer Price Index." By the same token, we probably also overestimated inflation in prior periods (although by less if technological progress was slower), which means some slowdown still occurred. For other views, see: Dean Baker, "The Overstated CPI—Can It Really Be True?" *Challenge,* 1996, vol. 39, no. 5, pp. 26–33; Bureau of Labor Statistics, "Measurement Issues in the Consumer Price Index," Report to the Chairman of the Joint Economic Committee, 1997; Audrey Freedman, "Presto Change-O! On the Consumer Price Index," *Challenge,* 1996, vol. 39, no. 2, pp. 60–62; Jim Klempner, "Fact and Fancy: CPI Biases and the Federal Budget," *Business Economics,* 1996, vol. 39, no. 2, pp. 22–29; Brent R. Moulton, "Bias in the Consumer Price Index: What Is the Evidence?" *Journal of Economic Perspectives,* 1996, vol. 10, no. 4, pp. 159–177; and Daniel Patrick Moynihan, *Miles to Go: A Personal History of Social Policy,* Cambridge, MA: Harvard University Press, 1996, p. 98.

14. It is important to understand that a lot is going on here, but some apparent inconsistencies can be explained. For a longer discussion of these issues, and specifically

the effects of fringe benefits on wage inequality, see Greg Acs and Eugene Steuerle, "Trends in the Distribution in Non-Wage Benefits and Total Compensation, 1979–1994," final report for the Department of Labor, Pension and Welfare Benefits Administration, July 1997.

15. Based on data from U.S. Bureau of the Census, Current Population Survey, the median age at first marriage for women increased from 20.8 years old in 1970 to 24.5 years old in 1995. Over the same period the median age for men increased from 23.2 to 26.9. Also, based on data from the U.S. Bureau of the Census, Current Population Reports, Series P20-495, "Household and Family Characteristics: March 1996," the average number of children in all families fell from 1.27 in 1970 to 0.92 in 1996. Also, even within families with children the average number of children fell from 2.28 in 1970 to 1.86 in 1996.

16. See Frank Levy, "Income and Income Inequality," in Reynolds Farley, ed., *State of the Union, Vol. I: Economic Trends*, New York: Russell Sage, 1995, p. 4.

17. It is also possible to use consumption instead of income to measure inequalities and well-being over time. According to the "American Enterprise Institute Conference Summary, Living Standards in the United States," March 1997, using consumption as a measure of well-being provides some different results, with living standards for both the rich and the poor continuing to grow after 1970.

18. The average income gain is slightly above the overall rate of increase of GDP per worker at this time because of the rise in labor force participation.

19. Data for 1979 from Frank Levy, "Income and Income Inequality," in Reynolds Farley, ed., *State of the Union, Vol. I: Economic Trends*. Data for 1992 based on data from *Statistics of Income—Individual Income Tax Returns*, with calculations by John O'Hare, The Urban Institute. It is also important to recognize that some, but only some, of this increase is attributable to greater recognition of income at higher income levels due to drops in tax rates and restrictions on tax shelters.

20. Levy, pp. 3, 32.

21. Robert H. Frank and Philip J. Cook, *The Winner Take-All Society*, New York: Free Press, 1995.

22. See Gary Burtless, "Rising Inequality: Sources and Remedies," in Robert Reischauer (ed.), *Setting National Priorities*, Washington, DC: The Brookings Institution, forthcoming.

23. See Robert Lerman, "The Impact of the Changing U.S. Family Structure on Child Poverty and Income Inequality," *Economica*, Vol. 63 (1996).

24. Data based on *Statistical Abstract of the United States, 1997*. It is important to note that these data do not take into account the presence or absence of children, although most data show that the incomes for people with children are even lower.

25. See Robert Lerman, "The Impact of the Changing U.S. Family Structure on Child Poverty and Income Inequality," *Economica*, Vol. 63 (1996).

26. See Census Brief, "Children with Single Parents—How They Fare," September 1997. It says that never-married parents are younger, have completed fewer years of school, and have lower levels of income than divorced parents on average. Specifically in 1995, 85 percent of children living with divorced parents lived with a parent that had completed high school; however, this was true for only two-thirds of children who lived with a never-married parent. Also, 60 percent of children living with only their mother are in poverty; however, this is true for only 45 percent of children living with a divorced mother and 69 percent of children living with a never-married mother.

27. In fact, the issue is more complicated because there should be some impact of tax rates on earnings. But even though there were large tax changes in the 1980s, over the

whole decade both average and marginal tax rates on different income quintiles were nearly the same at the end of the decade as at the beginning—average tax rates fell from 8.1 percent to 7.1 percent for the lowest quintile, from 15.6 percent to 15.1 for the next lowest, from 19.8 percent to 19.4 percent for the middle, from 22.9 percent to 22.1 percent for the next highest, and from 27.6 percent to 26.3 percent for the highest. There was a greater drop in marginal or last dollar tax rates, from 41.2 percent to 33.8 percent, for the highest quintile, and Feldstein (1995) feels that this change was very important in increasing labor supply and wage income in the highest quintile, but others are skeptical not about the direction but the extent of Feldstein's claim.

28. For a more detailed discussion, see Edward Gramlich and Mark Long, "Growing Income Inequality: Roots and Remedies," Future of the Public Sector Brief #3, The Urban Institute Press, June 1996.

29. See Frank Sammartino and Richard Kasten on the Congressional Budget Office estimates of the effective federal tax rate based on a tax simulation model in The Changing Distribution of Federal Taxes: 1975–1990 (CBO Report, 1997) and unpublished estimates.

30. Data from Rebecca Blank, "U.S. Labor Market and Prospects for Low-Wage Entry Jobs," in Demetra Smith Nightingale and Robert H. Haveman, The Work Alternative: Welfare Reform and the Realities of the Job Market, The Urban Institute Press, Washington, DC, 1995. Table 3-4. Also, similar shifts in earnings were found by Steven J. Davis, "Relative Wage Shifts and Households Consumption in the 1980s," Jobs and Capital, Winter 1997. He found that wages for men without a high school diploma fell by about 10 percent between 1980 and 1990, and that wages for men with a college education increased by over 10 percent during the same period. Davis, however, expands the discussion by illustrating wage changes by age group (birth cohort) and also relative household consumption by education level. He finds that the largest wage gaps by earning level occur for the youngest workers, and that the consumption data support the overall wage gap by education level that is illustrated by the income data. See also Stacy Poulos and Demetra Smith Nightingale, "The Aging Baby Boom: Implications for Employment and Training Programs," 1997, prepared for the U.S. Department of Labor, ETA. Exhibit II.11, p. 25, compares education and income levels of baby boomers and their parents and supports the increasing importance of education.

31. See Murray F. Foss, Shiftwork, Capital Hours, and Productivity Change, Boston: Kluwer Academic Publishers, 1997, p. 34.

32. See The Conference Board, "Heavy Computer Users Show Biggest Productivity Gains in Manufacturing," press release from Dec. 24, 1997.

33. See Fredric L. Pryor and David Schaffer, "Wages and the University Educated: A Paradox Resolved," Monthly Labor Review, U.S. Department of Labor, July 1997.

34. See Robert I. Lerman, "The Future of Work and Implications for Training Policy," keynote speech for the TEC National Council, Learning for Life Conference, September 4, 1996 (available from author), and "Meritocracy Without Rising Inequality," Series on Economic Restructuring and the Job Market, No. 2, September, 1997, Washington, DC: The Urban Institute.

35. While much work has been done in this area and there is still some dispute, the following articles are some examples of evidence on the role of technology in increasing the premium on education. See, for example, (1) John Bound and George Johnson, "Changes in the Structure of Wages in the 1980s: An Evaluation of Alternative Explanations," American Economic Review, June 1992, vol. 82, pp. 371–392, or (2) "Technology and the Wage Structure" by Steven G. Allen (1997), Working Paper, or (3) Robert Baldwin and Glen Cain, "Shifts in U.S. Relative Wages: The Role of Trade, Technology, and Factor Endowments" (1997), Institute for Research on Poverty Discussion Paper #11.

36. See Frank Levy and Richard J. Murnane, "U.S. Earnings Levels and Earnings Inequality: A Review of Recent Trends and Proposed Explanations," *Journal of Economic Literature* #0:1333-1381 (September 1992).

37. Based on data from the Bureau of Labor Statistics, March Current Population Survey. The civilian labor force increased from 100,873 in January of 1978 to 137,493 in January of 1998 (numbers in thousands).

38. A further bit of evidence dispels the notion that international competition is a primary cause of growing inequality here. If it were the cause, we might expect to see growing inequality in pay across all work. But overall, taking all hours of work of all workers together, inequality in *wages per hour* worked has hardly changed in the most recent decade. That is, much of the growth in inequality more recently has been reflected in changes in hours worked rather than pay per hour. This statistic does not dispute growth in inequality in wages per hour in the prior decade or continuing growth in inequality among workers and families. See Robert I. Lerman, "Reassessing Trends in U.S. Earnings Inequality," *Monthly Labor Review*, December 1997, pp. 17–25.

39. For a substantially richer and more detailed discussion of the issues dealt with in this section, see Daniel P. McMurrer and Isabel V. Sawhill, *Getting Ahead: Economic and Social Mobility in America* (Washington, DC: Urban Institute Press, 1998).

40. This is usually measured by comparing the positions of father and son based on either income or occupation (both of which have their flaws).

41. Data from the Bureau of Labor Statistics, Current Population Survey, annual unemployment rates for 1975–1997 based on average of monthly reports.

1975	8.5	1980	7.2	1985	7.2	1990	5.6	1995	5.6
1976	7.7	1981	7.6	1986	7.0	1991	6.9	1996	5.4
1977	7.1	1982	9.7	1987	6.2	1992	7.5	1997	5.0
1978	6.1	1983	9.6	1988	5.5	1993	6.9		
1979	5.9	1984	7.5	1989	5.3	1994	6.1		

42. Whether these patterns of long upswings and lower unemployment rates will continue on a more permanent basis is, of course, as yet uncertain.

43. *Economic Report of the President, 1997.*

44. See data on unemployment trends for 1975–1997 in footnote number 41.

45. U.S. labor force participation rates from 1979 to 1992 show an increase for women from 57.5 to 66.7 and a decrease for men from 86.2 to 83.7. This represents the rate across all education levels; however, the overall trend holds even within particular education levels. See Rebecca Blank, "U.S. Labor Market and Prospects for Low-Wage Entry Jobs," in Demetra Smith Nightingale and Robert H. Haveman (eds.), *The Work Alternative: Welfare Reform and the Realities of the Job Market*, The Urban Institute Press, Washington, DC, 1995.

46. See Center for Study of Social Policy and Philadelphia Children's Network, *Causes and Consequences of Black Male Joblessness*, monograph, 1994.

47. For a longer discussion of this issue see Rebecca Blank, "U.S. Labor Market and Prospects for Low-Wage Entry Jobs," in Demetra Smith Nightingale and Robert H. Haveman (eds.), *The Work Alternative: Welfare Reform and the Realities of the Job Market*, The Urban Institute Press, Washington, DC, 1995.

48. John C. Weicher, "The Distribution of Wealth: Increasing Inequality?" American Enterprise Institute, August 1996.

49. See Edward N. Wolfe, *Top Heavy: A Study of the Increasing Inequality of Wealth in America*, A Twentieth Century Fund Report, New York, 1995.

50. According to the Federal Reserve Board the percentage of wealth attributable to housing by family income is as follows: Less than $10,000—90.3 percent, $10,000 to $24,999—68.5 percent, $25,000 to $49,999—52 percent, $50,000 to $99,999—40.5 percent, and $100,000+—17 percent. The Federal Reserve Board also claims that if you consider Social Security and pension wealth as a percentage of total net worth, they make a very large, even primary source of wealth for many families.

51. Data on homeownership rates from the U.S. Census Bureau, *Housing Vacancy Survey—Annual 1997*, show that the homeownership rates for the United States increased from 63.9 percent in 1990 to 64.7 percent in 1995 and 65.7 percent in 1997.

52. In 1997 there were 3,973,000 people subsidized through section 8 housing vouchers and 2,859,000 people in public housing (based on data from HUD). In addition, the FY98 budget for HUD shows that there are many new but small initiatives for ownership, including $50 million more for homeownership zones and incentives for first-time homebuyers. Also 1996 had the largest increase in homeownership rates in 30 years because of the strong economy, low inflation, and innovative programs.

53. The number of private pension plans increased from 311,000 in 1975 to 733,000 in 1987 and then declined to 702,097 in 1993. For specific data on this and related trends see *EBRI Databook on Employee Benefits*, 1997.

54. Based on data from Susan Grad, *Income of the Population 55 or Older*, and SSA, *Income of the Aged Chartbook*, 1994. In addition, the *EBRI Databook on Employee Benefits*, 1997, shows that pensions and annuities accounted for 19.7 percent of the elderly's income on average, but that only half of that was from private pensions. They also found that 42.9 percent of the elderly's income came from Social Security in 1996. This last calculation excludes Medicare as a source of income.

55. Based on Health and Retirement Survey data (HRS). See James F. Moore and Olivia S. Mitchell, "Projected Retirement Wealth and Savings Adequacy in the Health and Retirement Study." For additional data on the wealth of elderly Americans see *Income of the Population over 55*, Social Security Administration, 1994.

56. Survey conducted and reported by Public Agenda, *Miles to Go: A Status Report on Americans' Plans for Retirement*, New York: Public Agenda, 1987, p. 10.

57. Data on money income from the *Statistical Abstract of the United States*, 1997. Based on 1995 median money income of persons with income. Data on financial and housing assets from the U.S. Census Bureau, *Asset Ownership of Households*, 1993. Based on median net worth.

58. Based on data for 1997 from the U.S. Bureau of the Census, Current Population Survey, March Supplement, "Fourth Quarter 1997 U.S. Housing Market Conditions."

59. See James P. Smith, "The Changing Economic Circumstances of the Elderly: Income, Wealth and Social Security." Center for Policy Research, Policy Brief #8, 1997. Based on data from the Health and Retirement Survey for people aged 51–61).

Chapter Three

FAMILY TRANSFORMATIONS

If it is true that all thought begins with remembrance, it is also true that no remembrance remains secure until it is condensed and distilled into a framework of conceptual notions within which it can further exercise itself.

—Hannah Arendt

Despite the important economic changes chronicled in preceding chapters, the last half of the twentieth century will probably be remembered as a time of even more profound changes for America's families. Family life and the wider market economy are closely intertwined. People's opportunities are powerfully affected by the families in which they live. We have already discussed how changes in family structure have added to growing income inequality since mid-century. We now focus in more depth on the family—including how we, as a people, have dramatically altered our patterns of consumption and leisure over our life spans.

Family issues are among the most difficult for government because, as an institution, the family takes priority over the state. The complication is that government really cannot avoid addressing "family" issues. Most of its benefit and tax programs are linked to the income and well-being of the family rather than the isolated individual. But what is today's family? Many programs are still built around yesterday's images of family—women who stayed at home, men who were sole breadwinners for their wives and children, children who were raised in two-parent families, and people who turned poor and frail at 62 or 65 or died even before reaching their 60s. These stereotypes grew out of the industrial order of 50 to 100 years ago. Yet they still control much of government policy. The rapid evolution of family life since World War II demands that we reconsider whether policies built around these stereotypes allow us to achieve the government we deserve.

We examine these various transformations in five overlapping areas: (1) marriage and other sharing arrangements, (2) women, work, and parenting, (3) men, work, and parenting, (4) elderly Americans and retirement, and (5) changing risks for children. While we sometimes discuss what is happening to individuals separately, depending upon their gender and age, most changes cannot help but affect all members of their extended families.

MARRIAGE AND OTHER SHARING ARRANGEMENTS

Individuals combine together in households for many reasons, almost all of which have to do with sharing. Even from a narrow economic perspective, there are clear advantages from the economies of scale that come when individuals share living space, television sets, cars, and cooking (among other household chores). People reap the benefits of such sharing in many social settings—schools, dorms, nursing homes, retirement communities, group houses, clubs, churches, shared apartments, and, of course, the family home. A major factor affecting the evolution of modern family life is the reduction in the direct economic dependence of women, the elderly, and young adults on other individuals. This has not only reduced the amount of sharing but has also made ways of sharing more complex.

Marriage is more delayed and more unstable. In the past few decades patterns of marriage have changed as people delay their first marriages, are more likely to get a divorce, and are less likely to remarry if they do divorce. After marrying unusually young at mid-century, young men and women have returned to and surpassed the average age of marriage 100 years ago.[1] But unmarried young adults are far less likely than they used to be to wait until they are married before leaving their parental home.

Many live alone or with housemates. But increasing numbers of Americans also live in marriage-type relationships. In 1960 and 1970, 2 percent of unmarried adults lived in such relationships. By 1990, almost 8 percent of unmarried men and 6–7 percent of unmarried women were cohabiting. For men and women in the 25- to 34-year-old group the proportions are much higher (13 percent for men and 16 percent for women).[2] It is also becoming more and more common for older adults, including elderly widows and widowers, to live together without being married.

The delay in marriage and the growth in cohabitation, as well as the aging of the large cohort of baby boomers (who have now hit middle age, when divorce is less prevalent) has led to a leveling off of the divorce rate since the mid-1980s. This does not translate into greater marital stability, however. The divorce rate (annual divorces per 1,000 married women) grew dramatically after 1960, from about 25 percent for couples who married in the 1930s to over 50 percent for couples who married in the mid-1980s.[3] The remarriage rate is also falling. In the early 1970s, about 20 percent of divorced men and 12.3 percent of divorced women remarried. By the early 1990s these rates had fallen to about 10.5 percent and 7.6 percent, respectively.[4]

Marriage is often discouraged by government. The increase in living with others in a variety of nonmarriage arrangements has been influenced partly by changes in societal mores. At the same time, government policy has been aiding and abetting the shift. In addition to taking advantage of the economies of scale of group living, cohabitation is a way to avoid large marriage penalties within the tax and public benefit systems.

These large incentives derive primarily from the way such systems treat household income. For example, as income rises in a married household—as opposed to almost all other living arrangements among adults—the income of one adult gets added to the income of the other adult in determining benefit eligibility and tax liability. Take a woman with two children earning $10,000 in 1998—typical of the situation into which welfare reform is pushing former welfare recipients. Although she is not eligible for cash welfare, such as Temporary Assistance for Needy Families (the TANF that replaced Aid to Families with Dependent Children, AFDC), she still is eligible for food stamps, Medicaid, and the earned income tax credit. If she marries someone earning $15,000, however, she (and therefore they) will lose her food stamps, her Medicaid support, and most of her earned income tax credit, at the same time as their total federal and state income tax burdens will rise. As a result of the loss of these benefits, their combined income will fall by almost 25 percent.[5] These large marriage penalties don't apply only to the poor. In the case of government retirement programs for the military or the foreign service, widows or widowers who remarry similarly see their retirement benefits fall or even disappear.

It is important to recognize what is being done here and why. Government effectively taxes the gains from the economies of scale achieved by married couples. It treats them as if they had income over and above what they would have when considered as single individuals. But it only taxes economies of scale when they are backed up by marital commitments, not other sharing arrangements. To complicate matters, it also provides marriage bonuses to many middle- and upper-income couples if their income is fairly unevenly split—so not everyone is unhappy with the existing system.

WOMEN, WORK, AND PARENTING

In 1996, one-quarter of all children lived only with their mothers. In addition to marrying later, divorcing more, and remarrying less, women are increasingly spending at least part of their parenting lives as single mothers. Higher proportions of women are also starting their parenting lives as single mothers. One-third of all births in the United States were to unmarried women in 1996 (up from only 4 percent in 1940).[6] This trend reflects both the decline in the fertility rate among married women and the modestly rising fertility rate among unmarried women. The level of single parenthood was even higher for black women, with 70 percent of black babies born to single mothers by 1994.[7] It is important to note that more than 25 percent of births to unmarried women were to households where both parents were present at least temporarily, even though unmarried.[8] And many single-parent households combine living arrangements with adults other than spouses, including living with grandparents, parents, boyfriends, girlfriends, and adult siblings. Even so, the presumption that mothers do not have to work outside the home because others will support them and their children is long gone.

The working woman has changed society's expectations and public policy. Women working for pay has become the prevailing expectation in most families and a pervasive fact of life. Although the movement for greater equality for women extends back to the earliest years of our nation, women's lives and life prospects, especially with respect to work, have changed profoundly since the 1950s. Women are now more likely to work in the marketplace full-time rather than part-time, as well as to have fewer breaks in their employment to raise children.[9] In addition to the benefits of additional life choices, this increased attachment to the workforce and longer work history has given modern women better prospects for retirement income than women of earlier generations (especially Social Security based on their own work record). This change in norms has accelerated for women of the baby boom generation and has been even more striking for married women with children than for women overall.

These new expectations for women's employment are held by men and women alike, and are illustrated by responses to a national survey on motherhood and women's work. In 1975 less than half of the respondents felt that working mothers could establish warm relationships with their children. By 1995 the share was up to 70 percent.[10]

Pre-1975 data are not available, but, if they were, we would almost certainly see even more dramatic changes on this question as compared to the 1950s.

Such changing attitudes—a mix of desires for personal fulfillment, economic necessity, and ever higher consumption levels—meant that by 1990 almost three-fourths of married mothers with school-aged children worked outside the home, compared to less than one-third of such mothers in the early 1950s. In the past three decades or so the change for wives with preschool children has been even more dramatic. The proportion of married mothers with children under 6 years of age and working rose over threefold between 1960 and 1995 (from 18.6 to 61.7 percent).[11] In fact, 55 percent of women today return to work within the first year after their child is born.[12] This shift to the workforce has increased the strain on women to balance careers and families and added to the demand for child care.

These changing attitudes have also had profound effects on policy. The demand for work requirements in welfare policy would have been unthinkable in a society expecting women to stay at home with their children. Similarly, the relatively new Earned Income Tax Credit (EITC)—first established in 1975 but increased several times since then—is available to parents and guardians only if they have earnings from work. These changes together are strong evidence of the growing expectation in America that mothers, even of very young children, will work outside the home.

Although women's opportunities have expanded, they are still more likely than men to give up career opportunities in order to spend time with their children. The movement into the paid workforce by women, which was brought on by both economic and social transformations, has been accompanied by other social changes in women's lives, including higher levels of education, career development, and the smaller size and later timing of their families. Women have closed much of the gender gap in formal educational attainment and have reduced occupational segregation by gaining professional training in fields once closed to women. College and advanced training are now as much a part of the life experience for women as for men, which helps to expand their horizons for employment and independent life choices.[13] While occupational segregation by gender has not been eradicated, the gap is closing. In 1960, for example, only 6 percent of new medical school graduates, 2 percent of new law school graduates, 4 percent of new business graduates, and virtually no dentists or engineers were women. Now women account for between 26 percent and 41 percent of graduates in law, business, medicine, and dentistry, although still few engineers.[14] These trends in careers and training for women, especially within the context of a workforce that is demanding more time and higher levels of skill, explain, in part, the decrease in income inequality by gender and other recent gains for women in the workforce. In 1995 women earned about 75 percent of what men earned in an average week, up from 62 percent in 1970.[15] Of course, not all the narrowing of the income gap is due to gains in earnings for women. Some portion of the gap results from the decline in male earnings. As we have already seen, the gains from earnings have not been evenly distributed, and for those without a college education, women's incomes are little different from 20 years ago, while men without college have seen declining wages.[16]

Hence, the economic roles of men and women are converging. But women are still in a weaker economic position in establishing and maintaining paid careers—a weakness that now has somewhat less to do with workplace discrimination and more to do with women continuing to have greater obligations for child-rearing.[17] Even though mothers are less likely than before to take time out of the labor force to raise their children, raising children still constrains the hours available for their jobs. One parent still needs to be available when children are sick or during the winter and long summer breaks children have from school. Typically, that parent is the mother. Balancing children and careers is a special problem for single-parent households, usually headed by women. In addition, women nearing retirement age spend roughly twice as much time as men caring for grandchildren as well as for parents (or in-laws).[18] Yet the additional flexibility at work required to care for both young and elderly dependents can inhibit advancement in a number of jobs. The women with absolutely the fewest choices and support in these situations, of course, are single and divorced mothers with little education.

MEN, WORK, AND PARENTING[19]

Just as expectations for mothers have changed, so, too, have expectations grown for fathers to take an active role not only in the financial support but also in the lives of their children. The research on fatherhood has increasingly focused on the multiple roles that fathers play within families, and the relative importance of these roles across cultures and history. The different roles of fathers must be viewed within the overall system of the family. This highlights both the direct interactions and indirect influences of fathers on children. The expectation that a man should mainly work and be the sole source of income for his family—an expectation that grew especially out of the industrial order—is no longer the norm. Fathers are being forced to establish new roles for themselves as co-earners, as co-parents, and, increasingly, as nonresident parents.

The economic positions of men and women are inextricably intertwined. What is happening to women in the world of work and in the family has strong implications for what is happening to men. As women entered the labor force in increasing numbers, men's increases in earnings slowed down. Women's earnings had been lower than men's, partly because of discrimination and partly because of typically lower pay in fields (teaching, nursing) where women represented above-average shares of the workforce. The gap between women's and men's earnings eventually began to narrow, reinforced by laws enacted to reduce workplace bias. It is worth repeating how some of these gains and losses were distributed. As we have seen, the narrowing of the total wage gap occurred in no small part through declining wages for low-skilled men, increasing wage rates mainly for higher-skilled women, and more hours of work for women in general. As more women have entered the workplace it has become easier for men to stay out of the labor force longer after a layoff, cut back on hours of work, or retire earlier—precisely because there are more earnings available from a spouse, and in some cases because the economic return from their own work has fallen below worthwhile levels.

Fathers' roles within the family are changing. Just as women are having to reconcile their roles as working women with the nurturing roles of their mothers, men today are also having to reconcile the "good provider" model of their fathers' generation with the new "nurturer" model required by today's society. Men are making progress in increasing the nurturing part of their fathering role in both absolute terms and in proportion to mothers.[20] In two-earner families, for example, even though child raising is still not shared equally between parents, almost one-quarter of employed mothers report that the father is the primary caregiver for children under five years old.[21] There are also encouraging signs of a modest increase in fathers' engagement with and accessibility to their children.[22] Recent estimates suggest that fathers spend on average 1.9 hours per weekday and 6.5 hours on Sunday in direct engagement with their children. Accompanying the shift in fathers' involvement in caretaking, employers are increasingly recognizing that issues related to flexible hours of work and pro-family work environments are not women's issues but parents' issues. Government policies, such as the 1993 Family and Medical Leave Act, are also extending parental rights to fathers and mothers alike.

While fathers' roles are changing, breadwinning is still an important part of many fathers' roles within their families.[23] It may also be closely tied to their own expectations for themselves. Studies of families during the Great Depression found that a father's interaction with his children was very closely tied to his perceived success in providing financial support for his family. More recent family studies have found that the same is true today.[24] This suggests that men's feelings about fathering are still very sensitive to changing economic forces in the workplace and to shifts in public policy related to employment and income.

Public policy is not currently well-designed to deal with this situation. The structure of income assistance for low-income families is an example that has already been noted but bears reemphasis. An employed man who marries an actual or potential welfare-participating woman with children reduces her income assistance, raises their joint taxes, and reduces the net economic prospects of the family remarkably—by the very act of marriage. "Better to avoid marriage, avoid regular work, or get a divorce," the government effectively pronounces to potential and actual low-income fathers. Thus, many fathers today have not only lost the role of sole breadwinner, they may not even *help* in the breadwinning task to the extent that their marriage into a family reduces, rather than increases, total economic resources.

Nonresident fathers are having to meet new demands for contact with and financial support for their children. While there has been a shift in court opinions in custody decisions in the past few decades, the majority of children in single parent families still live with their mother. And since about half of all American children spend at least part of their time growing up in a single-parent home,[25] this means that many fathers (and some mothers) are faced with the problem of being nonresident parents. A large proportion of fathers currently do little active parenting of their nonresident children, with what little contact they may initially have declining over time.[26]

Some structural barriers for fathers are created specifically by the marital conflict of a divorce. A negative relationship between divorcing parents can have direct negative effects for children, can directly influence fathers' parenting attitudes, and can result in the mother acting as a gatekeeper for the child.[27] Recognizing the growing importance of the interaction between parents, some courts are experimenting with mandatory parenting classes for divorcing parents as a way to help resolve their conflicts for the sake of their children.

Beyond the varying levels of direct interaction between nonresident fathers and their children, economic support (or lack thereof) is one way that noncustodial parents can influence their children's development.[28] What is happening to nonresident fathers again shows a strong link between fathering and the breadwinning role. Fatherhood programs have found, for example, that the more involved nonresidential fathers are with their children, the more likely they are to have a job, get a job, or remain employed.[29] While the direction of causation is unknown, the connection between financial security and father-child relationships is evident.

Child support awards, which are designed to ensure that both parents contribute to the economic support of a child, are frequently not made, and when made are frequently not paid in full. For mothers who are awarded child support, slightly under half receive the full amount, and one-quarter do not receive anything at all.[30] Receiving child support is especially difficult for never-married mothers because only about 33–40 percent of nonmarital births have paternity established.[31]

Another government policy that may foster irresponsible fathering actually encourages unmarried fathers to avoid paying any official child support in some situations because the majority of these payments go to the government. If a mother or her children receive welfare and other means-tested income assistance, for example, only a small proportion of any formal child support paid by the children's father actually goes toward increasing the mother's spendable income. The rest is used to offset the cost of the welfare benefits, leaving little net benefit to the family. If, in contrast, a father provides informal support, more of his contributions go directly to the mother and children. In either case, fathers who do not pay child support are less likely to be involved in their children's lives than the fathers who are paying at least some support. The quantitative impact of these public policies is unclear. What is clear is that government is sending plain signals to absent parents not to meet their legal financial responsibilities for their children.

ELDERLY AMERICANS AND RETIREMENT

Growing life expectancy and earlier retirement have dramatically changed the way we allocate work, responsibility, and leisure across our life spans. In 1940, the average life expectancies for men and women reaching age 65 were, respectively, 11.9 and 13.4 years. And many did not live to age 65. By 1996 those life expectancies had risen to 15.6 and 19.2 years and are projected to rise to 17.5 and 20.9 by 2040.[32] Even these projections may be low. The Japanese, among others, have already attained the longer life expectancy we are projecting for ourselves several decades into the future.[33]

Americans now spend, on average, one-third of their adult lives in retirement. Along with living longer, Americans are retiring earlier. Between 1950 and 1994, the average age at which men began to draw Social Security benefits fell by five years, from just under 69 to just under 64.[34] Between the end of the last century and today, the proportion of American men over the age of 64 who have retired has increased from 25 percent to 80 percent.[35] Elderly persons today spend close to a decade more in retirement than when Social Security first began. The surviving spouse of a typical married couple retiring today can be expected to receive Social Security benefits for about one-quarter of a century.

At the same time as the retirement period has been getting longer, Social Security benefits have been rising. Since World War II, the dribble of payments from the Social Security system has turned into a swelling flow of benefits to people who otherwise would never have been able to consider retirement.

Most of us now expect to spend a significant share of our adulthood in retirement, living off our retirement incomes. But this retirement expectation is a twentieth century phenomenon that has been built up by actions affecting the private as well as the public sector. The federal government gave a boost to private pension accumulation when, in holding down wage demands during World War II, it offered very favorable treatment to employers' retirement benefit contributions. The tax advantage of pension plans also rose over time as tax rates on cash compensation increased.

Retirement expectations have been further raised by a vast range of strong private and public incentives for earlier retirement. These include, among others, (1) seniority pay scales that make some older workers more costly to employ than younger workers; (2) health insurance costs that are higher for older workers than for younger workers paid the same cash wage; (3) traditional pension design, which bases benefits on years of work and highest wages received within the firm, making an additional year worked by an older worker much more costly to the pension plan than a year worked by a younger worker at the same cash wage; (4) designated retirement ages in Social Security and elsewhere that are independent of life expectancies; (5) "earnings" tests in Social Security that hint, sometimes incorrectly, that work will substantially reduce Social Security benefits; and (6) benefit formulas in Social Security that provide almost no additional lifetime benefit for working longer and contributing substantially more taxes both to Social Security and to the general revenues of government. The expectation of earlier and earlier retirement has been built into an enormous range of public and private institutions and arrangements. These have evolved and reinforced each other for over half a century.

The consumption levels for tomorrow's elderly are scheduled to rise much faster than for the population, further promoting a low national savings rate. Government policy toward the elderly was originally designed to raise their typically very low standards of living. One of the most remarkable successes of social policy in the industrial world has been the removal of many elderly from poverty (including generous provision of medical care). In 1960–61, 70-year-olds in the United States consumed on average about 97 percent of what was consumed by 20-year-olds, 71 percent of the consumption of 30-year-olds, and 64 percent of the consumption of 40-year-olds. By 1987–90, these proportions had risen to 164 percent, 118 percent, and 94 percent (figure 3.1). Much of this growth is due to rising medical care service use and costs. Under existing government policy, consumption by the typical elderly and near-elderly continues to rise much faster than for the rest of the population.

Accounting for consumption patterns by age in this way sends a new message about why the U.S. national savings rate is low. The young may not be saving less of their income from work and assets than previous generations. Rather, the elderly and near-elderly are consuming increasingly more relative to their incomes from those same sources.[36] Thus, the resulting large cash transfers from the non-elderly to the elderly and near-elderly in the form of pension and health benefits are at least partly responsible for the lower personal savings rate, which has dropped from 8 percent in the early postwar period to around 5 percent today.

Some of the public financial support of the elderly is unrelated to their needs. One of the implications of longer lives in retirement and higher levels of support and consumption is that larger shares of society's total income are increasingly directed to its members when

Figure 3.1 ANNUAL CONSUMPTION FOR THE ELDERLY AND YOUNG

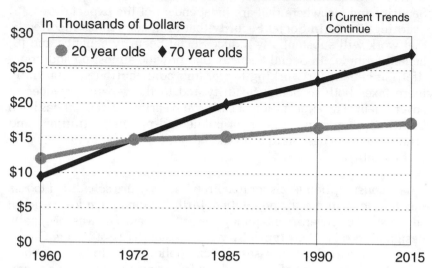

Source: Based on data from *Understanding the Postwar Decline in U.S. Saving: A Cohort Analysis*, by J. Gokhale, L. Kotlikoff, and J. Sabelhaus. NBER Working Paper #5571, May 1996. Data shown are for males in 1960–1961, 1972–1973, 1984–1986, and 1987–1990. Data after 1990 simply extrapolate current trends, and do not rely on programmatic data.

they are older, rather than when they are young, or when they are raising children. But the implications extend much further. Increasing resources to ourselves when older gives us greater independence from those who are younger. Few would argue that this is a negative development. But it has fostered much greater separation of parents from their adult children, and grandparents from their grandchildren, leaving the oldest elderly more vulnerable when they need the care of others. Meanwhile, lower birth rates are reducing the numbers of children and grandchildren providing care.[37]

At the same time as the elderly and near-elderly as a group are receiving increasing fractions of the nation's income, our public and private retirement systems leave a significant number of the very old much poorer than the rest of the population. Elderly poverty is concentrated among the very old, especially among widowed women.[38] This is partly because our retirement benefits increase from one generation to the next and partly because retirement benefits on net are loaded more into early retirement years rather than the later years when incapacity and widowhood are more likely.

To be more specific, Social Security benefits are adjusted only for inflation after retirement. But each new generation of retirees starts with higher real benefits than previous generations because pre-retirement accumulations of Social Security benefits grow with average wages. And wages outstrip prices unless the economy is totally stagnant. Thus, those retiring twenty years from now at age 65 will receive annual benefits 23 percent higher than retirees today.[39] In the case of private pensions, payments often are not even adjusted for inflation, in which case their real annual value can fall by one-half or more between a person's retirement at 65 and 20 years later when he or she is 85. Finally, many public and private pension plans have benefit levels that fall significantly when one spouse dies. All these factors together lead to substantially higher poverty rates and lower relative incomes among the very old than among the elderly as a group.

The number of workers transferring resources to the elderly and near elderly will soon fall dramatically relative to the number of elderly and near-elderly recipients. The huge rise in fertility in the 1946–1965 period, when combined with the abruptly dropping birth rates in the periods both before and after, has led to a unique age structure for the population today (figure 3.2). The baby boom is one of the most dramatic demographic events in the history of the United States. Just as one can trace a fish being digested by a snake, one can follow the impact of the baby boom generation on American society. In the 1950s and 1960s the baby boom meant unusually large expenditures for public schooling. By the mid-1960s higher education expenditures were exploding. By the early 1970s housing demand was growing dramatically. Today baby boomers are in their high earning years and, as a consequence, swelling pension plan deposits. Beginning about the year 2008 (when the first of the baby boomers turn 62), retirement costs for Social Security and withdrawals from private pension plans will begin to grow rapidly.

Under current retirement age standards, by the time most baby boomers have left the workforce (about 2030), the number of workers in the economy relative to beneficiaries will fall from a ratio of about 3 to 1 today to 2 to 1. It will stay there or below unless fertility rates rise (figure 3.3). Social Security taxes will need to rise 50 percent by 2030 if the current ratio of benefits to wages is to be maintained. Alternatively, benefits must drop by more than 30 percent if today's tax rate is to support cash transfers from the young to the elderly and near-elderly in 2030. The situation is even worse for health benefits, which are affected by all the same forces—the drop in workers relative

Figure 3.2 BABY BUST, BABY BOOM, BABY BUST

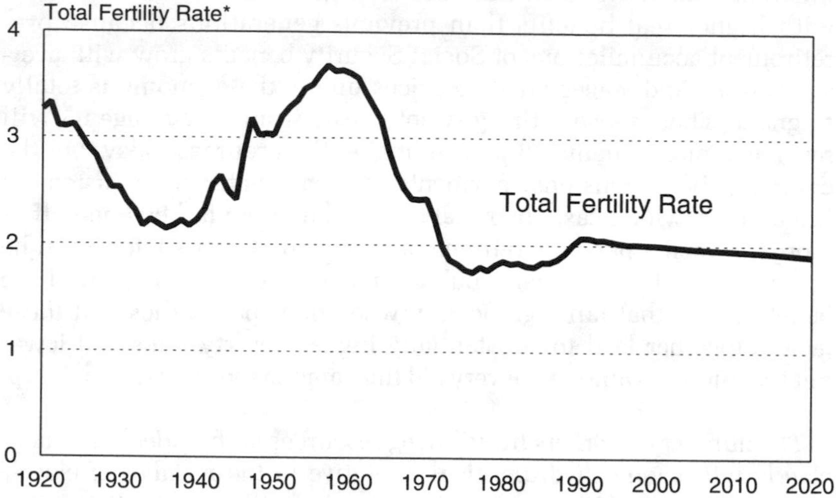

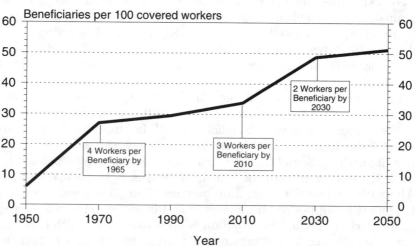

Source: Historical data from the Social Security Administration, Office of the Actuary
(1992) and the annual report of the Board of Trustees of the OASDI Trust Funds (1997).
*The total fertility rate for any year is the average number of children who would be
born to a woman in her lifetime, if she were to experience the birth rates by age,
observed or assumed, for the selected year, and if she were to survive the entire child-
bearing period.

Figure 3.3 NUMBER OF SOCIAL SECURITY BENEFICIARIES PER WORKER
          GROWS

Source: Based on data from the Social Security Administration, Office of the Actuary
(1997).

to beneficiaries and longer life spans—but also by the inability of government to contain spiraling costs.[40]

CHANGING RISKS FOR CHILDREN

Children have been the most vulnerable to the side effects of our changing economic and social conditions. Whatever the overall gains for society, many children have not fared well on fronts that range from rising poverty rates and decaying inner cities to victimization and violence. Increasing rates of divorce, out-of-wedlock birth, and the absence of fathers have reduced the percentage of time children spend with parents. These trends increase risks to children's healthy development. Risk does not guarantee detriment, of course, because children are resilient and because both individuals and society compensate in other ways. But the accumulation of risks does increase the possibility of negative outcomes. Only by facing up to these risks for children—including those that derive from economic and social developments that on their own might be positive—can we better channel government policy toward meeting the needs of the young.

Children's economic poverty is increasing, especially relative to older generations. The increasing proportions of economically vulnerable one-parent families, combined with the increased generosity of entitlement programs for the elderly, have drastically changed the age distribution of the poor. Over the past 25 years, the proportion of children who are poor has risen by 35 percent while the proportion of elderly persons in poverty has dropped by almost 50 percent.[41]

Children also represent a disproportionate percentage of America's poor overall.[42] While 30 years ago 15 percent of children under age 18 were poor, by 1996 that share was 20.5 percent, even after a very long national economic expansion.[43] Over the same period the poverty rate for the population as a whole fluctuated between 11 percent and 15 percent. The story is even worse for particular groups of children. Poverty rates for children under 6 are about 25 percent, and the poverty rate for children with parents under 30 is around 40 percent.[44]

Children also make up a disproportionate percentage of welfare recipients, with 7.7 million children receiving welfare in early 1997.[45] Under the welfare reforms implemented by many states following the federal welfare reform legislation passed in 1996, many families have been removed from one or more sources of welfare, but not from all income assistance.[46]

The ultimate impact of these threats to children, and more broadly to society, has yet to be fully realized. The risks that children who grow up poor, without two parents, or on welfare today could develop into negative outcomes 10–20 years from now when they reach young adulthood, 20–30 years from now when they are raising their own children, or 30–40 years from now when they are older workers. If large fractions of our children have reduced opportunities, this fact alone throws a damper on prospects of future economic growth. When risks to children are also disproportionately placed on low-income and minority households, it may have a long-run impact on our ability to reduce inequality, including inequality among races. Put another way, generating greater equality in outcomes among adults requires, more than anything else, greater equality in opportunity among youth, and fewer risks among those youth who are most vulnerable.

Children's poverty extends beyond economics. The economic vulnerability of single-parent families is associated with other risks for children, including the effects of family disruption. Whether the mother is divorced or never married, children have a harder time developing a strong attachment to their fathers if they live elsewhere.[47] As we noted earlier, many absent fathers have little to do with their children. While the presence of a father by no means guarantees a more favorable outcome, there is still little doubt that the absence of one parent deprives children of crucial attachments and guidance. Overall, the many studies in this area have found that paternal involvement has many positive consequences for children in cognitive and social competencies.[48] The absence of a strong, positive father also may rob boys of a role model as they grow up and define their own social roles and rob girls of a model for finding nurturing spouses of their own.

One consequence of many of these factors—absent fathers, increases in maternal employment, single-parent families, and the inadequacy of alternative support systems—is that increasing proportions of school-aged children are left unsupervised on a regular basis.[49] Between 2.5 million and 7 million children are left on their own after school, according to national estimates. Local estimates indicate that 20 percent to 70 percent of children are in self-care. (The wide range of estimates at both the national and local levels may be explained, at least in part, by the tendency of parents to underreport self-care because they don't like to admit that their children are left by themselves.[50]) We may debate which factors are dominant, but the basic facts of self-care by children remain.

Being left alone while parents work has many possible adverse consequences for children. Most children are spending increasing amounts of time on their own watching television.[51] TV is not necessarily bad in itself. But excessive TV viewing has been documented to have negative effects on children, especially when there is no parental monitoring of program content. Certainly there can be more productive uses of much of their time. In addition, many children left alone live in neighborhoods that are not safe and where the social outlets often include gangs and drugs. Children in bad neighborhoods are harmed even more than other children by lack of supervision, and single parents who have to work are not able to fill that gap.

Crime affects many children's lives. Among the most disturbing of all statistics is the rate of crime by and against children. These patterns are at least partly associated with lack of supervision in after-school hours, because most of the crime by youth as well as the victimization of youth happens between the hours of 2 p.m. and 7 p.m. on school days.[52] Some cities are experimenting with curfews as a way to curb juvenile crime, but curfews will do little good before 10 p.m., when most are enforced. The arrest rate for 15- to 20-year-olds is almost four times as high as for those over 25 years of age.[53] In addition, juveniles aged 12–17 are nearly three times as likely as adults to be the victims of violent crimes.[54] Finally, the number of reported cases of child abuse has been rising significantly. Whether there are more cases or simply more reported cases does not make such statistics any less alarming for the overall well-being of children.

The demands on schools have increased, and schools are still not institutionally prepared to meet those demands. Schools increasingly are required to meet the diverse and changing educational and developmental needs of children from different backgrounds. These changing needs are partly the consequences of family changes such as divorce, single parenthood, and poverty at different stages in a child's development.

Society has been slow to adapt its educational structure to the new challenges. Currently children spend almost 90 percent of their total time, and the majority of their waking hours, in out-of-school activities.[55] This is at least in part because school schedules are still based on 6-hour days and 180-day years. This schedule may have been appropriate for an agrarian society but it does not fit the needs of many of today's families. There is even some evidence that part of the gap in educational achievement among those in different economic and social classes is due to differential access to out-of-school time in supervised enrichment and extracurricular activities, with the poor remaining at a substantial disadvantage relative to higher-income students.[56] Evidence also indicates that the drop in knowledge and overall educational level from summer vacations disproportionately affects students from low-income families.[57]

Besides the function of school time within the lives of children, education in general is of rising importance in a society increasingly based on knowledge and evolving technology. Schools need to be able to prepare children for the workforce of today and tomorrow. Exactly how this should be accomplished is still open to much debate over tracking, vocational training, smoothing school-to-work transitions, competition among schools through vouchers and contracting out, and related issues. We also expect more of schools in terms of providing mentors, counseling, and guidance, while preparing students in such sensitive areas as teaching values and life skills. But teachers often have no additional time to spend with students.[58] And extracurricular activities, Boys and Girls Clubs and the like, can only reach the children who join them, often to the exclusion of those who most need such organizations.

Finally, schools have been asked—usually without additional resources—to try to involve parents more directly in the education of their children. Activities here include more integrated services for the entire family, and promotion of adult literacy so that parents can serve as their children's first teachers.

*   *   *

That much is changing in our family life is obvious. Like economic changes noted earlier, many of these changes have been for the better—longer lives, better health care, less poverty among the old, greater equality of earnings between men and women, increased sharing of parental roles. Other problems have become worse or at least stand out more as problems in our richer society—unacceptable rates of poverty for children; a large upcoming decline in the number of workers able to finance each retiree's benefits, high out-of-wedlock birth rates, high absentee rates for noncustodial parents, large government marriage penalties, and lack of parental and adult supervision for many of our children.

Can government solve all these problems? No. Should government sit still as these changes occur? The answer is also "No." But before we can begin to assess possible alternatives, we must examine the fiscal capability of the government to respond.

Notes

1. For discussion see, Sara McLanahan and Lynne Casper, "Growing Diversity and Inequality in the American Family," in Reynolds Farley, ed., *State of the Union, Vol. II: Social Trends,* New York: Russell Sage Foundation, 1995, figure 1.1, p. 7. Data from the U.S. Bureau of the Census, Current Population Survey for median age at first marriage, shows an increase from 22.8 and 20.3 in 1950 for men and women respectively to 26.9 and 24.5 in 1995. These numbers exceed the 1890 medians of 26.1 and 22.0 respectively.

2. *Ibid.,* pp.7–8.

3. Theresa Castro-Martin and Larry Bumpass, "Recent Trends and Differentials in Marital Disruption," *Demography* 26, No. 1, 1989.

4. Based on data from the *Monthly Vital Statistics Report,* Vol. 43(12s), from the National Center for Health Statistics, July 14, 1995.

5. See Eugene Steuerle, "The Effects of Tax and Welfare Policies on Family Formation," unpublished paper prepared for Family Impact Seminar, Conference on Strategies to Strengthen Marriage: What Do We Know? What Do We Need To Know? Washington DC, June 1997.

6. Based on data from the *Statistical Abstract of the United States,* 1997.

7. *Ibid.*

8. Based on data from the U.S. Department of Health and Human Services, 1995, cited in William Doherty, Edward Kouneski, and Martha Farrell Erikson, *Responsible Fathering: An Overview and Conceptual Framework,* Final Report prepared for the Administration for Children and Families, Office of the Assistant Secretary for Planning and Evaluation, September 1996.

9. For example, in 1996 only 22 percent of working women 16 and over usually worked part-time. Based on calculations from the U.S. Department of Labor, Bureau of Labor Statistics, *Employment and Earnings,* January 1997.

10. Anthony Astrachan, *How Men Feel,* Garden City, NY: Anchor Press/Doubleday, 1986.

11. Sara McLanahan and Lynne Casper, "Growing Diversity and Inequality in the American Family," in Reynolds Farley, ed, *State of the Union, Vol. II: Social Trends,* New York: Russell Sage Foundation, 1995, table 1.4, p. 13. Also, based on data from the Children's Defense Fund, the proportion of women working outside the home has increased to 59 percent for women with children under 3 years old.

12. Based on data from the U.S. Census Bureau, Current Population Survey for 1995—women 15–44 years old who have had a child in the last year and are in the labor force.

13. Robert D. Mare, "Changes in Educational Attainment and School Enrollment," in Reynolds Farley, ed., *State of the Union, Vol. I: Economic Trends,"* New York: Russell Sage Foundation, 1995, figures 4.3 and 4.4, pp. 163, 164.

14. See Suzanne Bianci, "Changing Economic Roles of Women and Men," in Reynolds Farley, ed., *State of the Union, Vol. I: Economic Trends*, New York: Russell Sage Foundation, 1995.

15. See Cynthia Fraser and Kristin Ward (eds.), *From the Wage Gap to the Gender Gap: A Political and Economic Handbook*, Institute for Women's Policy Research, Washington, DC, 1996.

16. As we saw earlier, from 1979 to 1989 the wages of men without a college education fell by over 12 percent, while for women they fell by less than 1 percent. For longer discussion see Rebecca Blank, "U.S. Labor Market and Prospects for Low-Wage Entry Jobs," in Demetra Smith Nightingale and Robert H. Haveman (eds.), *The Work Alternative: Welfare Reform and the Realities of the Job Market*, The Urban Institute Press, Washington, DC, 1995.

17. Victor R. Fuchs, *Women's Quest for Economic Equality*, Cambridge: Harvard University Press, 1988, p. 4.

18. Philip B. Levine and Olivia S. Mitchell, "Women on the Verge of Retirement: Predictors of Retiree Well-Being," Pension Research Council, Wharton School of the University of Pennsylvania, January 1997, table 7.

19. For a much more extensive review of the literature and theories in the research on fatherhood, see Michael E. Lamb (ed.), *The Role of Fathers in Child Development*, 3rd edition, John Wiley & Sons, Inc., New York, NY, 1997.

20. See Joseph Pleck, "Paternal Involvement: Levels, Sources and Consequences," in Michael E. Lamb (ed.), *The Role of Fathers in Child Development*, 3rd edition, John Wiley & Sons, Inc., New York, NY, 1997.

21. See O'Connell, M. (1993) *Where's Papa? Fathers' Role in Child Care*. Washington, DC: Population Reference Bureau, cited in Michael E. Lamb (ed.), *The Role of Fathers in Child Development*, 3rd edition, John Wiley & Sons, Inc., New York, NY, 1997, p. 74.

22. According to Joseph Pleck, "Paternal Involvement: Levels, Sources and Consequences," in Michael E. Lamb (ed.), *The Role of Fathers in Child Development*, 3rd edition, John Wiley & Sons, Inc., New York, NY, 1997, paternal engagement increased from 1/3 of mothers' engagement a decade ago to over 2/5s today, and accessibility increased from 1/2 to 2/3, also in proportion to mothers.

23. See Michael E. Lamb, "Fathers and Child Development: An Introductory Overview and Guide," in Michael E. Lamb (ed.), *The Role of Fathers in Child Development*, 3rd edition, John Wiley & Sons, Inc., New York, NY, 1997.

24. Study data for the Great Depression from Glen Elder, J. Liker, and C. Cross (1994), "Parent-Child Behavior in the Great Depression: Life Course and Intergenerational Influences," in P. Baltes and O. Brim (eds.), *Life Span Development and Behavior* (Vol. 6, pp. 109–158), Academic Press, Orlando, FL. An example of a more recent study is R. Harold-Goldsmith, N. Radin, and J.S. Eccles (1988), "Objective and Subjective Reality: The Effects of Job Loss and Financial Stress on Fathering Behaviors," in *Family Perspective*, 22, pp. 309–325.

25. Patrick Fagan, in "The Breakdown of the Family: The Consequences for Children and American Society," *Issues 96*, The Heritage Foundation, Washington, DC (forthcoming), suggests that the proportion of children entering broken families, either at birth or because their parents divorce, has quadrupled since 1950 to over 50 percent. His data are from the National Center for Health Statistics.

26. See William Doherty, Edward Kouneski, and Martha Farrell Erikson's paper, *Responsible Fathering: An Overview and Conceptual Framework*, prepared for the Administration for Children, Youth, and Families in September 1996.

27. For a longer discussion of the idea of mothers as gatekeepers to children and references to specific studies in this area, see E. Mavis Hetherington and Margaret M. Stanley-Hagan, "The Effects of Divorce on Fathers and Their Children," in Michael E. Lamb (ed.), *The Role of Fathers in Child Development*, 3rd edition, John Wiley & Sons, Inc., New York, NY, 1997.

28. See Michael E. Lamb, "Fathers and Child Development: An Introductory Overview and Guide," in Michael E. Lamb (ed.), *The Role of Fathers in Child Development*, 3rd edition, John Wiley & Sons, Inc., New York, NY, 1997.

29. Many studies have looked at the connection between paternal involvement and payment of child support. For one source see William Doherty, Edward Kouneski, and Martha Farrell Erikson's paper, *Responsible Fathering: An Overview and Conceptual Framework*, prepared for the Administration for Children, Youth, and Families in September 1996.

30. Based on Factsheet from the U.S. Department of Health and Human Services, November 1996.

31. For data, see C.F. Landsbergen and D. Hecht (1994), "Organizational Impediments to Paternity Establishment and Child Support," *Social Science Review*, 72, 109–126.

32. The data on life expectancies come from the 1997 Annual Report of the Board of Trustees of the OASDI Trust Fund, with projections based on intermediate assumptions.

33. See Samuel H. Preston, "American Longevity: Past, Present, and Future," *Policy Brief*, No. 7, Syracuse University, Maxwell School of Citizenship and Public Affairs, Center for Policy Research, 1996.

34. Data on the average age of retirement come from the Social Security Administration, Office of Research and Statistics, 1995.

35. See Dora L. Costa, "The Evolution of Retirement," *NBER Reporter*, Fall 1997.

36. See John Sabelhaus and Ulrike Schneider, "Measuring the Distribution of Well-Being: Why Income and Consumption Give Different Answers," Working Paper, Washington, DC: The Urban Institute, 1995.

37. Dora L. Costa, in "The Evolution of Retirement," *NBER Reporter*, Fall 1997, reports that close to one-half of retired men in 1880 were living in the households of their children or other relatives, whereas today that figure is only 5 percent.

38. See C. Eugene Steuerle and Jon Bakija, *Retooling Social Security for the 21st Century: Right and Wrong Approaches to Reform*, The Urban Institute Press, Washington, DC, 1994.

39. Based on calculations from Steuerle and Bakija, *Retooling Social Security for the 21st Century: Right and Wrong Approaches to Reform*, The Urban Institute Press, Washington, DC, 1994, table A-1.

40. Some are even anticipating falling saving rates if baby boomers begin to sell off their assets to support themselves in retirement. See Sylvester Schieber and John Shoven, "The Consequences of Population Aging on Private Pension Fund Saving and Asset Markets," NBER Working Paper #4665, 1994.

41. Data from the Child Welfare League of America, based on Census data.

42. As reported by the Child Welfare League of America based on Census data for 1995, children make up only 27 percent of the population but represent 40 percent of America's poor.

43. Based on data from the U.S. Bureau of the Census, Current Population Survey, 1996.

44. The data on the poverty levels of young working families come from "Rescuing the American Dream: Halting the Freefall of Today's Young Families with Children," The Children's Defense Fund, 1997.

45. Data from the Administration for Families and Children, Office of Family Assistance, *AFDC/TANF Flash Report*: February 1997.

46. The 1996 reforms could also raise the number of children in poverty. See Sheila Zedlewski, Sandra Clark, Eric Meier, and Keith Watson, 1996, "Potential Effects of Congressional Welfare Reform Legislation on Family Incomes," Washington, DC: Urban Institute, July 26. On the other hand, CBO estimates that 1997 reforms are likely to raise the number of children covered by publicly funded health insurance by an estimated 2.3 million by 1999. "Expanding Health Insurance Coverage for Children under Title XXI of the Social Security Act," Congressional Budget Office (1998).

47. For a longer discussion of the effects of single-parent families on children, see the works of Andrew Cherlin, such as *Divided Families: What Happens to Children When Parents Part*, with Frank Furstenberg, Harvard University Press, Cambridge, MA, 1994.

48. See Michael E. Lamb, "Fathers and Child Development: An Introductory Overview and Guide," in Michael E. Lamb (ed.), *The Role of Fathers in Child Development*, 3rd edition, John Wiley & Sons, Inc, New York, NY, 1997.

49. See Edward Zigler and N. Hall, "Day Care and Its Effects on Children: An Overview for Pediatric Professionals," *The Journal of Developmental and Behavioral Pediatrics*, Vol. 1, 1988.

50. See Michele Seligson, "Care for School-Aged Children," a paper presented as the American Academy of Pediatrics Day Symposium in Washington, DC, 1991.

51. On average, children spend 40 hours a week watching television and playing video games. Also, children from low-income households are estimated to spend 50 percent more time watching TV than their affluent peers. See National Institute on Out-of-School Time, Fact Sheet on School-Age Children.

52. Youth are most likely to commit crimes on school days (57 percent) compared to all other days. In addition, the peak time is between 2 p.m. and 7 p.m. Data based on *Juvenile Offenders and Victims: 1997 Update on Violence*, by the Office of Juvenile Justice and Delinquency Prevention.

53. Based on data from the Bureau of Justice Statistics.

54. Based on *Juvenile Offenders and Victims: 1997 Update on Violence*.

55. See Beth Miller, Susan O'Connor, and Sylvia Wolfson Sirignano, "Out-of-School Time: A Study of Children in Three Low-Income Neighborhoods," Child Welfare League of America, 1995.

56. See Duncan Chaplin and Jane Hanaway, "The Second Curriculum: Trends of Disengagement," paper presented at the Annual Meeting of the American Educational Research Association, 1995.

57. While much work has been done in this area, it was introduced by Barbara Heyns, *Summer Learning and the Effects on Schooling*, with foreword by Christopher Jencks, Academic Press, New York, NY, 1978.

58. See the U.S. Department of Education, "Prisoners of Time," April 1994, for a more comprehensive explanation of the many challenges facing schools within their current time structure as they attempt to meet the goals for 2000.

Chapter Four

GOVERNMENT'S CHANGING CAPACITY TO RESPOND

Laws and institutions must go hand in hand with the progress of the human mind. As that becomes more developed, more enlightened, as new discoveries are made, new truths discovered and manners and opinions change, with the change of circumstances, institutions must advance to keep pace with the times.

—Thomas Jefferson

Many of the forces that affect our economy, our families, and our lives cannot be controlled directly by government. But we often use government to respond to and channel these forces. And the way we govern ourselves can itself be a powerful force for change. A crucial part of getting the government we deserve, therefore, is to understand how fiscal transformations over the past 50 years have shaped government's capacity to act. What we can do in the future is limited inherently by commitments made in the past. Efforts to accommodate the demands of the twenty-first century—demands that derive from our changing economy, families, and lives—are likely to fail without a simultaneous effort to master and manage the public priorities that have already been set.

FISCAL TRANSFORMATION[1]

For almost a generation now, deficit reduction has preoccupied the federal legislative process. Virtually all major new spending initiatives have been set aside as impossible given the federal budget constraints. "We all want to get the American economy moving again, and we all realize to achieve this we must cut federal deficits," said House Speaker O'Neill (D-MA) amid the deficit reduction efforts of 1982. "We have more will than wallet," said President Bush in his 1988 inaugural address. Between 1982 and 1997, the president and Congress—mainly Democratic presidents with Republican Congresses and Republican presidents with Democratic Congresses—agreed to six major budget agreements (1982, 1984, 1987, 1990, 1993, and 1997). At the end of the century the consensus is increasingly strong that the budget will go into surplus—barring new tax or spending legislation. The bipartisan nature of the many budget agreements since 1981 and their dominance of federal policymaking are testimony to the widely shared public concern that government has been on a debt spree that had to be stopped.

Despite the possibility of modest budget surpluses for a brief period, budget concerns remain preeminent in federal policymaking—and rightly so. Deficits spiral upward once the baby boom generation begins to retire (figure 4.1). In that sense, we are in the eye of the storm between large past deficits and the large future deficits that are inevitable if we tried to meet all the promises for spending growth scheduled under current law.

And deficits are only a small part of the story. Regardless of the amount of federal debt, the proportion of government revenues available for new domestic initiatives that respond to the needs of the time—the discretionary money in the federal budget expenditures—continues to shrink. Almost 60 percent of the federal budget is already committed to spending obligations (mandatory spending or entitlements in budget language) that are built into public policy. Thirty-five years ago, only 30 percent of the federal budget was so obligated.[2] The shadow of prior policy commitments now largely determines how the federal government spends new revenues. Today's laws and policy-making institutions no longer provide the financial maneuvering room that would allow current voters and their representatives to make spending decisions that would accommodate their changing lives. Meanwhile, the costs of previous promises made for the future continue to soar, although they only show up as large projected deficits when the baby boom generation is about to retire.

How have we reached this point where our budget priorities under current and future law have been set primarily by policymakers no longer on the scene? Why do we find ourselves in a straitjacket that continues to constrict the use of public money for important public purposes? The answer is that we did it to ourselves, through a multitude of separate decisions and choices over many decades. And we are going to have to un-do it to ourselves. The first step is to understand what has happened to America's fiscal landscape.

GOVERNMENT GROWTH: 1900 TO MID-1970s

The twentieth century stands out as an unprecedented period of growth in government relative to growth in the economy as a whole.[3]

Figure 4.1 DEFICITS—PAST, PRESENT, AND FUTURE

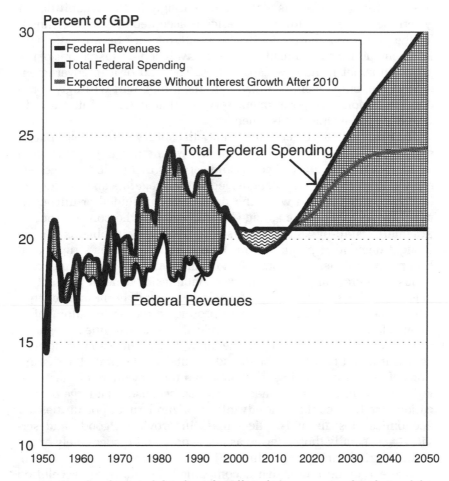

Source: Based on historical data from the Office of Management and Budget and data
for 1997 and beyond from GAO's model for long-term growth, with no legislative action
and no economic feedback (Feb. 1998).

This period is almost certainly neither repeatable nor reversible.
Those who would like to repeat it will be disappointed, if only because the past growth was so significant that there are fewer resources
left to tap. Those who would like to reverse it are equally unlikely to
succeed. Government growth in any period reflects a response to
broad popular demands. In the twentieth century these included the
democratic demand for greater equality of opportunity and better

protections against certain risks. What democratic government does in each time and place is also related strongly to the capabilities of government as an institution. Americans accepted bigger government for the first three-quarters of the twentieth century because the public's demand for government services outweighed its suspicions of the power inherent in its new capabilities. The goal of lean government is laudable, but it seems unlikely that the public will willingly abandon the majority of government services that it has wanted and to which it has become accustomed.

The United States entered the twentieth century with a small public sector. But as vast new private markets were emerging to provide a rapidly increasing array of goods and services in a period of vigorous economic growth, government moved to both regulate and participate in these markets. Even when the steps were misguided or uncoordinated, what we now see as Big Government was the consequence of pragmatic, step-by-step, responses to particular problems people thought demanded public action. Voters and politicians struggled to find public policies to respond to a dramatically changing America.

Business grew largely to achieve economies of scale in production of goods and to take advantage of newfound ways of harnessing energy. It was cheaper and much easier to produce a thousand automobiles in one plant, to take an obvious example, than one at a time in separate firms. Government grew simultaneously. It grew in response to new concerns about how to establish and maintain order amid the disruptions of an industrializing workplace and the movement of the population to the cities. Government grew also because, as a large organization itself, it could take advantage of modern opportunities for economies of scale and critical mass in providing goods and services—especially those viewed as being provided inadequately or not at all in private markets. Feeling vulnerable to new concentrations of private economic power that accompanied the industrial revolution (the threat of "big business"), people often turned to government for protection.

Imposing Order on a Burgeoning Industrial Capacity

Until the Great Depression, federal domestic policy efforts were primarily regulatory. From the turn of the century through the presidency of Woodrow Wilson—the Progressive Era—the increased demands placed on government were met, first by civil service reforms and antitrust policy, and later by consumer protection initiatives and the setting of standards in the workplace. Neither federal expenditures nor federal taxes grew much as a proportion of gross domestic product (GDP).[4] The major federal spending category, as in the late nineteenth century, was expenditures for war and war veterans (who commanded large proportions of federal peacetime budgets).

In the Great Depression, the industrial and economic expansion broke down. The unemployment rate surged to as high as 24.9 percent.[5] Almost all groups suffered as real GDP per worker shrank—from almost $24,000 in the last year of the boom (1929) to less than $21,000 in the depth of the slump (1933)—and doubts grew about democratic government's ability to manage the situation without stronger state dictatorship. The New Deal was the label given to government's response to the crisis. Rhetoric notwithstanding, this response often followed a regulatory path that had already been blazed. National planning, for example, had already begun under Herbert Hoover; the New Deal simply expanded it. Many of the regulatory initiatives traceable to the New Deal remain: regulation of securities trading and margin requirements, national enforcement of workers' rights, and the creation of deficit insurance and such regulatory agencies as the Federal Deposit Insurance Corporation (FDIC).

With respect to fiscal and budgetary efforts, most attention was devoted to the alleviation of individuals' problems related to the Depression itself. It is worth noting that this response to the emergency began before Roosevelt. Federal domestic expenditures, both in real terms and especially as a percentage of a declining gross domestic product, rose significantly under Herbert Hoover (see table 4.1), implying both a public demand and a sense of government capability that transcended political parties.

The focus of these efforts—reflecting the obvious political importance of massive unemployment combined with evolving ideas of social insurance—was on wage replacement rather than direct meeting of economic need. In other words, the needs of workers, not the needs of the disadvantaged *per se*, provided the rationale used to sell these programs to the electorate. Unemployment compensation, worker compensation, veterans' benefits—all fit this description. Even programs designed to help needy groups who were not expected to work, at least in that era, were described in the rhetoric of the workforce. Social Security, for example, was described as based on "workers' contributions" and "earned" pension rights, even though (a) benefits went to elderly and disabled Americans, (b) payment to beneficiaries as a group far exceeded their contributions for many decades, and (c) the payment formula from the beginning built in substantial redistribution from beneficiaries who had been highly paid during their work-

Table 4.1 BIG-SPENDING PRESIDENTS ON DOMESTIC GOVERNMENT: CHANGE IN
FEDERAL DOMESTIC OUTLAYS AS A PERCENTAGE OF GDP

President	Domestic Outlays
Nixon	5.0
Hoover	4.0
Eisenhower	2.9
Truman	2.1
Bush	1.6
Johnson	0.9
Wilson	0.8
Kennedy	0.7
Carter	0.4
Coolidge	0.1
Ford	0.1
T. Roosevelt	0.0
Clinton, both terms	0.0
Taft	−0.2
Harding	−0.3
Clinton, 1st term	−0.5
Reagan	−2.0
F. Roosevelt	−3.6
Total[1,2]	**12.8**

Source: C. Eugene Steuerle and Gordon Mermin, "The Big-Spending Presidents," *Future
of the Public Sector* briefs series, no. 11, 1998.
[1]Assuming passage of the Administration's fiscal year 1999 budget proposal.
[2]Federal domestic spending was 1.3% of GDP in 1902 and is scheduled to grow to 14.1%
of GDP in 2001. The total change in federal domestic outlays, therefore, is 12.8% of
GDP.

ing lives to those who had been poorly paid. What is now known as
welfare is another case in point. Aid to Dependent Children (later Aid
to Families with Dependent Children, now Temporary Assistance for
Needy Families) was from the beginning a program that helped poor
single mothers and their children. But it was justified as a program
that replaced the wages of workers who had died and left their "widows" and children without support.

World War II forced the reorientation of government spending toward war and defense and led to substantial increases in federal
revenue. But *domestic* spending did not immediately regain its former
share of national product even when the war was over. In fact, *federal
domestic spending as a percentage of national product was actually
smaller at the end of the Roosevelt/Truman era than at its beginning
two decades earlier.* Indeed, much of the domestic spending of the
Roosevelt years—in particular, jobs programs and other wage-
replacement efforts—was dedicated to specific needs of the time, not

to permanent programs with large, built-in growth rates. Where there were exceptions, such as Social Security, they were smaller in size[6] than programs such as the large public jobs programs that peaked briefly from 1936 to 1939 (figure 4.2). Whether or not their establishment was intended to be permanent, their relative size was clearly meant to be temporary—to decline as unemployment rates declined.

One must be careful, then, in overblaming current budget programs on some big, pro-government "mistake" made in the distant past—on the Progressives' faith in government regulation as a response to the accrual of power in parts of the private sector, on Herbert Hoover's faith in planning, or on the New Deal. Such a view of history discounts all the separate fiscal choices made along the way, in response to new perceptions about what government could and should do and not do.

Unprecedented Optimism and Fiscal Good Luck

The period between the end of World War II and the mid-1970s combined unprecedented optimism about the capacities of government with a string of fiscal good luck that together were unique in our history.

Figure 4.2 GOVERNMENT EMPLOYMENT AS A PERCENTAGE OF TOTAL EMPLOYMENT IN U.S. ECONOMY

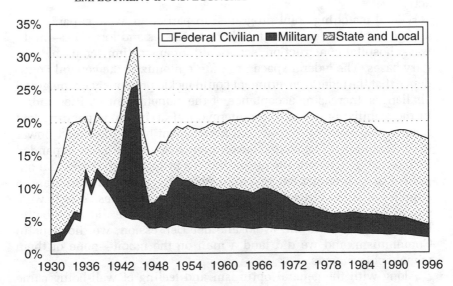

Source: Calculations based on data from the Bureau of Economic Analysis, *loc. cit.*

Optimism.[7] If the Depression had created doubts about the viability of the democracy, winning World War II gave Americans new faith in their power to work together as a nation. The forces of evil and good had been clearly arrayed—reinforced by the end-of-war revelations of genocide—and evil had been conquered. The general euphoria over victory and the new role of the United States as the unchallenged leader of the free world stimulated a surge of patriotic nationalism. It also raised high expectations about the nation's ability to make the middle-class American dream of financial, employment, and family security come true. In the words of Robert Samuelson, expectations rose so far that "the American dream became the American fantasy."[8]

Although the postwar period began with some fear of a return to the prewar economic slump, it was in fact a period of vigorous economic growth. This growth reinforced Americans' optimism both about the nation and about government itself. Battles were fought about how strong government should become and in what areas. But pro-centralizing policy forces won many important victories—victories made easier and less contentious by the environment of easy financing discussed below. In the process, as Martha Derthick has said, "the place of place [became] much attenuated in American politics and government."[9] Centralization accompanied growing federal domestic policy. But federal preemption took a variety of forms, including judicial, direct legislative, regulatory, and grant-in-aid activity.

Federal matching grant programs, in particular, were expanded in a number of areas once left totally to the states and localities—highways, hospital construction, school aid for areas "impacted" by military bases. The federal space program epitomized the general confidence that the federal government could tackle previously unimagined challenges. Increasing acceptance of the monetary authorities and/or in the stabilizing power of countercyclical taxing and spending lent further credence to the view that government had widespread power to find solutions. The federal government also dramatically expanded its international commitments, becoming by default the principal opponent of communist expansion, a police force for the world, and a supplier of aid to struggling nations. And many of these efforts were successful, even if less than perfectly executed. We did get a better highway system, we did avoid another Depression, we did contain Communism, and we did land a man on the moon—none of them trivial achievements.

Along with the general optimism and feeling of well-being came new demands on Washington for domestic problem-solving in such areas as poverty, urban decay, crime, health, and the environment. Much of the vast expansion of domestic policy during the postwar period was for income security and poverty alleviation—activities that started out as only a modest part of the federal budget.

Here began a subtle change that was to greatly influence the direction of social policy formation. In effect, society gave itself a new commitment—to eradicate a poverty that was considered unacceptable in a nation of such great wealth. As a result, the political discourse changed from emphasizing benefits to workers (and insurance against what Franklin Roosevelt called the "vicissitudes" of the labor market) to calling for guaranteed minimum living standards for all. Social welfare policy became increasingly inclusive. The political need to tie arguments for assistance to some presumption of work history began to give way; income *guarantees* rather than income *replacement* became the theme. The presumption that income needs were primarily temporary support in times of macroeconomic disaster yielded to the rhetoric of entitlements. The expectation that government expenditures would rise and fall to compensate for cyclical macroeconomic swings gave way to the expectation of social benefit programs with built-in expenditure growth.

During this period, for instance, Congress adopted Medicare as an entitlement that was virtually unrelated to need or contributions made during prior work history. The Medicaid program was also introduced, a health care entitlement for the poor that provided matching federal dollars for whatever states chose to spend on health care for welfare recipients and other needy persons. Many Medicaid provisions were allowed to vary by state, as was the case with AFDC cash welfare payments. But the federal government imposed eligibility and coverage minimums that states had to meet to qualify for the federal matching funds. Unlike programs such as unemployment insurance, demand for health care would expand in both good times and bad.

Social Security was somewhat of a hybrid in this transition. Workers' contributions and earned pension rights were still the language used for its rationale. But decisions were made to increase the liabilities of the system with no corresponding action to ensure full current financing of these future liabilities. Social Security tax rates rose, but they were never set high enough for each generation to cover its own retirement costs, building up ever greater liabilities for generations of workers yet to come.

Between the Korean War and the late 1970s, federal domestic expenditures exploded—growing from 6 to 15 percent of GDP. State and local expenditures grew from 7 percent to 13 percent over the same period (figure 4.3).[10] Domestic public spending by all levels of government as a share of GDP increased by close to 15 percentage points. In today's dollars, this involved an annual increase of more than $1.2 trillion and an increase in average annual spending per person of about $4,500 and per household of about $12,000. The United States was not alone in this. Domestic public expenditures grew at the same or higher rates throughout most of the developed world. Nor was the expansion in government related to political party. The most significant federal domestic spending growth in the period since World War II occurred on the Republican watch—under Presidents Nixon and Eisenhower (table 4.1). As a percentage of GDP, the growth in federal

Figure 4.3 GOVERNMENT DOMESTIC SPENDING, 1902–1994

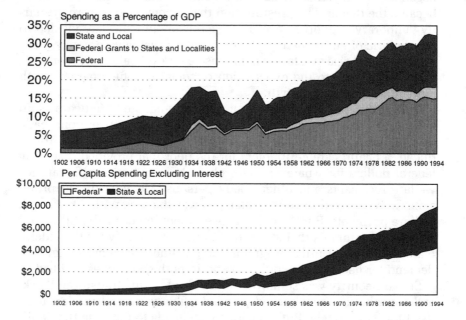

*Includes federal grants to states and localities.
Source: Calculations based on finance and population data from the Bureau of the Census, *loc. cit.*, and GDP data from the Office of Management and Budget, *loc. cit.*, and Professor Robert J. Gordon, Northwestern University. Note that domestic spending includes interest in the top chart but not in the bottom chart. These spending figures are greater than National Income and Product Account and Office of Management and Budget figures because the Census of Governments treats government enterprises and interest on a gross basis, counts the sale of land and property, and does not reduce expenditures by certain offsetting receipts. Government spending does not include utility, liquor store, and postal expenditures.

domestic spending under these two presidents accounts for nearly 60 percent of the total growth in the federal government's domestic spending over the entire history of the United States.[11]

Writing as domestic policy advisor to the newly elected President Nixon—whose presidency would come to outpace all others in domestic expenditure growth—Daniel Patrick Moynihan captured the belief of the period when he spoke of national policy almost without borders: "[T]here is no significant aspect of national life about which there is not likely to be a rather significant national policy. It may be a hidden policy. . . . But it is policy withal."[12]

Fiscal good luck. How could a spending increase of 15 percentage points of GDP at the federal, state, and local levels in less than a quarter of a century be financed? The mere fact of faster economic growth cannot be the answer because the question refers to growth *in excess of* the growth rate of GDP. What made it all possible was the unprecedented ease with which government could find money—so much money that it would finance many tax cuts along with the new public expenditures.

At the federal level, federal revenues as a percentage of GDP were relatively constant (figure 4.4), so they could not be used to finance domestic spending as a higher proportion of GDP. Instead, four sources of easy finance—over and above the healthy rate of growth of revenues that accompanied economic growth—dominated at the federal level.

Most important was a cyclical but long-run decline in the defense budget, from a peak of about 14 percent of GDP at the end of the Korean War, to below 5 percent by the late 1970s, to 3 percent at the end of the twentieth century and even lower as we enter the twenty-first century.[13] Each drop of 1 percentage point alone translates to over $80 billion per year in today's dollars that could be converted from defense to domestic spending without increasing tax rates at all. Nixon, Eisenhower, and later Bush, were big domestic-spending presidents because they had large peace dividends to spend: post-Korea, post-Vietnam, and post-Cold War.

But defense reductions were not the only easy source of finance. Social Security tax rates to cover old age, survivors, disability, and Medicare income climbed, with little public objection, by about 3 percentage points per decade from 1950 to 1990.[14] Each percentage point in the Social Security tax rate today amounts to over $40 billion in annual revenues to the government.[15] The combined increases, therefore, amount to hundreds of billions of dollars above what would be obtainable through economic growth alone. In addition to the So-

Figure 4.4 GOVERNMENT REVENUE AS A PERCENTAGE OF GDP, 1902–1994

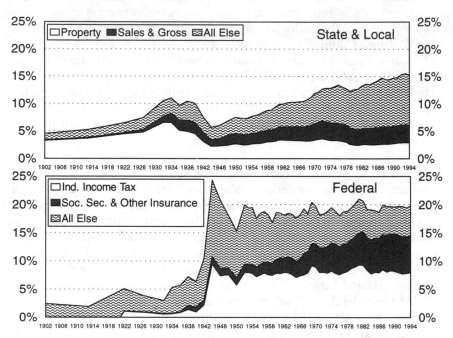

Source: Utility, liquor store, and postal revenue are excluded. Calculations based on finance data from the Bureau of the Census, *Government Finances, 1990–1991*, series GF/91-5, 1993, unpublished tables, and GDP data from the Office of Management and Budget, *Budget of the United States Government Fiscal Year 1997*, and Professor Robert J. Gordon, Northwestern University.

cial Security tax rate increases, there were tax base expansions as a greater share of earnings became subject to the Social Security tax, again leading to tax receipts that increased faster than the economy as a whole. (See figure 4.4 for Social Security's increasing share of total federal revenues.)

One reason there was so little objection to this tax was that for several generations there really was no *net* Social Security tax over the lifetime of beneficiaries. Benefits would be far in excess of taxes paid by almost every member of those generations. In effect, the government operated the Social Security system like an insurance company that charged higher and higher premiums to new policyholders, which it then immediately paid out in benefits to older policyholders who had paid in at a much lower premium rate. As a consequence, all beneficiaries, rich and poor, received lifetime Social Security benefits well in excess of what their taxes could have financed if they had been converted into an annuity for later payment. The strong rate of growth, both of the economy and of the population, added to the system's short-term ability to pay increasingly higher lifetime benefits and a higher internal "rate of return" on workers' Social Security contributions than could be justified by the taxes they paid. This was true even for high-income workers, who historically received benefits far in excess of taxes paid (figure 4.5).

For the first generation of Social Security beneficiaries this was inevitable, of course, because there had been no program in place to levy contributions from them during their working years. The rate of growth of benefits was not inevitable, however, nor was the failure to

Figure 4.5 LIFETIME SOCIAL SECURITY BENEFITS AND TAXES
(FOR HIGH-INCOME COUPLES UNDER CURRENT LAW)

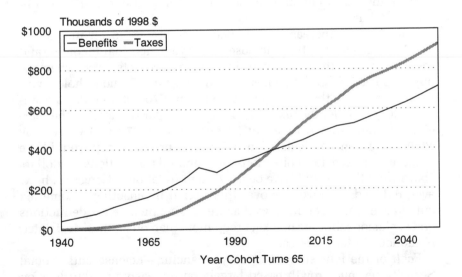

Source: C. Eugene Steuerle and Jon Bakija, *Retooling Social Security* (Washington, DC: Urban Institute Press, 1994). All amounts are discounted to present value at age 65 using a 2 percent real interest rate. Adjusts for chance of death in all years after age 21. Includes actuarial value of all OASDI worker's, spousal, and survivors benefits payable over a lifetime. Includes both employer and employee portions of the OASDI payroll tax. Couples are assumed to be the same age and to have two children born when the parents are ages 25 and 30. Assumes retirement at the normal OASDI retirement age. Projections are based on the intermediate assumptions from the 1993 OASDI Trustees Report. OASDI tax rate is assumed to be set at 10.65 percent after 1992.

ensure that future liabilities could be paid without continually raising tax rates on future generations.

Meanwhile, the economy became steadily more inflationary. Between the end of the Korean War and 1966, the consumer price index rose on average less than 2 percent a year. By 1980, the annual inflation rate had risen to 13.5 percent.[16] This acceleration brought two additional financing boons to the U.S. Treasury.

The first was an indirect tax on government bond holders. The example of a holder of government bonds earning an interest rate of 4 percent makes the point. As soon as the inflation rate rises above 4 percent a year, the real interest rate on this bond becomes negative. The higher the inflation rate, the more negative the rate of interest, allowing the government to increase its nominal deficit at the same time as inflation is eroding its outstanding debt. For a government whose debt is about half the value of the GDP, an unexpected increase in inflation of 1 percentage point is equivalent initially to an annual revenue increase of about 0.5 percent of GDP (close to $40 billion in today's dollars).[17]

Inflation also increased real income tax rates. In an unindexed system, a rise in inflation increases taxpayers' nominal incomes, and therefore moves them to higher income tax brackets, even when the buying power of those incomes remains stagnant. For households with incomes at twice the median income (about $70,000 in today's economy), for example, the tax rate on the last dollar of income (the marginal tax rate) rose from about 22 percent in 1967 to 43 percent by 1980.[18] In absence of legislative action, this bracket creep would have eventually raised tax collections by hundreds of billions of dollars above what they would have been without inflation.[19] Congress, however, reduced tax revenues over this period by enacting income tax cut after income tax cut, as well as increasing income tax deductions and exclusions. But the bracket creep more than offset these legislated reductions in tax revenue.

Each of the four sources of easy financing—defense cuts, Social Security revenue growth based largely on increasing net burdens on future generations, capital losses on holders of old government debt, and bracket creep in the income tax—eventually provided hundreds of billions of dollars per year. Benefits were increased. Tax cuts were passed to offset many of the revenue increases. Then the next Congress took its turn at passing still more benefit increases and tax cuts.

Very importantly for politics and attitudes toward government, everyone seemed to be a winner in the legislative process. Some won with higher benefits and some with tax cuts, but seldom was anyone designated to pay for those changes through tax increases or benefit cuts elsewhere in the system.[20] Everyone could be happy. In contrast to later years, the public was able to believe that it was getting higher government benefits *and* lower government costs at the same time.

This heady fiscal period not only stimulated extraordinarily high expectations but also created legislative habits that would be hard to break. Programs expanded but little attention was paid to the need for coordination, so duplication and multiplication of agencies and functions was inevitable. Equally little attention was paid to how the built-in growth rates of different programs benefiting different groups were diverging. Social Security was indexed to grow with wage growth and life expectancies. Medicare's reimbursement practices ensured that it would grow with the rapidly rising costs of medicine on the technology frontier. Some public assistance programs—Medicaid, AFDC—were designed to grow with increases in the eligible population, although AFDC payments to beneficiaries often fell in real terms. Other programs, such as housing assistance, could grow only as stipulated in annual appropriations.

The programs with the most rapid built-in growth turned out to be those oriented to the elderly and to consumption in old age, rather than to the young and to human capital investment. As long as programs for children grew, that they were growing more slowly than programs for the near-elderly and elderly attracted virtually no attention. And no one seemed concerned that high built-in growth rates in some programs could threaten all discretionary domestic expenditures in leaner times.

TIGHTENING THE FISCAL STRAITJACKET: MID-1970s TO THE PRESENT

By the mid-1970s, economic growth was slowing and easy financing over and above economic growth was dwindling. At the same time, the level of public financial commitments continued to rise—by now even without new legislation. Causes included burgeoning entitlement and other automatic spending obligations (including interest payments on a newly rising debt). Drops in fertility rates since the mid-1960s began to look like a longer-term trend, signaling an eventual aging of society and a further increase in future spending commitments relative to what was being earned by workers. The combined effect was to put Americans in a fiscal straitjacket from which we are yet to work ourselves free.

Economic Slowdown

Between 1973 and 1997, real U.S. economic output per worker grew at 0.9 percent a year on average, compared with annual average growth between 1947 and 1973 of 2.2 percent (see figure 2.2 in chapter 2). Had GDP per worker grown at the same rate between 1973 and 1997 as between 1947 and 1973 and tax policy followed the same course as it in fact did, government revenues today would be almost 40 percent higher than is the case.[21] Politics being what it is, this money almost certainly would not have been allowed to build into a permanent surplus. Even so, the fiscal crisis would have been less severe, if only because additional spending likely would have lagged the revenue growth somewhat and because individual incomes would have risen more, reducing slightly the demand for income-related public assistance.

The End of Easy Finance

Slower economic growth alone does not trigger a fiscal crisis. Certainly the growth of government revenues slowed with a slower growing economy, but there was still real growth in both revenues and the expenditures they would finance. What gradually led to a crisis was the progressive drying up of all four sources of easy financing—defense cuts, Social Security revenue growth, capital losses on old government debt, and income tax bracket creep.

Defense. The proportion of GDP going to defense has dropped by 10 percentage points between the mid-1950s and today, notwithstanding the brief period in Reagan's first year as president when the share allocated to defense increased.[22] All budgets today, whether set by Democrats or Republicans, assume further drops in the percentage of GDP going to the defense budget, simply to offset increases elsewhere in the budget. But defense now accounts for only a minor fraction of the federal budget (figure 4.6). As it approaches zero, it will become impossible, simply as a matter of arithmetic, to depend on future declines.

Social Security. The 3-percentage-point increase per decade in Social Security tax rates came to a halt in 1990, making the 1990s the first decade since the 1940s in which no such increase was scheduled.[23]

Figure 4.6 CHANGE IN THE COMPOSITION OF THE FEDERAL BUDGET, 1950–2002

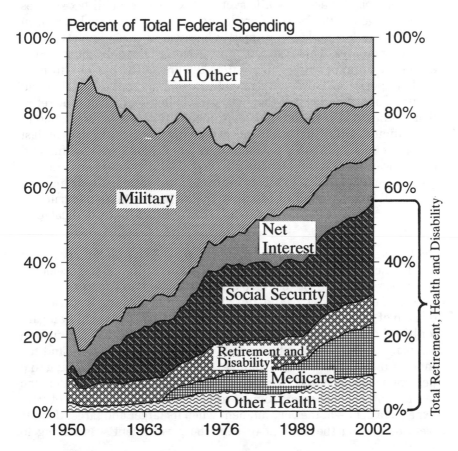

Source: Calculations based on data from the president's budget proposal in the *Budget of the United States Government Fiscal Year 1998*, OMB (1997).

Congress can still tinker with the tax base, as when it eliminated any cap on earnings subject to the Medicare tax in 1993, and some rate increase may eventually be adopted to deal with the baby boomers' upcoming retirement. But the pressures against raising Social Security taxes significantly more, even to meet upcoming demographic pressures when the baby boomers retire, had grown considerably by the late 1970s.

First, the Social Security system is now enormous. For over two-thirds of workers, the Social Security taxes they pay (including the taxes their employers pay on their behalf) are larger than the income taxes they pay.[24] Second, while average tax rates from all tax sources have changed little for the population as a whole, they have risen dramatically for workers—primarily because of these Society Security tax increases. This rise, too, must eventually end, because taxing each generation of workers more than the preceding one is arithmetically impossible. Third, government can no longer promise all Social Security beneficiaries that they will get a better deal when they retire than if they had invested their own money with an insurance company (figure 4.5). That someone eventually had to pay has at last become obvious. Finally, Social Security and Medicare benefits and other government retirement, health, and disability programs are now quite generous relative to most government programs, absorbing over half of all federal spending (figure 4.6). Raising the taxes dedicated to Social Security would further reduce the share of funds dedicated to society's other needs.

Real interest changes on old government debt. The inflationary tax on bondholders worked only as long as inflation continued to accelerate. But toward the end of the 1970s, inflation rates fell in response to Federal Reserve policy (and possibly to other factors, such as the erosion of union power). These declining rates caused a windfall gain for bondholders. Long-term bond purchasers who started out making a 2 percent real rate of return when inflation was 10 percent and the interest rate 12 percent, for example, saw their real returns rising to 6 percent when inflation dropped to 6 percent. All of a sudden the federal government went from a world of cheap debt to one of very expensive debt—at the very moment when its larger and larger deficits were escalating the amount of debt the government was having to sell.[25]

Real tax rate changes. The tax revolts of the late 1970s to the early 1980s stemmed largely from higher income and property rates, as inflation moved individuals into higher income tax brackets. In 1981, as part of the Economic Recovery Tax Act, Congress decided to remove this inflationary bracket creep by indexing tax brackets for inflation beginning after 1984. That meant that average income tax rates would no longer increase for an individual whose real income stayed the same.[26]

As noted, individual income taxes remained remarkably constant over the postwar period as a whole, because the inflation-caused bracket creep was largely offset by legislated tax cuts. Even the individual tax cuts of the early 1980s merely offset a very large rise in average tax rates in the late 1970s, when inflation rates peaked. Without automatic bracket creep, however, there was no longer the easy financing to support such legislated tax cuts, much less an increase in government expenditures.

Built-In Real Spending Growth

Even the combination of slower economic growth and the drying up of all easy financing would not have been enough to cause the large deficits of the 1980s and early 1990s. The U.S. economy continued to grow, if more modestly, and so did the resources available to government. In real terms—that is, correcting for inflation—federal government revenues per capita grew from $3,789 in 1973 to $5,165 in 1993. State and local revenue per capita (excluding federal transfers) grew from $2,583 to $4,121.[27] Since our tax system holds overall average tax rates roughly constant in real terms, government revenues grow at about the same rate as the economy. Even if the slower growth environment of the post-1973 period continues, future government revenues per capita will still double in half a century, which under normal circumstances would yield significant fiscal slack. To understand the full explanation for the deficit crisis, therefore, we need to look beyond tax revenues to the spending commitments we have made far into the future.

The truth is that policymakers have essentially squandered more than all of the growth in the economy and in government revenues, by building more and more automatic growth into public programs. It would be one thing if they merely bought too many goods and services in the current year. Instead, they bought more and more goods and services for decades into the future. At first these commitments, building on a small base, remained small in comparison to defense and other discretionary spending—although we should not forget that President Eisenhower's railing against the military-industrial complex was partly a reaction to the ways special interests were creating semi-automatic growth, even in discretionary defense programs. But the die was cast. It was only a matter of time before larger and larger shares of any new revenues were consumed by these growing real spending commitments.

Two distinctions are important here. The first is the distinction between automatic built-in real growth and inflation adjustment. Programs that are indexed to keep pace with inflation do not necessarily build in real growth. Social Security recipients, for example, have come to expect increasing benefits each year to offset inflation and preserve the buying power of their benefits. But proper inflationary indexing does not cause real growth in Social Security spending.[28] It merely prevents automatic real declines in spending. For perspective, compare a world with no inflation to a world of 5 percent inflation a year and accurate indexing. In the latter world, the indexing would add 5 percent to program spending to offset the 5 percent real drop caused by inflation. Real program spending would be the same as in the world of no inflation. What contributed to the deficit crisis was automatic real program growth that outpaced even the real growth in the economy and the real growth in wages.

The second important distinction is between regularly appropriated program growth and automatic entitlement growth. Growth can be built into almost any program. But entitlements and many tax preferences avoid not just an annual appropriations process but any requirement for periodic review. Legislation literally designates these programs to exist eternally and even to have eternal growth. Some programs in the law today have already been scheduled to grow faster than the economy for the twenty-first and twenty-second centuries and beyond.

Never before in our history has the law pre-ordained so much of our future spending. Never before have dead and retired policymakers so dominated officials elected today. And never before has so much policy bypassed the traditional set of brakes applied throughout the history of democratic decisionmaking.

Two areas have dominated the built-in growth picture within the industrial nations: health care and retirement security. The demand for health care is virtually unlimited to the extent that we do not recognize any costs when we go to the doctor or hospital, or when we buy insurance. Not that the costs don't exist; they are simply shifted to other insurance buyers and taxpayers. Most government insurance—and until recently, most private insurance—has yet to impose adequate constraints on price and use to slow down the extraordinary growth in health costs—including growth in payments to doctors and other health care providers.

Social Security and other retirement payments by government, in turn, have grown faster than the economy largely because of improvements in health and longevity.[29] A larger share of the population is living to retirement, and individuals are spending more of their lives in retirement. These longevity cost increases are added to programs already scheduled to grow significantly, because annual benefits to new retirees are indexed to grow as fast as average wages in the economy.[30]

While mandated spending has grown as a share of the federal budget, the discretionary portion has fallen. In 1962 discretionary government spending (spending subject to the annual appropriations process) was almost two-thirds (63 percent) of total spending, twice as much as mandatory spending (31 percent). (The remaining 6 percent was net interest on the national debt.) By 1984, mandatory spending had just surpassed discretionary spending (45 percent versus 42 percent), with 12 percent going to net interest on the national debt. Mandatory spending has now grown to 60 percent and discretionary spending has fallen to 34 percent of total spending.[31] And the divergence will increase under current law.

But depending upon this type of decline in discretionary spending to continue—even independently from its corrosive effect on the democratic process—has no theoretical or empirical justification. It only becomes possible even on paper through a mechanical calculation that ignores foreign threats, transportation demands, the needs of the impaired and disabled, or any other future domestic concerns. In his fiscal 1999 budget, for instance, President Clinton showed how continual declines in discretionary spending could pay for some of the growth in mandatory spending (he wanted to argue that there could be "surpluses as far as the eye can see"). But the assumption required to make that claim for huge mandatory spending growth was that discretionary spending would continue to fall relative to the size of the economy.[32] (Figure 4.7 shows both historic and hypothetical changes in mandatory and discretionary expenditures under this impossible scenario.)

In effect, mandatory spending in recent years has been growing so much faster than the economy that there are not even enough resources to pay off old commitments, let alone meet new ones. Even recent budget agreements, which reduced Medicare entitlement spending in particular, have had only modest effects on this extraordinary growth path in mandatory spending.

Compounding Interest Payments

Although not typically counted as such, interest payments on the national debt are in fact mandatory expenditures. Absent these inter-

Figure 4.7 CURRENT PATH OF MANDATORY AND DISCRETIONARY SPENDING

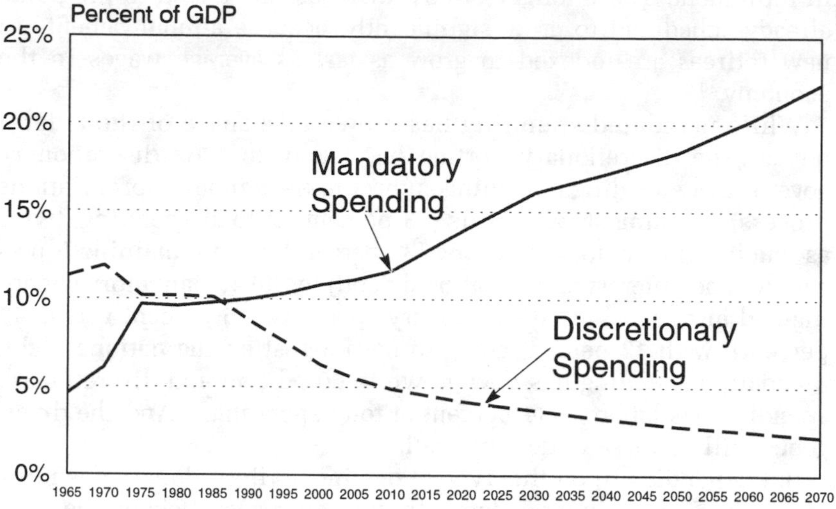

Source: Based on data from the *Budget of the United States Government, Fiscal Year 1999*. Assumes passage of President Clinton's budget proposal without long-run reform.

est payments, our budget would have been in surplus by 1995. From about 1974 to 1997 these payments became an increasingly important part of the automatic obligations budget of the U.S. government— rising from less than 7 percent of total spending in the 1960s and early 1970s to more than 14 percent in 1997. They are scheduled to fall again to 8 or 9 percent by 2008 if we maintain close to zero deficit for a few years.[33] But in a couple of decades, if the deficit again rises, as scheduled, interest costs could again grow dramatically.[34] As they rise, one of these things must happen. Taxes must eventually increase, other spending must fall even further to meet the obligations, or the national debt must increase.

In the Eye of the Storm: The Demographic Revolution

When the baby boomers retire, as we saw in chapter 3 (figure 3.3), the proportion of the population that is elderly will increase drastically, with truly gigantic implications for our fiscal condition, given that retirement and health spending are already on an extraordinary growth path.[35] Within three decades, according to projections by the Social Security and Medicare actuaries, the pension and health demands of retiring baby boomers, combined with the rising costs of health care and interest on the debt, will eat up close to 100 percent of the projected revenues at current tax rates—leaving *literally* nothing for any other public expenditure (whether it be highways, defense, education, the environment, public safety, or the safety net).[36]

When the impacts of the deficits implied by these projections are factored in and more realistic assumptions are made with respect to discretionary spending, the overall federal deficit is projected by GAO to rise from 0.2 percent of GDP in 1997 to 10 percent of GDP in 2050. (Figure 4.8 gives a crude depiction of the interaction of the demographic shifts with the fiscal implications of current law.) This projected increase is based on programmatic growth alone and could reach more than 16 percent of GDP if economic feedback effects from declining national savings are included. The heart of the matter is that such programs as Social Security, Medicare, and Medicaid (including nursing home care) will rise by as much as 7 percentage

Figure 4.8 LONG-TERM FEDERAL EXPENDITURES AND RECEIPTS AS PERCENTAGE OF GDP

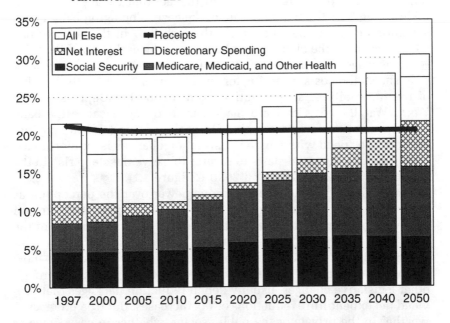

Source: General Accounting Office (1998) model of long-term growth with no legislative action and no economic feedback. Assumes discretionary spending grows with GDP after 2008.

points of GDP and, if deficits are rising, net interest payments will compound from 3 percent to 9 percent of GDP.[37] Surely changes will have been made by then to ensure that such a picture never becomes reality. But just as surely, the aging of the baby boom generation will put the nation under huge fiscal pressures in the interim.

LEGISLATION IN AN ERA WITH NO FISCAL SLACK

All this adds up to a set of enormous and increasing pressures squeezing the discretionary side of the budget—the side of the budget that is subject to annual appropriations. As long as retirement and health costs are not brought under control, the pressures on the rest of the budget will be extraordinary and growing, no matter which political party is in power or what the political leanings of our elected representatives are. Our cash flow accounting systems, however, do not reflect accruals of future liabilities or the fact that we are only in the middle stages of the national budget squeeze. The aging baby boom generation does not begin to strain the cash flow in the budget until a few years after the oldest baby boomers hit the early Social Security retirement age beginning about 2008. This is because such accounting only shows the costs of paying for the retirement and health benefits of the unusually small generation born during the Depression and World War II—costs that are made easier to pay because the baby boom generation is now entering its peak earning (and tax-paying) years.[38] The speed with which the situation changes is extraordinary, however, once the trend starts to reverse (observe the steep rise in the deficit between about 2010 and 2030 in figure 4.1).

Fiscal conditions exercise enormous power over the perception as well as the reality of government. The period of enormous expansion in government created the legislative habit of thinking mainly of the new—new programs, new initiatives. In the period of fiscal constraint, policymakers tended to focus mainly on what existed—how to finance or constrain the built-in growth of old programs through other legislative changes, usually deficit reduction packages that provided net expenditure reductions or tax increases. But true progress—whether in the private or the public sector, whether in easy times or hard—requires attention to both old and new. New needs require new responses, and this inevitably means selective replacement of the old with the new on a gradual but steady basis.

The few remaining years of the 1990s and the first decade of the twenty-first century give modest breathing room. Legislation in 1997 was unique in the way it took advantage of this breathing room. It created some deficit reduction, but then it offset many of those gains, modest at best, by sugar-coating the pill with tax cuts, some of which will have significant costs ten, twenty, and thirty years down the road. The apparent flexibility provided when one ignores longer-term obligations must be transformed into real flexibility for the future. It is time to reconsider our straitjacket and to loosen its knots. Since the jacket is constructed of promises we made to ourselves, it is one that we can remove. But first we must understand at least some of the structural transformations our government has undergone in parallel to the fiscal transformation just discussed.

RESTRUCTURING AND REINVENTING: THE CASE OF SOCIAL INSURANCE

As we have seen, federal government domestic spending grew faster than the economy for much of this century, with its major growth spurt taking place between the end of World War II and the mid-1970s. Meanwhile an era of extraordinarily easy financing has been replaced by an extraordinarily tight one. This fiscal transformation bears a strong relationship to the way government policymaking itself has been structured.

Asking how a typical family is likely to react if its income quadruples is a useful way to set the stage for the discussion. The family members in charge of spending the family's income in the event of such a bonanza will focus mainly on deciding how to spend the new three-quarters of their current income, not on reexamining how they are spending the original quarter. And so it was with government. Reshuffling existing commitments in the face of new demands and plentiful funds was simply not the primary question facing government in the three decades after 1945. Instead, domestic public programs proliferated and bureaucracies grew. Federal initiatives stimulated formation of new state and local coordinating organizations to handle the increasing maze of programs. New stakeholders were created with each new program, and lobbying by these stakeholders multiplied as well.

A backlash to this increasingly dense and complex institutional environment was almost inevitable, irrespective of fiscal conditions.

First, large organizations are subject to diseconomies (as well as economies) of scale, which become more evident as size increases. They have more trouble handling the flow of information as more layers of hierarchy are added. As more needs are met, additional expenditures are likely to go to less and less crucial needs. And as total spending on less crucial needs increases, it attracts more scrutiny. When old age programs were established in the 1930s, for example, they supported the elderly at minimum levels for the last decade of their lives, on average. Now these programs provide much higher real levels of support for closer to two decades.[39] The second reason for an inevitable backlash is that larger government automatically calls more attention to its costs. Those costs deserve more attention because they are a larger portion of what we spend. Interest groups grow in number and intensity because there are more resources at stake. At the extreme, in an entirely socialized economy "government becomes the problem" simply because there is no private sector.

As either a nation or a family moves beyond a period of substantial income growth, it turns more attention to income reallocation. With fewer easy sources of financing available, reallocation and redesign—reinventing government in today's vernacular—become ever more necessary to finance anything new. The challenge is both to reduce the costs and size of government and to improve performance and efficiency. Here one paramount structural issue affecting fiscal policy has come into prominence—the allocation of social risks among people.

Who Risks What?

Federal social insurance policies have become so large that almost no major budgetary action can be taken without reference to them. The 1997 budget legislation, for instance, was sold to the public as a tax cut, but the largest changes were attempts to add further controls on social insurance spending in Medicare, backed up by promises that a Medicare commission would address even more fundamental structural change. Given the large deficits now scheduled, it was inevitable that the country would become engaged in a major debate over social insurance. The debate is not new, but it is newly driven by the requirement to reorder what has become large, risky, and uncertain in itself—government social insurance as it exists today.

Social insurance, now the predominant federal responsibility, is designed to provide public protection against the risks that society decides should not be left entirely up to individual planning or the marketplace. The twentieth century has seen U.S. society, and the developed world generally, respond to demands to provide such protection against an increasing variety of risks. These include old age, widowhood, and disability (Social Security); sickness in old age (Medicare); and unemployment (unemployment insurance). For all these anti-risk programs, individuals or employers contribute directly. Even antipoverty programs financed out of general revenues (primarily cash public assistance and Supplemental Security Income) can be thought of within a social insurance framework. In this view, all members of society contribute according to their means, to cover the risk that unforeseen circumstances may leave us without the means to fend for ourselves.[40]

Three problems with the existing structure stand out. First, our centralized government has become very good at creating pools that reduce risks—the basic goal of insurance—but in a way that shifts costs increasingly from older generations to generations yet to come. Rising tax rates for Social Security and Medicare provide the prime example. Second, new challenges to the work-based insurance system (unemployment insurance, disability insurance, and worker compensation—all developed in the industrial age) have arisen with new patterns of labor market work. For example, the two-earner couples that are now in the majority face a type of risk and need a type of insurance different from those of the one-earner couples that used to dominate our social landscape. And as the structure of the labor market and the nature of jobs have changed, only about one-third of today's unemployed qualify for unemployment insurance as it is currently designed.[41] Third, when advocates, legislators, and program managers become good at protecting their constituents by shifting risks to others—regardless of wider assessments of societal needs—the whole system loses the capacity to respond to change.[42] Even if automatic growth in one program reduces risk for one faction, it is seldom without increasing risks for others.

Patterns of Growth

Large-scale insurance, both public and private, is a comparatively recent phenomenon. It can be traced partly to the same factors of industrialization and urbanization noted earlier: development of sophisticated accounting systems that grew along with the size of both private and public organizations. Insurance by nature requires a large pool of individuals to insure, reasonable costs of administration, and ways of accounting for and reconciling payments and eligibility rules with the aggregate obligations being placed on the insuring organization. Insurance has also grown in response to the increasing demand for risk protection from a more affluent consumer-oriented society.

In the United States, the first significant private pension policies did not begin to emerge until the end of the nineteenth century. In 1871, the Bureau of Labor Statistics recorded only five mutual benefit systems known as "establishment funds"[43]—relief funds that paid out pension and death benefits financed by voluntary employee dues. The first industrial pension plan in the United States was established in 1875 by the American Express Company. Even by 1932, only 15 percent of American workers were even eligible for retirement pension coverage.[44]

Government involvement in pension policy came from several sources. Disability payments to Civil War veterans evolved into the first major public pension policy in the United States. Government gave a further boost for employers to establish pension plans with tax regulations and laws that exempted employee benefits from taxation until they were actually paid (that is, until the employee retired). The Great Depression was a powerful political catalyst for the adoption of a more universal pension system. Some private retirement annuities went bankrupt. Others suspended payment. And the widespread hardship of the era focused public attention on the large proportion of the population with no pension coverage.

Health insurance, at least as we think of it today, is an even newer concept than old age insurance. In industries where accidents were relatively common, such as railroads and mining, firms would often have medical help available on the job. But the first significant modern health insurance in the United States was not offered until 1929, when a Blue Cross plan was created between Dallas public school employees and Baylor University Hospital. In the same year, Los Angeles city government employees entered into an agreement with two physicians for medical services for the employees and their families. This plan is often cited as the first prepaid group practice.[45]

The U.S. government first got heavily into health insurance through its veterans' provisions. For most of the nonelderly, however, government assistance still comes mainly in the form of tax incentives, again an almost unintended consequence of the adoption of taxes on incomes and wages, while health insurance premiums remained an untaxed benefit.[46] This incentive was magnified, first, when wage and price controls were placed on cash wages but not health insurance during World War II and, second, as income and Social Security tax rates rose. The most dramatic recent change in social insurance came in 1965, with passage of Medicare for the elderly and Medicaid for the poor—both major direct health expenditure programs.

The link between private and public insurance growth is close. For example, employer supplements to wages and salaries grew from around one-half of 1 percent of GDP in 1929 to just under 11 percent by 1994.[47] Private pension and welfare funds (primarily pensions and group health insurance) grew at almost the same rate as employer contributions to public social insurance (mainly Social Security and Medicare, but including such items as unemployment compensation). Tax incentives only partly explain the simultaneous growth. Also at play have been rising demand for insurance by an increasingly affluent population and the rising capabilities of large organizations (government and big industry) to pool risks, do the accounting, and supply the insurance services—with public insurance filling huge gaps in the private insurance market and laying the foundation for further expansion.

Problems of Design

Government officials and analysts have spent countless hours refining the basic social insurance framework for pensions over the past half century. This framework now includes national laws mandating that private plans maintain enough assets to cover future liabilities, that employees be vested more quickly, that private pension plans be insured through the Pension Benefit Guarantee Corporation, and that Social Security benefits be indexed for inflation. Government has also made modest efforts to build in controls on public health care costs. The Medicare program now includes a managed care option to control service use and costs, and sets standard reimbursement rates per diagnosis to control provider reimbursement. But Americans have spent more time tinkering around the edges of the social insurance system than fundamentally rethinking its design.

As one consequence, the social insurance system has made promises far in excess of revenue available to it. At the same time it lacks flexibility to adapt and meet emerging needs. Our expectations have become out of line with reality and we must begin the task of rethinking, keeping in mind that the overpromising of our social insurance system today is not due solely or even necessarily to fiscal and political bias against future generations. Many of the features of social insurance that are most out of control are almost accidental—the consequence, in no small part, of public programs copying design features from private programs.

Social insurance for retirement, for example, followed the model of defined benefit pension plans based upon a notion of wage replacement. In other words, pensions in retirement would be targeted to attain a given percentage of wages prior to retirement. Changes in expected life span, ability to work, or demographic trends were not, as they ideally should have been, figured into the picture.

Likewise, public health insurance followed the typical design for employer-provided health insurance in two ways. First, at time of treatment patients paid little, if anything. The treatments that generated higher costs were decided by doctors and patients but paid for by insurers (private or public). The lack of a clear link between decisions on treatment and the associated costs invited overuse and cost escalation. But "insurers" did not absorb the costs of inflation. They ultimately shifted them elsewhere. In the case of employer-provided insurance, in-kind health benefits to workers substituted for higher cash wages. In the case of government, taxpayers footed the bill. Hiding the true cost of insurance policies continues to dilute the incentives for workers and taxpayers collectively to keep health costs under control.

Both public pension and public health costs rose dramatically, too, as people lived longer. With respect to pensions, the focus on annual replacement wages guaranteed that annual benefits for each cohort of workers grew as fast as per capita wages in the overall economy. But increasing life spans made lifetime benefits grow even faster. With respect to rising health costs, built-in incentives toward higher-cost treatments and higher-cost providers were exacerbated by additional years of Medicare coverage from increased years of life and by government subsidizing almost every health dollar spent rather than some basic level of service. These rising costs to social insurance schemes are reflected in figure 4.9, which shows in current dollars the lifetime value of benefits for Social Security and Medicare recipients. Lifetime Social Security and Medicare benefits for an average-wage couple retiring in the mid-1990s approach half a million dollars, a figure that is growing rapidly in real terms for future retirees.[48] Note again that these figures do not take into account rising numbers of beneficiaries relative to taxpayers. Future costs rise not only because of growth in benefits per beneficiary but also because of increasing numbers of beneficiaries.

Getting around these problems is easier for private companies than for government. In the private pension field, firms are turning more

Figure 4.9 LIFETIME SOCIAL SECURITY AND MEDICARE BENEFITS FOR AN
AVERAGE-WAGE ONE-EARNER COUPLE (1998 DOLLARS)

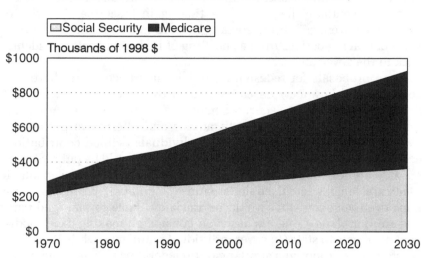

Data are discounted to present value at age 65 using a 2% real interest rate. Assumes
survival to age 65 and retirement at the OASI normal retirement age.
Source: C. Eugene Steuerle and Jon Bakija (1994), *Retooling Social Security for the 21st
Century*. Adjustments to 1998 dollars based on GDP deflator from the Bureau of Economic Analysis, National Income and Product Accounts (base year 1992).

and more toward "defined contribution" pension plans.[49] Under such
plans a given percentage of wages is paid into retirement accounts,
and the retirement benefit depends entirely on these contributions.
This change turns at least some of the risks of living longer back to
the individual and the rest of the risk back to the government safety
net. But private pension plans to date cover only a fraction of
retirement-income needs for most individuals. And the baby boomers
have yet to retire.

In the health field, private employers are outsourcing many of their
activities, while more workers and employers are simply choosing
cash wages over health coverage. Both trends are contributing to the
downward trend of employer health coverage in recent years—adding
to the 40 million persons who already lack health insurance.[50] At the
same time, private employers have led the way in the use of managed
care, such as health maintenance organizations and preferred provider
organizations. These new organizational forms are designed to remove
the incentives to overtreat and overreimburse by paying a fixed

amount per insured family irrespective of that family's health or use of care. By making health insurance more affordable, reductions in cost can eventually help turn the tide against declines in private insurance coverage. But the social gains are much smaller if the private cost saving derives from a shuffling of high-cost health incidents back to the government.

Some proposals for redesigning public insurance would have the government follow new developments in the private sector. For the first time since Social Security began, the Social Security Advisory Council of 1994–96 offered split advice and alternative proposals: Two of these proposals would give individuals defined contribution accounts into which mandated savings or taxes would be put.[51] Strong consideration is also being given in the public debate to conversion of Medicare benefits into fixed dollar sums ("capitated" payments), perhaps even vouchers, that would be made available to managed care and similar plans. Congress has even considered making fixed Medicaid payments to states to cover individual recipients, while President Clinton once proposed a similar cap on federal payments to states on a per recipient basis.[52] Such proposals are modeled on efforts being implemented in the private sector, models that rely mainly upon the notion of paying a fixed or limited sum up front to cover all "basic" medical care and then forcing some intermediary to ensure that total costs for the entire plan stay within the fixed sum.

But the wisdom of merely following private-sector practice—such as defined contribution plans and managed care—has to be examined with great care. Many individuals may remain inadequately covered from society's perspective. And those who are covered may not have the types of protection—even at the same cost—that are appropriate from the standpoint of assuring adequate retirement and health conditions. For example, it can be argued that public pensions oversubsidize the near-elderly while providing inadequate coverage to the truly old. Simply paring retirement benefits across the board would do nothing to solve this problem. The public sector can learn from private practice, as long as it fully recognizes the difference between public and private costs and benefits.

In addition to distinguishing between the public and private goals of social insurance, those who would redesign our social insurance system must worry about how it fits with private insurance. The retirement age as determined by Social Security, for example, is the base upon which private retirement insurance is designed. As the age for receipt of full Social Security benefits rises, this link needs to be kept in mind. The tax preference for employer-provided health insurance, in turn, exacerbates the cost problems in health care by denying assistance to those who obtain insurance outside the employer network, while placing no limit on the size of subsidy for those who have employer-based insurance.

Perhaps an even tougher issue in reforming social insurance is considering what risks to cover. Are risks of the new marketplace becoming more important relative to the traditional risks associated with health care and old age? Can unemployment insurance and workers compensation designed in an industrial age handle the newer risks of a technological, knowledge-based workplace? When workers can more often replace their wages with the wages of a spouse, has the relative size of different social risks changed? And do we have the right mix of responsibilities among employees, employers, and the government for dealing with those risks?

The toughest issues of all may be those associated with who "deserves" benefits from social insurance and who should pay. By constantly shifting higher and higher tax burdens onto future generations, for example, Social Security and Medicare have allowed several generations—including the very rich of these generations—to avoid responsibility for how to pay for the system that has benefited them so much. Similarly, welfare programs, at least until recently, have suffered from an unbalanced emphasis on recipient rights rather than responsibilities. Once the government sets certain minimum standards for the public benefits it will provide, whether to the elderly or the nonelderly needy, the public must scrutinize the payment obligations for those benefits to ensure that all persons pay in a fair and efficient form that does not give the greatest rewards to those who dodge responsibility. At the same time, we must be aware of the effects of imposing undue hardship on the poorest in society and decide on a fair social safety net.

Clearly, a one-design-fits-all-times approach to social insurance is dangerous. That mentality from the past is one of the major sources of today's fiscal crisis. Fiscal and economic pressures now combine to force government to reform not only how much insurance it will provide but also how this insurance will be redesigned at a more fundamental level. New choices will inevitably be made in the ways taxes or premiums are collected, benefits paid, and providers covered. Unless flexibility and adaptability are *built into its very structure*, social insurance can insure us only against yesterday's risks, in a world without yesterday's easy financing.

Timing has become all important. The upcoming retirement of baby boomers forces the economy to adjust within one generation to demographic changes that really stretched over three generations (baby bust/baby boom/baby bust). We know we must pay the piper, but there is a very real cost to procrastinating. Acting sooner rather than later makes changes less painful—allowing long-term growth in the economy to prevent large drops in real benefits from one year to the next, even when promised benefits become a smaller part of a larger economy. The fundamental issues are what we can afford, what risks most require social insurance, and how rights and responsibilities are matched—not how to sustain the promises past generations of policymakers made to future generations they never knew.

Notes

1. Some of this section represents an extension of Steuerle (1996),"Financing the American State at the Turn of the Century," in W. Elliott Brownlee (ed.), Funding the Modern American State 1941–1995.

2. Calculation for current data is based on data from the Congressional Budget Office, January 1998, The Economic and Budgetary Outlook: Fiscal Years 1999–2008, Washington, DC: U.S. Government Printing Office. Historical data for 1963 come from the Budget of the United States Government, Fiscal Year 1999, Historic Tables, OMB (1998).

3. For illustration see figure 4.3.

4. For data see figures 4.3 and 4.4.

5. Based on data from the Bureau of Labor Statistics.

6. Expenditures replaced a much smaller percentage of wages for many fewer workers than today.

7. For a longer discussion see James T. Patterson (1997), "Grand Expectations: The United States, 1945–1974," Oxford University Press.

8. See Robert Samuelson, 1996, The Good Life and Its Discontents, for an expanded argument over the build-up of expectations.

9. See Martha Derthick, "Whither Federalism," Future of the Public Sector Brief #2, June 1996, The Urban Institute Press.

10. Grants from federal to state and local government are included in federal expenditure and excluded from state and local expenditure. From the 1950s to the mid-1970s federal grants increased from less than 1 percent to 3 percent of GDP.

11. It would be a mistake to attribute the growth in spending under President Nixon merely to a continuation of Lyndon Johnson's policies. Nixon sought to solve welfare, added a Food Stamp program, and favored a significant expansion of Social Security, among other activist policies.

12. National Goals Research Staff, July 4, 1970, "Statement of the Counselor to the President," in Towards Balanced Growth: Quantity with Quality, Washington, DC: Government Printing Office (pp. 5–6).

13. Based on outlay and GDP data from the Office of Management and Budget, 1998, *Budget of the United States Government, Fiscal Year 1999*.

14. For data see Steuerle and Bakija, *Retooling Social Security for the 21st Century: Right and Wrong Approaches to Reform*, The Urban Institute Press, Washington, DC, 1994.

15. Author's calculation based on the fact that the Social Security tax base is approximately half of GDP and therefore a 1 percent tax on the wage base is equal to a ½ percent tax on GDP.

16. Based on CPI-U data from the Bureau of Labor Statistics, 1996, Internet site. Inflation in a given year is defined as the percent change in the annual average CPI-U from the previous year to the current year.

17. The gain here declines over time as outstanding bonds are rolled over into new ones paying the higher interest rate.

18. C. Eugene Steuerle, 1992, *The Tax Decade*, Washington, DC: The Urban Institute Press, p. 24.

19. The Treasury estimates that indexing between 1984 and 1989 reduced revenues by $57 billion for fiscal year 1990. Inflation over this 5-year period equaled 19.2 percent. Inflation over the period from 1960 to 1984, on the other hand, was 250 percent, based on the implicit price deflators for GDP, as reported in the *Economic Report of the President*, 1994.

20. Federal taxes remained fairly constant relative to GDP because the federal tax increases in Social Security and bracket creep were offset by legislated tax cuts and more automatic reductions in corporate and excise taxes, e.g., due to a decline in corporate profits and a relative erosion of the excise tax base. State and local taxes actually rose, at least until the late 1970s (see figure 4.4), as states expanded the types of taxes collected, increased rates of existing taxes, moved increasingly into the income tax field, and benefited from bracket creep. Although states also benefited from the growth of federal grants (see figure 4.3), net state and local expenditures rose in part to meet the demands for education of the baby boomers and, later, to finance the nonfederal share of rising health care costs.

21. Calculations are based on the assumption that revenue and GDP increase proportionately.

22. Data based on the historical tables of the *Budget of the United States Government, Fiscal Year 1999*. Defense decreased as a percent of GDP from 13.0 percent in 1954 to 3.2 percent in 1998.

23. The tax rate of 15.3 percent in 1990 was actually determined in the Social Security Amendments of 1977.

24. In this example, we treat employer taxes paid on behalf of the workers as effectively being paid by the worker in the form of commensurately lower wages.

25. In the postwar era, the nation actually hit a low of debt-to-GDP in 1974. One reason the turnaround comes even before inflation starts to decline is that the inflationary tax was more effective the larger the stock of outstanding debt. As debt-to-GDP fell considerably over the early postwar period, there was less of a base on which to assess the inflationary tax. As an extreme example, when debt-to-GDP approaches zero, there can be no inflationary tax upon it. In effect, even with rising inflation in the mid-to-late 1970s, the inflationary tax no longer is offsetting the nominal deficit enough to reduce the debt-to-GDP ratio.

26. Note, however, that some so-called "bracket creep" would remain. Even where individual earnings did not increase, the household's tax rate could rise because more hours were worked or there was an increase in workers in the family.

27. See footnote to figure 4.3.

28. To the extent that inflation is overstated, of course, there will be real growth.

29. For a further discussion of the issues relating to Social Security and Medicare see C. Eugene Steuerle and Jon Bakija, 1994, *Retooling Social Security for the 21st Century: Right and Wrong Approaches to Reform*, Washington, DC: Urban Institute Press.

30. Other types of transfer programs have also grown because of an increase in the number of individuals who become eligible automatically. These are typically welfare-type programs such as AFDC, which until recently usually saw the eligible population grow with the number of single-parent families. Payment levels per person in AFDC, however, did not grow as fast as the economy, so its impact on the entitlement budget has been small relative to health and retirement programs.

31. Data based on *The Economic and Budget Outlook: Fiscal Year 1999–2008*, Congressional Budget Office, Washington, DC, January 1998.

32. Mechanically, this was done by assuming further extension of the types of budget caps agreed to in recent legislation, followed by no real growth as the economy and population expand.

33. Data based on *The Economic and Budget Outlook: Fiscal Year 1999–2008*, Congressional Budget Office, Washington, DC, January 1998.

34. This is not merely a problem in the United States. Among the so-called G-7 or principal industrial countries, gross interest payments have risen from 1.9 percent of GDP in 1970 to 5.0 percent in 1994. See Vito Tanzi and Domenico Fanizza, 1996, "Fiscal Deficit and Public Debt in Industrial Countries, 1970–1994," in C. Eugene Steuerle and Masahiro Kawai (eds.), *The New World Fiscal Order: Implications for Industrial Nations*, Washington, DC: The Urban Institute Press, table 10.4, pp. 242–243.

35. Because our birth rate is declining, the United States would be forced to deal with a declining ratio of workers to retirees anyway. But the retirement of the baby boomers will confront us with the need to deal with the demographic shift within the span of a single generation, rather than in two or three.

36. By another measure, the additional annual Social Security and Medicare commitments to the elderly and near-elderly rise by 3 percent of GDP by about 2030, if health costs per person are brought immediately under control. If they remain out of control, then the commitments to the elderly and near-elderly rise by 6 or more percent of GDP. See C. Eugene Steuerle and Jon Bakija, 1994, *Retooling Social Security for the 21st Century: Right and Wrong Approaches to Reform*, Washington, DC: The Urban Institute Press. Also see Bipartisan Commission on Entitlement and Tax Reform, 1994, *Interim Report to the President*.

37. Data based on GAO model of long-term growth based on no federal action and no economic feedback.

38. See U.S. Board of Trustees of Federal Old-Age and Survivors Insurance and Disability Trust Funds, 1996, *Annual Report*, Washington, DC: U.S. Government Printing Office, p. 111.

39. For a more detailed discussion of the trends in Social Security and longer spans of benefits see Steuerle and Bakija, *Retooling Social Security for the 21st Century: Right and Wrong Approaches to Reform*, The Urban Institute Press, Washington, DC, 1994.

40. See John Rawls, 1971, *A Theory of Justice*, Cambridge, MA: The Belknap Press of Harvard University Press.

41. For a longer discussion of this issue see Wayne Vroman, *The Decline in Unemployment Insurance Claims Activity in the 1980s*, Occasional Paper 91-2, U.S. Department of Labor, Employment and Training Administration, 1991. Data are based on an average

percentage of recipients for the 1990s, based on data for total unemployment from the U.S. Census Monthly Labor Force Survey and data for the number of insured unemployed from the *Handbook of Unemployment Insurance Financial Data*, by the Unemployment Insurance Service.

42. See, for instance, Mançur Olson, 1982, *The Rise and Decline of Nations*, New Haven, CT: Yale University Press.

43. This history of pension and health plans is recounted in more detail in Gregory Acs and C. Eugene Steuerle, "The Corporation As a Dispenser of Welfare and Security," in Carl Kaysen (ed.), *The American Corporation Today*, New York: Oxford University Press, 1996.

44. See, for instance, William Graebner, 1980, *A History of Retirement*, New Haven, CT: Yale University Press.

45. Marilyn J. Field and Harold T. Shapiro, 1993, *Employment and Health Benefits: A Connection at Risk*, Washington, DC: National Academy Press.

46. Eventually the tax exclusion for employer-provided health insurance was codified in the 1954 Tax Code.

47. Data from the Bureau of Economic Analysis. For a longer discussion, see Gregory Acs and C. Eugene Steuerle, "The Corporation As a Dispenser of Welfare and Security," in Carl Kaysen (ed.), *The American Corporation Today*, New York: Oxford University Press, 1996.

48. The amount paid in has also risen over time, but, in general, most individuals retired today still receive more than they have paid in. Particularly for higher-income future retirees, however, this is not true for Social Security. See Steuerle and Bakija, *Retooling Social Security for the 21st Century: Right and Wrong Approaches to Reform*, The Urban Institute Press, Washington, DC, 1994.

49. Data from the *EBRI Databook on Employee Benefits*, Employee Benefits Research Institute, Washington, DC, 1997, p. 84. Total defined benefit plans decreased from 103,000 in 1975 to 84,000 in 1993, while defined contribution plans increased from 208,000 to 619,000 over the same period.

50. In 1995, 40.6 million people were without health insurance according to the U.S. Census Bureau, "Health Insurance Coverage: 1995," released September 26, 1996.

51. See the Report of the 1994–1996 Advisory Council on Social Security, Washington, DC, 1997, chaired by Edward M. Gramlich.

52. To achieve savings of $9.3 billion over 5 years, President Clinton proposed limiting federal spending on Medicaid with a per capita cap to the states based on state Medicaid expenditures for 1996.

Chapter Five

OUR CHANGING POLITICAL PROCESS

Washington is more open, less corrupt, and more accountable than at any time in history. Its principal problem is not that it listens too little, but that it listens—and is shouted at—too much. . . . American government is in touch with everyone, moving in synch with the opinion of the moment as gracefully as blackbirds rising in unison from a field. The blackbirds, of course, often go nowhere.

—Michael Wines, 1994[1]

Earlier chapters describe how powerful forces many years in the making have now converged. These forces—in our economy and family life, in the budget and organization of government—render today's domestic policy choices uniquely confusing and difficult. This is true for public officials and citizens alike. No one can fully understand the forces at work or their many interactions. Nor is there sufficient evidence to know which changes, left to themselves, might be temporary or even self-correcting. Yet public choices have to be made.

The means available to Americans for dealing with these transformations is their political process. Politics and government do not have the answer to every problem. But "politics"—broadly understood—is the tool Americans together possess to cope with their common problems (and this may as easily mean doing less as doing more through government). Stripped down to its essentials, the American political process expresses a faith in self-government. It is the democratic faith that through argument, deliberation, and persuasion people are, in the long run, capable of discovering and promoting their common good. Consider the alternatives. If one rejects democratic self-rule through public debate and deliberation, the only alternatives are rule based on the will of the most powerful, or rule based on deference to experts, insiders, whoever is seen as specially anointed to tell other people what to do. All America's complex institutional forms and political procedures trace back to this basic idea of government by discussion as the best means of arriving at policy choices.[2]

And yet our political process—the method we have for dealing with all the other transformations—has itself undergone a sea change in recent decades. These changes add up to a simultaneous triumph of democratization and distrust. The paradox is remarkable. On the one hand, politics has become more sensitive than ever to the public's opinions and anxieties. On the other, the public has become increasingly cynical about and alienated from this political system. A development that should increase a sense of legitimacy in public affairs has been accompanied by just the opposite response. American democracy may be more open, inclusive, and information-rich than ever before. But today's Americans typically report feeling more victimized than accommodated, more like subjects than citizens.

All the challenges described in previous chapters are now being encountered in a novel political context. An unwritten constitution of polls, policy activists, media-based politics, and advocacy groups has grown up around the written Constitution and traditional ideas of parties, interest groups, and elected representatives. In this chapter we examine how these various political tendencies fit together at century's end and their overall implications for domestic policymaking.

THE TRIUMPH OF DEMOCRACY

The home-grown "pro-democracy" forces that have come to dominate the landscape are a good place to begin. The collective result is peculiarly a creation of our own times, a "hyper-democracy." We use hyper-democracy to mean the expanding and quickening circuitry through which publics and public officials interact incessantly, even hourly, over the shaping of American life through public policy. There is now Big Democracy to go along with Big Government. Hyper-democracy offers the *opportunity* to represent the people's genuine interests more effectively, but whether it does so in fact depends largely on the quality of deliberation that evolves. Four key features of our Big Democracy stand out. As we discuss each, we focus particularly on areas where we think the quality of public deliberation is threatened.

Inclusive Democracy: The Multiplication of Voices

American politics has been heading toward greater "democracy" from the beginning. There have been zigs and zags along the way, as with the imposition of segregation after the end of slavery, but the inexorable tendency has been to expand "the people" to mean all the people.

Legal formalities are one part of this story. Constitutional mechanisms to "refine" public participation and hold it at arm's length from government (the electoral college, indirect election of senators) faded progressively into insignificance. Within a generation of the Constitution's ratification, property qualifications for white male electors were being dismantled. Women gradually acquired the vote—at the state level in the late nineteenth century and at the federal level through constitutionally guaranteed suffrage in 1920. However, the culmination of formal political inclusiveness occurred only after the mid-twentieth century, with the national guarantee of voting rights for minorities, young adults, and the principle of "one person, one vote" throughout all U.S. political jurisdictions.[3] This historical trajectory has taken us from a time when the momentous issue of ratifying the Constitution was put before an electorate that included less than 5 percent of Americans to today's mass democracy in which virtually any nonincarcerated adult can register and vote (although declining proportions of Americans are availing themselves of that right).

Legal barriers excluding diverse voices have also fallen dramatically since the mid-twentieth century in the courts—the least popularly based branch of government. New legislation and more activist judges made the legal process far more accessible than ever before.[4] Expansive changes in the rules of standing, class action lawsuits, and recovery of legal expenses have allowed more groups to press their policy claims through the judicial process. Rules of administrative law that once mainly protected business from government have been broadened to ensure access to administrative decisionmaking for a host of advocacy groups. In these and other ways, once marginalized groups—women, minorities, environmentalists, consumers, the disabled, and many others—are explicitly included in the formal political processes of government.

And the informal forms of democratic inclusiveness have been at least as impressive as the formal in recent decades. Policy activists in proliferating groups have appeared on the scene, particularly since the tumultuous 1960s. If average Americans had been asked in 1955 about "the movement," they would probably have made mental reference to the communist movement of then-recent McCarthyite fervor. Asked the same question 20 years later in 1975 they would almost certainly have asked "which movement—civil rights, feminist, environmentalists, consumers, farm workers, abortion rights, conservative Christian, gay rights . . . or what?" One indicator of this change is the rapid growth in the number of interest groups since 1960. Roughly 70 percent of Washington-based political associations have opened their doors since that year.[5] America has experienced other periods of high group agitation in the past, the turmoil leading up to the Civil War being a particularly unhappy example.[6] What is new is not simply the number of groups, but the adversarial, well-organized, permanent

maze of advocacy groups enveloping the comparable maze of government policy responsibilities that has grown up over the past half-
century. Growing consciousness of politics as providing policy
choices and growing demands for inclusiveness have gone hand in
hand. Given the immense stakes in all manner of modern policy
issues—touching virtually every aspect of Americans' lives—the
complexity and diversity of modern-day group agitation is without
historical precedent.

The mid-twentieth century's civil rights movement served as something of a bellwether for many subsequent developments in the new
group politics. What often began as rather fluid social movements
enlisting enthusiasts for given policy causes gradually became more
organized, more media savvy, and more enduring lobbying presences.
All became part of a growing consciousness of and preoccupation
with public policy. Every new government initiative raised the stakes
for more groups to become active. Semi-dormant groups such as the
Sierra Club and Audubon Society, for example, have become ener-
gized on national policy issues in partial competition with new, more
strident groups such as Friends of the Earth and Greenpeace. Advances in communication technology obviously did much to facilitate
the organization of political claims by like-minded interests that
might otherwise never have been mobilized in cohesive lobbying
groups. When new "public interest" lobbies (for consumers, the environment, etc.) organized against older entrenched interests, opponents were spurred to counter-mobilize as more effective business
lobbies. When complex public policies produced different impacts for
different groups, this served to divide once united constituencies and
caused ever more differentiated groups to form. Health care policy is
a good example, splitting hospitals, doctors, and insurers into different groups as well as reconstituting umbrella organizations.

Compared to the blanket racial, gender, and other exclusions of the
past, hyper-democracy does represent a triumph of inclusion. We can
celebrate its success without naively dismissing its own tendency to
exclude in a modern way. In an era when everything of public concern
tends to be translated into issues of public policy, the new inclusiveness favors the organized, the funded, the loud-voiced, and the politically active. Precisely because hyper-democracy allows more people
and groups to participate formally and informally, those who are not
activists are perhaps further "outside" than ever before.

In this post-sixties environment, the growing cadres of policy activists who have taken advantage of the increased opportunities for participation are not generally representative of average citizens. They

show little of ordinary Americans' desire for nondoctrinaire, moderate, workable policy processes.[7] The presumptive voices of various American publics, in other words, have been multiplied and amplified in a way that is more than merely additive, more than simply putting more chairs at the table. It is an inclusiveness of "agendized" groups—voices advocating and defending distinctive social causes with which they are *permanently* identified. Compared with 50 years ago, policymaking is infused with activists and groups pursuing some permanent ideological agenda to shape public affairs. Falling into this category are defense funds, coalitions, action groups, forums, and networks, along with many think tanks and policy institutes that have the label nonpartisan but in fact push highly partisan agendas. In such agendas, specific issues often matter less on their own merits than as markers in the group's permanent campaign of policy advocacy. "Framing the issue," "setting the agenda," "sending messages," and the like can be at least as important as striking a particular "deal" to achieve a policy settlement. Long-term settlements may actually be the last thing wanted by those active in advocacy politics.

Open Democracy: The Repeal of Public Privacy

Earlier in this century it was possible to carry on a good deal of policymaking behind the scenes, with relatively little publicity for the people or processes involved. Today publicity, exposure, investigation, revelation, and campaigning for policies through the media has become the norm.

For example, at mid-century the classic study *Presidential Power* portrayed a relatively insulated world of Washington bargaining. Public attention was at a distance, an external backdrop of "prestige" that could slowly change and might be indirectly used, for bargaining and persuasion, by the men governing public policy among themselves inside the "Washington community."[8] In more recent decades, the community has become more of a goldfish bowl of constant exposure and "going public."[9] The 1935 Social Security Act and its subsequent amendments over the next several decades were framed in what now seems a remarkably nonpublic way, especially when compared with the more recent attempt of President Clinton to propose that Social Security reform evolve from a set of public meetings around the country in 1998, or the massive level of input into the 1993–1994 health insurance reform debate.[10] Policymaking is now porous and exposed to public view. "Behind the scenes" scarcely seems to exist except as a slogan for publicizing the latest exposé of what is "really" going on in the political game.

Again, the tumultuous events of the 1960s were associated with this insistence on greater exposure and participatory openness in the political environment. Formal barriers insulating policymaking and the people involved fell dramatically. In Congress, publicly recorded votes, open committee meetings, more democratic procedures, televised debates, and other such changes became the order of the day. Throughout government new Freedom of Information laws, public disclosure, public hearings, and reporting requirements were put into place. After Richard Nixon resigned from the presidency, the most sustained and comprehensive effort at ethics reform and public disclosure in American history began.[11] With not only the policy process but policymakers themselves subject to public scrutiny and exposure, appearances and the technicalities of behavior have grown in importance.

Informal forces have been even more important than these formal varieties of openness. In the wake of the Vietnam and Watergate experiences, investigative reporting and media exposures have become the stock and trade of covering public affairs. Along with the new openness of competing leaks, press conferences, and staged media events has come a dominant form of coverage that seeks to unmask the "real" meaning of events as attempts by one side or another to gain political advantage over its rivals.[12] In contrast to the earlier, more genteel environment of deference to public officials, it became the norm after Vietnam, Watergate, and similar experiences to report all policymaking as plebiscitary—oriented predominantly to electioneering strategies for short-term political gain and public favor.

The newfound democratic openness has been aided, not least of all, by innovations in communication technology, which have taken place with remarkable and accelerating speed over the past century. Figure 5.1 shows just how quickly most households have become accustomed to the new devices as they became available. These changes in communications and media generally are improvements in economic well-being, but they have also altered the types of messages we receive in ways that may not be improvements. As one example noted by Daniel Boorstin, historically almost all communications were messages sent to specific addresses. The radio and television changed that by broadcasting to no one in particular.[13]

With the help of this new technology, invasive journalism and pervasive exposure are now taken for granted. Widespread use of TV mini-cams, videos, Xerox machines, concealable tape recorders,

Figure 5.1 COMMUNICATION TECHNOLOGY IN AMERICAN SOCIETY

(percentage of households possessing various technology)

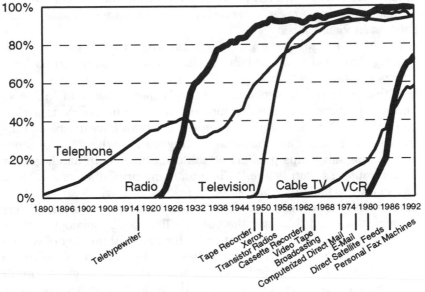

Year Device Became Commercially Available

Source: Urban Institute, calculations based on data from Bureau of the Census, *Historical Statistics of the United States*, 1975, *Statistical Abstract of the United States 1994*, and *Datapedia of the United States* (Lanham, MD: Bernan Press, 1994). Data before 1920 are upper-bound estimates. Commercial introduction dates are approximations rather than precise dates.

faxes, and the Internet have made it virtually impossible for political authorities to monopolize information and control criticism. To take one seemingly small example, with no Xerox machines there would be much less material to leak and far shorter stacks of files for investigators to pore through—from the Pentagon Papers revealing official deceptions in the Vietnam War to the saga of special prosecutors investigating Iran-Contra, Whitewater, campaign finances, and White House interns. The overall result is a remarkable dissolving of boundaries that once insulated politicians and other policymakers from public attention. Leading college textbooks can now take as their organizing theme the idea that our political system is far more exposed to popular pressures than it ever was at mid-century.[14]

Obviously, the new openness has positive and negative features. Such an environment offers access to voices that would not previously have been heard. It also facilitates the exposure of failures and wrongdoing throughout the political system. But at the same time it is an environment offering ever more opportunities for dispute, delay, and preemptive strikes through policymaking in the media. The politics of disclosure encourages a pervasive sense of contentiousness, mistrust, even viciousness.

We are not arguing the case for returning to the type of policy-making that used to occur behind closed doors. But the gains from openness cannot be fully captured unless we understand the frustration that is bound to accompany today's more open and inclusive political process. Case studies indicate that in one policy area after another, large, seemingly homogeneous coalitions have dissolved during recent decades and become battlegrounds where many more groups and subgroups publicly attack each other with much greater contentiousness than before.[15] The contemporary public arena, thus, has many participating voices—but few leaders who can count on bargaining quietly together and "delivering" major blocs of supporters through thick and thin over the years.[16] To argue by analogy, today's policymaking marketplace is not one where a small number of whole-salers can do business on a regular basis, but one where a multitude of merchant-salesmen must bark their wares in a permanently floodlit midway. And since American voters themselves have become more "independent" and less tied to party labels over the years,[17] customer loyalty in the political midway, as in the private marketplace, can no longer be counted on. In that sense the openness that prevails is one of uncertainty and public contentiousness on all sides.

The debit side of hyper-democracy for policymaking comes into even clearer focus when we consider the final two characteristics of the changing political process.

Media-Based Democracy: The Distortion of Attention

Innovations in the means Americans have for paying attention to their public affairs have occurred with breathtaking speed over the past century. Thanks to the communications revolution, a constant flux of information now radiates into and out of the public forum. And with communication on questions of policy and political conduct instantaneous, continuous, and pervasive, ever more frenetic efforts are needed to capture attention and "send messages" amid the din.

The gains are extraordinary from a communications technology revolution that can claim a significant share of the credit even for the downfall of communism in Russia and Eastern Europe. Other consequences of technology, however, have done much to turn public affairs into a daily or hourly spectacle to be passively consumed by a mass spectator audience. In terms of a generic sense of "what is going on," Americans today are obviously more quickly and intimately informed about more things than ever before. But as Walter Lippmann observed 75 years ago as the age of electronic communications was beginning, no data speak for themselves. More than ever before, what the public knows of the larger world are mental images constructed out of media representations of the environment, a fictional "pseudo-environment" that may bear greater or lesser correspondence to the underlying reality.[18] But it is on the basis of this indirect, imagined world that contemporary citizens must typically judge and act. For example, during the run-up to the 1992 election, official figures on the economy were mixed, with inflation and interest rates low and unemployment rising moderately by historic standards. This mixed statistical story of strength and weakness was no match for the more dramatic news accounts of economic distress. And media coverage of the economy remained overwhelmingly negative throughout the 1992 recovery, as was the public perception of economic trends.[19]

Modern communications might be said so far to have yielded not so much a highly informed as a highly exposed public.[20] And it is exposure of a particular kind. While the communications technology undergirding our contemporary form of democracy brings a tremendous volume of information before the public, it also tends to portray policymaking as a constant drumbeat of unresolved, if not unresolvable, policy problems. Common sense suggests what many research studies are now showing: that even with the best of intentions, the exposé approach to policy issues in the modern communication system can be quite misleading. In particular, it plays to short attention spans, immediate reactions, and the inevitable human demand for simplified dramatics.

Attention spasm. Media scrutiny of public policy issues and choices is spasmodic in three respects. First, media attention typically lurches from one topic area to another, giving extensive coverage and then moving on to the next "hot" subject. Second, for any given episodic topic, attention usually focuses sequentially on one side of the issue— positive or negative, enthusiasm or fear—at a time. Rarely do many aspects of the same issue receive simultaneous focus, and many faces of complex policy issues remain hidden.[21] Finally, within a given presentation of an issue, electronic technology provides the public with a continuous flow of information, but precisely for that reason communication must be broken into short morsels to hold people's attention. Thus, even with news extending to a daily 24 hours, CNN stories average only about three minutes compared to a two-minute average for the stories on the three major networks' 22-minute news broadcasts.[22] Fitfulness and morselization are endemic to the electronic mass forum.

On-line responsiveness. In the past, physical difficulties of communication meant that policymakers had to exercise some version of independent judgment on a good many issues. Of course, judgment could still be poor, and decisionmaking in the proverbial smoke-filled rooms was no guarantee of unclouded thinking. But lacking a modern system of virtually instantaneous communication, policy deliberations had time, so to speak, to gestate and ripen internally before wider public reactions could be registered. The pace was contemplative even if the decisionmakers did not want to be.

Today's technology has been rapidly shrinking the time delay between inside decisionmaking and outside reactions. Call-in talk shows register public responses while a major event is still unfolding. Moreover, the 24-hour news cycle of the modern media is a tapeworm that needs continuous feeding. Most congressmen by the late 1990s were offering their constituents "home pages" with Webworks. And with the rapidly expanding Internet, anyone with a computer has minute-by-minute access to pending legislative committee agendas, congressmen's voting positions, e-mail facilities, and bulletin boards. Computer-enhanced call-in campaigns to policymakers[23] abound, and fax campaigns are so prevalent that many members of Congress constantly change or hide their fax numbers to deter interest groups from jamming them with instantaneous, often pretended popular reaction to events.[24] For those with interests in a particular issue, on-line policy decisionmaking seems destined to grow.

Feeding tastes for the dramatic. Modern media technology exposes much. But it does not expose all things even-handedly. As competitors for attention, modern media are apt to associate immediacy and "liveness" with importance, intensity of feeling with seriousness. A dull-looking congressional vote, agency announcement, or treaty signature may signify an important change in our world. But such things cannot compete for public attention with a plane crash or personality clash. Walter Lippmann's 75-year-old observation about the print media has been vastly magnified by today's electronic media. Drama—emotive, visual intensity—easily displaces substantive importance in reporting on and thinking about what is going on in the world. Pathology is the privileged content in communicating information for society's self-understanding. In the current media vernacular, "if it doesn't bleed it doesn't lead."[25] In this environment, the communication of information about public policy choices gravitates toward human interest "story lines" involving dramatic conflict, visual imagery, and personally compelling hopes and fears.[26] To attract attention and audience shares, media discussion of public affairs is typically cast as a two-sided, adversarial debate, when in fact there may be many sides or no predetermined sides at all for complex policy issues. If media politics helps expose more people to more information, it also nurtures conflict and distorts perceptions of public "problems," which may not have been problems in the first place.

Milder critics surveying this scene contend that today's high-tech instruments of public communication could do more to live up to their educational potential. More severe critics argue that such instruments are actually making us dumber. What is undeniable is that each of us has a limited attention span, a desire to respond quickly if that makes our voice more likely to be heard, and an inclination to favor dramatic entertainment over substantive information. What today's communication technology does is to enlarge and recast these individual proclivities into patterns of public thinking at a societal level. Far from being a source of solace or shield against despair, "the social order" is experienced vicariously through the mass media as a neverending series of adversarial arguments about social pathologies and a gnawing presence in everyday life. Like marbles falling out of a chute, policy problems in media democracy seem to drop on the public mind as sharp, self-contained, serial headaches about which experts and policymakers do little but disagree.

Crafted Democracy: Manipulation and the New Political Technology

Given developments toward a more inclusive, open, media-based democracy, it is not surprising to find that those wishing to govern have developed coping strategies. Building and maintaining public support in the policymaking process has become a fine art. First Lady Hillary Clinton speaks for a whole political generation that now understands that "you have to run a campaign for policy just like you do for elections."[27] There are in fact hundreds of permanent policy campaigns constantly under way across the American political landscape.

Remarkable developments in what can be called "political technologies" represent an array of sophisticated techniques for studying, manufacturing, organizing, and manipulating public voices in political support of candidates and causes. The techniques are by no means fool-proof devices for persuading a supposedly gullible public, and competitors' techniques for shaping public opinion can cancel each other out. But the cumulative impact of the new political technology gives a much more calculated, contrived quality to the whole political process than anything that prevailed even as recently as the 1950s. Much of the democratic conversation about policy is now talk crafted by professional opinion managers.[28] It is important to appreciate how recently this development of sophisticated, manipulative techniques has occurred.

Polling

Modern polling proved to be the midwife of hyper-democracy. Public opinion research in the United States is often traced back to nineteenth-century straw votes and newspaper straw ballots, later expanded to include mail questionnaires. The unreliability of these methods eventually led to more statistically valid public opinion polling, which began in the late 1930s under such names as Gallup and Roper. Expanding on consumer research methods developed in the 1920s largely for purposes of advertising and marketing, polling gained momentum especially after World War II.[29] Statistically reliable polling became a prominent part of public life after the 1950s, complementing the growth in mass communication technology.

Polling techniques have advanced considerably in recent decades. But their potential for informing has yet to be realized, as they are still rarely used to examine policy issues in any depth. Most polls that Americans hear about are routinely conducted by major media outlets. These media-inspired polls, which occupy center stage in public attention, are produced not so much to probe public views on policy issues as to create "news" stories reporting the poll results. Such stories typically describe the popularity of particular viewpoints and personalities, as well as dramatize current events.[30] For complex policy choices, the questions are usually too simplistic to provide anything more than off-the-top-of-the-head opinions. Nonetheless, since the early 1960s, as figure 5.2 suggests, reporting the public's alleged opinion to itself has become a prominent and enduring way of presenting public affairs through the media.

Polling that Americans do *not* hear about is conducted continuously and privately by politicians and groups active in the political process. These are typically used to design media campaigns, target fund-raising opportunities, or plan other aspects of political strategy. Pri-

Figure 5.2 PUBLIC OPINION POLLS IN THE NEW YORK TIMES

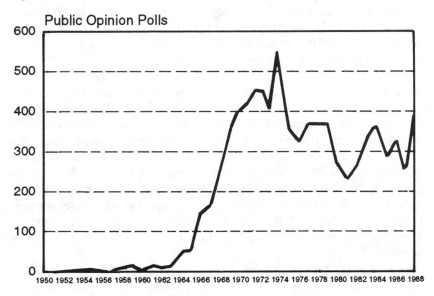

Notes: Figure shows the number of days cited under "public opinion" in the *New York Times*. According to John Brehm the cited public opinion stories "by and large report poll results, and only rarely reflections on public opinion in the broader sense."
Source: John Brehm, *The Phantom Respondents* (Ann Arbor, MI: University of Michigan Press, 1993): p. 4.

vate poll and focus group results are often used for "issue position-ing," for example, whereby a public figure can take an agreeable but substantively vacuous public stand on a variety of otherwise contro-versial topics. The result of all this fairly superficial probing of mass opinion can resemble an empty canyon of ricocheting echoes, none of which say anything of substance about public policy choices.[31] But today's all-pervasive polling does have the effect of supplying day-by-day readings that track the public's snap viewpoints about politicians' and other policymakers' performance. Such almost instantaneous per-formance monitoring adds powerful impetus to the "on-line respon-siveness" of media-based democracy.

Political Marketing

From opinion polling about what the public thinks, it has been but a short step to new political technologies for telling people what they want to hear. Politicians and what were then quaintly called "advertising men" discovered each other in the 1950s. The first efforts were a simple technology transfer from advertising campaigns for consumer products to the "marketing" of candidates in elections. Then recognition grew that the citizen did not so much vote for a candidate as make a psychological purchase of him.[32]

Since the 1950s, therefore, more and more specialized political consultant services have developed to cover every imaginable point of contact between leaders and the governed. The basic features of this landscape now include the overlapping techniques of survey research, strategic planning, direct marketing, image management, media materials production, "media buying," event management, targeted "grassroots" mobilization, research against opponents (full-service "oppo firms" being the fastest growing segment of the consultant industry in the 1990s), as well as the extensive fund-raising services needed to pay for all these other services. In 1994, the 15 most expensive Senate campaigns spent 70 percent of their funds on consultants' services.[33]

In this arms race of professional opposition politics, consultants and politicians have also had strong incentives to turn seasonal work—election-time services—into long-term employment. The tools of polling, marketing, and orchestrating public support now extend to full-time consulting on policy issues (health care, tax reform, etc.) as these rise and fall on the media agenda. In fact, the handiwork of professional, consultant-based politics often creates the only picture of public affairs that the average American experiences.

The pervasiveness of political marketing means that policymaking now takes place in a context of permanent, professionally managed, and adversarial campaigning to win the support of those publics upon whom the survival of the political client depends.[34] Into the pseudo-environment of the media are poured massive amounts of what historian Daniel Boorstin began to perceive early in the age of TV politics in 1961 and called "pseudo-events."[35] These are not spontaneous, real events but orchestrated happenings that occur because someone has planned, incited, or otherwise brought them into being for the purpose of being reported upon and swaying opinion. Leaks, interviews, trial balloons, opinion reports, reaction stories, staged appearances, and camera-ready confrontations are obvious examples we hardly notice anymore. Pseudo-events have become so pervasive that it is now difficult to see anything reported about public affairs that is not an orchestrated happening for ulterior motives of professionals in politics or the media (a distinction that itself disappears in hyper-democracy). In political management, the greatest art of all is to make the counterfeit appear candid and unrehearsed. In society's continuously open "feed" of media politics, the greatest sin of all is silence and "dead time." Hence modern democracy's demanders and suppliers of pseudo-events thrive in a permanent love feast of co-dependency.

The heavy infusion of political management into hyper-democracy has the effect of transforming politics and public affairs into an unending stream of pseudo-events for citizens' consumption. As Boorstin shrewdly predicted, in this montage of orchestrated happenings ordinary people are confused, not so much by the artificial simplification as by the artificial complication of experience. Political news—including news about public policy—is largely news made to happen. Meanings are spun. The performance becomes more significant than what is said. Pseudo-events generate counter-pseudo-events and thus, in defiance of the laws of nature, generate larger outputs of emptiness from whatever small amount of spontaneous happenings might have actually existed. What happened becomes enmeshed in ambiguities of what really happened, what might have been the motives, and whether any statement really means what it seems to say. In short, the distinction in reality between the actual train wreck and the interview about the train wreck tends to evaporate.

The crafted politics of modern democracy cost huge amounts of money to create and distribute, hence the importance of fund-raising. In turn, the buying and selling of political happenings through the media means that a great many people have a strong financial stake in promoting pseudo-events. This is one reason that artificial happenings tend to drive out authentic ones in public affairs, but it is far from the only reason. In contrast to the complexities of policy and politics, pseudo-events are more dramatic, more easily disseminated, more predigested for easy absorption. They provide the "issues" for common discourse with a minimal expenditure of mental energy on the consumer's part.

In sum, the modern American political process is highly inclusive of those who are able to organize. It is also porous to public scrutiny and exposure, saturated by media concerns, and constantly crafted as a public presentation by skilled professionals. This configuration presents at least three general problems as an environment for deliberating on and making public policy choices. These features are not invariably present in all policymaking circumstances, but all three are pervasive tendencies that capture the general drift of things in our modern political process. First, policy debate occurs without deliberation. Second, public mobilization occurs without a public. Finally, the public tends to be taught that nothing being said can be trusted. Other than this, the system works well.

THE PUBLIC'S POLICY CONVERSATION

Talk—not power, expertise, or deference to authority—is the essence of democratic self-government. Precisely for this reason freedom of speech, press, and assembly is given the highest legal protection among Americans' cherished natural rights. And for the same reason it is important to consider the kind of public policy debate that is encouraged by today's political environment. Whatever the country might do about its changing economic and social condition will have to be done through a vast, ongoing conversation among the people— both by those who participate directly in a more open political process and by those who participate indirectly by silently acquiescing in or griping about whatever happens.

The process of government by discussion has always been a messy mixture of emotion, reason, and a good bit of chicanery. Indeed, U.S. historians have trouble pointing to any golden age of purely rational policy debate. Yet, our changing political processes are reshaping the possibilities of argument, deliberation, and persuasion that lie at the heart of the nation's democratic faith. What has developed is certainly not direct citizen engagement and control over policymaking. But neither is it the traditional picture of policy debate, in which constitutional structures and limits in communication technology tended to hold expressions of popular opinion at arm's length from policy arguments within government.

Policy Debate without Deliberation

The political environment of hyper-democracy systematically discourages substantive policy arguments that test and refine competing truth claims. This is because good policy argumentation is bad political management—the central, orienting insight of which was expressed by one of the ablest founders of the profession in a landmark strategy memo of 1967:

> The natural human use of reason is to support prejudice, not to arrive at opinions. . . . [W]e have to be very clear on this point: that the re-

sponse is to the image, not to the man. . . . It's not what's there that
counts, it's what's projected—and carrying it one step further, it's not
what he projects but rather what the voter receives. It's not the man we
have to change, but rather the *received impression.* Reason requires a
high degree of discipline, of concentration. . . . [I]mpression can en-
velop him, invite him in, without making any intellectual demand.
(italics in original)[36]

In the media contest for control of public impressions, it is generally
less effective to inform than to construct strategies to "frame" issues
and images, to shift focus and counterattack rather than answer, to
avoid admissions of ignorance or uncertainty, and to exaggerate policy
conflict for dramatic impact.[37] As a leading practitioner in the profession put it, "Let's face it, there are three things that the media are
interested in: pictures, mistakes, and attacks."[38]

Winning policy debates in the world of consultant politics and
hyper-democracy is defined as coming out on top in a series of dis-
connected, adversarial contests where results are measured by vote
percentages and "moving the [poll] numbers." Doing whatever will
win on these terms has become the accepted norm, not because consultants and their clients are bad people but because all participants
realize that this is the principal way they are judged and rewarded.
To gain attention, raise funds, and be newsworthy amid a glut of
information, problems need to be framed in terms of dramatic, black-
and-white conflict. As experienced by the average citizen, the likely
result of this activity is an atmosphere of generalized contentiousness
without the payoff of seeing contending claims about policy problems
tested, refined, and moved toward conclusions.

The politics of agendized groups reenforces the same pattern.
Among the unrepresentative corps of activists who have taken advantage of the system's increased openness, policy disputes are likely to
begin with presumptions, not of good-faith bargaining in search of
agreement, but of confrontation with adversaries who are presumed
hostile to one's cause (else they would be on "our" side). Exaggerating
their differences with opponents, followers choose leaders who are
more extreme than they are to fight the good fight, thereby encouraging
a self-fulfilling prophecy of adversarial conflict.[39] Since they, in turn,
have to mobilize members and contributions around dramatic, easily
understood threats to the cause, group leaders are ultrasensitive to
negotiating anything that could be seen as a sellout. Leaders' incomes,
moreover, are often enhanced when they can make contributors feel
more, not less, threatened. The curious result is that policy activists
often won't even agree when they agree, lest they be charged with

compromising the group's cause and identity or reducing the permanent demand for their role as agents.

For these reasons, a great deal of policy debate is not really concerned with "making policy"—in the sense of finding a settled course of public action that people can live with. It is aimed at crusading for an agenda by confronting power with power, fund-raisers with fund-raisers, media campaigns with media campaigns. With differences ever magnified and opponents demonized, any discussion of public policy is likely to leave ordinary Americans feeling that all politics is a matter of watching scorpions in a bottle. On the matter of race relations, for example, there is not only the normal friction inherent in any change that accompanies progress. As Orlando Patterson points out, mobilized political groups on all sides of the issue have a stake in exaggerating the idea that no progress has been made, thus inhibiting average Americans' understanding of what has actually happened.[40] On welfare, one side will point to declining AFDC or TANF benefits while ignoring expansions in other income-conditioned programs, while the other side will allude to the cost of all social insurance (such as Social Security), most of which does not go to low-income individuals. Other policy debates on affirmative action, foreign trade, abortion, crime, business regulation, and environmental crises are rich in examples of debate without deliberation.

The overall result distorts underlying policymaking realities. First, the public is commonly presented with a picture of deeper disagreement among policy experts and a general contentiousness in policy arguments than may in fact be true when the cameras and microphones are turned off. Second, immense reenforcement is given to the natural human tendency to overestimate sudden and dramatic risks and underestimate the long-term consequences of chronic problems. Finally, attention is focused on attention-grabbing renditions of what has gone wrong in America for which somebody else can be blamed. The process of debating policy thus constantly reenforces a culture of complaint where seemingly dramatic conflicts never really settle anything or lead anywhere.

Public Mobilization without a Public

Polling and other modern political technologies now make it possible for politicians, consultants, and the media to "know" the public without having an actual political relationship with it. Politics in practice tends to bifurcate. On the one hand are the ad-packaged images for broadcasting to faceless consumers of the mass media. This is the political theater average Americans experience in the daily news:

sound bites, horse race stories, political ads, and the like. The public is courted but not mobilized through engaged political commitments.

On the other hand is a never-ending series of customized micro-campaigns tailored to subgroups of the population with distinctive demographic profiles. In terms of actually mobilizing people to participate, consultant-managed politics shifts the strategic incentives from support-gathering to support-hunting. Payoffs (votes, poll numbers, fund-raising) are most effectively achieved by concentrating resources on narrowly targeted groups of predisposed supporters rather than by developing general coalitions. One example: Modern political management techniques allow "list vendors" to assemble computer-generated lists of potential supporters profiled by demographic, consumer, and political characteristics. From such lists "personalized" mailings and other direct contact "hits" on individuals are organized, which in turn can serve as the database for organizing periodic "grass-roots" letter-writing, call-in, and other mobilization campaigns.

All of this makes for a public policy conversation in which it is ever more feasible to cater to the like-minded and inject the voice of "our people" into policymaking contests.[41] Obversely, such targeting excludes from political contact and mobilization those people who are not precommitted true believers—ordinary folks who, as one leading consultant has put it, "are not profitable to work."[42] The modern political process is rich with incentives to promote differences and mobilize factions. Far fewer are the incentives to bridge differences and build coalitions through negotiated compromises. The result, as Harvard political scientist Morris Fiorina has put it, "is unnecessary conflict and animosity, delay and gridlock, and a public life that seems to be run by wackos."[43] It is an environment in which the American public as an authentic citizen presence—a body politic linking past and future—becomes easy to ignore.

These features of our hyper-democracy give vast new dimensions to an age-old problem. Consent of the governed has always been a manipulated contest, persuasion always a skirting of the difference between image and reality. The Founding Fathers had it right. The people's will is not the same thing as the public's interest. The new age of superficial opinion and politically crafted talk has grossly widened the gap between the two.

The Triumph of Distrust

From the very beginnings of American politics, democracy and distrust have gone hand in hand. The generation of people who transformed themselves from colonists into Americans created an unprecedented form of popular government and made powerful claims on such government to secure their rights and actively legislate for the public good. Yet, they were also deeply suspicious of government's power to subvert their liberties. This dual outlook found expression in our first moments as a nation, when the Declaration of Independence began with a list of complaints about too little government— the British king's obstruction of good legislation and administration— and ended with complaints about the royal government abusing its powers by doing too much.[44]

This venerable love-hate relationship with government continues. But it seems to have taken a new type of debilitating turn. The good news is that Americans remain deeply attached to the symbols of their constitutional regime. There is little evidence that they have withdrawn patriotic feelings toward their basic form of government and its founding values.[45] The bad news is that a long-term downward trend in political trust reflects not simply a skepticism toward authority but a much more negative cynicism toward anything that happens in politics. To doubt and question public authority is a time-honored American tradition. Always to expect the worst is not.

While Americans continue to express hope for their nation and communities, a large majority have become alienated and cynical about the entire political process—no matter who is in charge or in which direction policy changes are made. From the late 1950s onward, Americans have expressed a mammoth loss of faith in politics and government (see figure 5.3). Even after long economic expansions in the 1980s and 1990s, by self-report Americans remain angrier at government and the political process than at any period in recent memory.[46] And although hard data are lacking, retiring congressmen and other public officials frequently note that the past several decades have witnessed a significant decline in a sense of trust, comity, and civility among participants in government themselves. Some believe that such declining political trust is connected to a more general decline in interpersonal trust among people in their everyday lives. That most people could be trusted was believed by a majority of Americans three decades ago, as opposed to one-third in recent years.[47] But the loss of confidence in government and the political process began earlier and dropped further than any general decline in personal trust over the past several decades.

Declines in public trust have also occurred for other nonpolitical institutions of American society (business, labor, media, and the like), and the same trend is true in other advanced democracies of western Europe (figure 5.4).[48] But these facts are hardly a source of comfort.

Figure 5.3 TRENDS IN POLITICAL ALIENATION INDICATORS

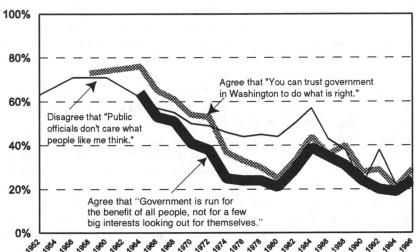

Source: University of Michigan's Survey Research Center–Center for Political Studies' National Election Studies.

Figure 5.4 CONFIDENCE IN SELECTED INSTITUTIONS: PERCENT RESPONDING THEY HAVE A GREAT DEAL OF CONFIDENCE IN THESE INSTITUTIONS

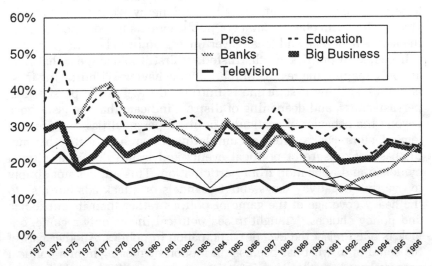

Source: Karlyn Keen-Bowman, The American Enterprise Institute (1998, forthcoming). Based on data from the NORC.

Political institutions and processes are especially important in the United States because they are some of the few historically unifying points of reference among an otherwise highly diverse people. More than any other nation, Americans define themselves not by some common bloodline, ancient national boundaries, or cultural heritage but by belief in their democratic form of government.

Thus the paradox: While on the surface America has become more democratic, dramatically shrinking the apparent distance between the governed and those who govern, most Americans feel increasingly distrustful of their government and political processes. Cynical views of government have undoubtedly been encouraged by national leaders' poor performance in office.[49] Watergate and Vietnam, for example, were used for years as shorthand explanations for failures of leadership. But distrust is at least as great among younger generations who know of these events only through history books. Changing party control of the White House in 1992 and Congress in 1994 appears to have done nothing to dispel public distrust and cynicism.[50] Public confidence and the popularity of elected officials clearly rise and fall with the economic cycle, but interestingly enough, what may be the longest economic expansion in U.S. history has still left trust at low levels. Trust and approval ratings do not go hand in hand. What might occur with the next cycle of economic disturbance and recovery will be another story. In any event, the real issue is the overall trend of recent decades that has left the American public more or less uniformly distrustful of whatever is being done by whoever is doing it. Washington is an obvious target of public cynicism about politics, but the fact is that state and local governments do little better.[51]

If people in politics are distrusted, at first it may appear that they are only reaping the results of their own behavior. Withdrawing trust is not a bad thing if someone is untrustworthy. But the persistence, pervasiveness, and deepening of distrust indicate that the issue goes beyond the behavior of particular political personalities to more systemic factors. For example, accumulating research indicates that media-based exposure of political events and issues does fuel citizen cynicism and alienation from participation. This applies not simply to overtly "negative" news about scandals or attack ads but also to the heavy coverage of the game of politics rather than its substance and policy choices.[52] Taught to see political life as only a game, onlookers often reject the idea of participation in politics. Another part of the spiral of distrust has been set in motion by moving from a political process based on the labor-intensive work of political parties toward one based on capital-intensive forms of political management and mass marketing. Media-based politics and its associated political technologies require huge amounts of money and, thus, equally huge fundraising efforts. The resulting special interest and special access politics easily alienates many ordinary citizens, who see a kind of auction house "openness" spreading that denies a true sense of public order.

The political order they do see is created by politicians, group activists, and media people whose individual maneuverings in the system, skilled as they are, have the cumulative effect of sowing public disgust. As political professionals become more skilled at mobilizing target constituencies, people are taught to expect pandering and to disrespect those who do it. The oversimplifying and overpromising needed to gain attention in a media-saturated society easily lead to disillusionment later on. Stridency and the demonizing of opposition works well to mobilize unrepresentative groups of policy activists. But it also works effectively to alienate ordinary citizens who like to see themselves as people of good will, moderation, and who, even in the best of circumstances, dislike the open political conflict of democratic debate and bargaining.[53] In short, many different syndromes seem to point in the same direction—teaching people that the political process is inauthentic and literally untrustworthy. While withdrawing trust from a deceitful person is not a bad thing, doing the same thing for the accumulated institutional means of self-government is a huge danger sign for democracy.

The economic and social conditions highlighted earlier in this book provide ample grounds for public concern. Taken on their own terms, these growing challenges offer good reason to think Americans need more, not less, confidence in their governing processes. The issues involved are complex and long-term. To deal well with such challenges, public trust may not be sufficient, but it surely is a necessary condition in the public policy conversation. It is the oxygen needed to sustain genuine policy deliberation in a much more openly "democratic" era. Public trust nurtures forbearance and improves the atmosphere for bargaining in good faith. Trust increases room for talking honestly and weighing alternatives, exactly the deliberative "slack" needed to make the difficult discernments required of complex policy choices in a complex world. Trust offers a kind of safe haven for talking about genuine uncertainties in the data and outcomes—and admitting that no one has all the answers. And when the inevitable disappointments and failures occur in an uncertain world, trust is vital for sustaining the commitment to try again. A self-governing political society trying to work at its complex, long-term problems—which is surely healthier than an indifferent society that turns a blind eye to them—requires these qualities and a good deal of patience on all sides. What was said about us at the beginning of this century remains no less true at its end:

> With people whom we distrust, it is as difficult to do business as to search for scientific truth, arrive at religious harmony, or attain justice. When one must first question words and intentions, and start from the premise that everything said and written is meant to offer us an illusion in place of truth, life becomes strangely complicated.[54]

Public policymaking in a society at once more "democratic" and more distrustful has indeed become strangely complicated. It is a paradox that cripples political leadership as well as ordinary citizenship. Contending leaders are led into circumlocutions, carefully restricting their comments, or placing remarks in a particular rhetorical context, almost as if to say, "Read between the lines and you'll understand how I really feel, what I really mean, how I am distinguished from the PR front that is put up for me." But they are generally not allowed, they believe, to acknowledge the costs of what they favor or the benefits of what they oppose. Anticipating oversimplified counterattacks in the public media, to which reasoned responses attract little attention (and take too much time to report), leading politicians often shun such serious discussion, rally ditto-heads, and try at best to do good by indirection and stealth—democratic leadership with a wink and a nod. In all of this there is a kind of "tragedy of the commons" in the public conversation—a remorseless working of things so as to produce, through each participant's doing what is individually "sensible," a collectively impoverishing result that none in their hearts might really want.[55]

Earlier chapters have described where problems of our changing economic, social, governmental, and fiscal structures intersect. The challenges Americans face in a postindustrial society hardly constitute an emergency crisis, at least not by the standards of this nation's eventful history. The challenges are more like slow-motion crises that eat away at us even as they are easily exploited for short-term political purposes. This is especially true in an atmosphere of pervasive distrust and paralyzing cynicism about the capacities of government to do anything helpful in dealing with pressing social problems. Despite all the hype of hyper-democracy, indifference is something like the political society's default setting. And yet domestic policy problems, if they are real problems, are likely to be complex and require sustained efforts to address. This is not easily conveyed in sound-bite debates, competing public relations campaigns, and the short, simple dramas of good guy/bad guy policy debates.

What we are experiencing, then, is a policy environment that is more democratically open both to contending voices and to ruthless manipulation. The public increasingly seems to perceive its increased access yet lack of control over what is happening, its ability to join special interest groups yet its loss of ownership over policy choices, its increased opportunities to "vent" without really governing. In a world of hyper-democracy, the American public seems to sense both that it is being courted more ardently than ever before and that it is not really being heard or respected.

Notes

1. *The New York Times*, October 16, 1994, 4–1.

2. See for example Alexander Hamilton's introductory comments in *The Federalist*, Number One. The historical development of "Government by discussion" is summarized in Samuel H. Beer, *To Make a Nation* (Cambridge: Harvard University Press, 1993), and described analytically in Charles E. Lindblom, *The Intelligence of Democracy* (New York: The Free Press, 1963). The recent revival of attention to the deliberative nature of democracy, particularly with regard to moral disagreements, is found in Amy Gutmann and Dennis Thompson, *Democracy and Disagreement* (Cambridge: Harvard University Press, 1996).

3. The references are to the Voting Rights Act of 1965, 26th Amendment (1971), and Supreme Court cases *Baker v. Carr* (1962) and *Gray v. Sanders* (1963).

4. R. Shep Melnick, *Regulation and the Courts* (Washington, DC: Brookings, 1983); George Hoberg, *Pluralism by Design* (New York: Praeger, 1992); Richard Stewart, "The Reformation of American Administrative Law," *Harvard Law Review*, 88 (1975).

5. Kay Lehman Schlozman and John T. Tierney, *Organized Interests and American Democracy* (New York: Harper and Row, 1985); Jeffrey M. Berry, *The Interest Group Society* (Boston: Little Brown, 1984).

6. Daniel Webster voiced a seemingly modern complaint that "we have a race of agitators all over the country. Their livelihood consists in agitation . . . their capital, their all in all, depend on the excitement of the public mind." Speech in Buffalo, New York, 1851, quoted in Paul Finkelman, *Dred Scott v. Sandford* (Boston: Bedford Books, 1997, p. 135).

7. Nolan McCarty, Keith Poole, and Howard Rosenthal, *The Polarization of American Politics* (1998, forthcoming); E.J. Dionne, Jr., *Why Americans Hate Politics* (New York: Simon and Schuster, 1991).

8. Richard E. Neustadt, *Presidential Power* (New York: The New American Library, 1964, pp. 45–47 and chapter 5).

9. Samuel Kernell, *Going Public: New Strategies of Presidential Leadership*, 2d ed. Washington, DC: CQ Press, 1993; Bruce Miroff, "The Presidency and Public Leadership as Spectacle," in Michael Nelson, *The Presidency and the Political System*, 4th ed. (Washington, DC: CQ Press, 1995).

10. Compare, for example, Edwin E. Witte, *The Development of the Social Security Act* (University of Wisconsin Press, 1963), with Paul Light, *Artful Work: The Politics of Social Security Reform* (New York: Random House, 1985), and Theda Skocpol, *Boomerang: Clinton's Health Security Effort and the Turn against Government* (New York: Norton, 1996).

11. Peter W. Morgan and Glenn U. Reynolds, *The Appearance of Impropriety* (New York: Free Press, 1997).

12. Thomas Patterson, *Out of Order* (New York: Knopf, 1993); James Falloffs, *Breaking the News* (1996).

13. See Daniel J. Boorstin, *Cleopatra's Nose: Essays on the Unexpected* (New York: Vintage Books, 1995, p. 148).

14. Morris P. Fiorina and Paul E. Peterson, *The New American Democracy* (Allyn and Bacon, 1998).

15. Frank R. Baumgartner and Bryan D. Jones, *Agendas and Instability in American Politics* (Chicago: University of Chicago Press, 1993, pp. 179ff).

16. Theodore H. White, *In Search of America* (New York: Harper and Row, 1982).

17. Warren E. Miller and J. Merrill Shanks, *The New American Voter* (Cambridge: Harvard University Press, 1996).

18. Walter Lippmann, *Public Opinion* (New York: Macmillan, 1922).

19. "The Boom in Gloom: TV News Coverage of the American Economy, 1990–1992," *Media Monitor* 6, 8, October 1992; *Roper Reports*, 92–98, December 1992.

20. Eric Smith, 1989, *The Unchanging American Voter*, Berkeley: University of California Press; Michael Delli Carpini and Scott Keeter, 1991, "Stability and Change in the U.S. Public's Knowledge of Politics," *Public Opinion Quarterly*, vol. 55. Low levels of information do not necessarily mean the public in aggregate behaves irrationally with regard to its most general policy preferences over time. Benjamin I. Page and Robert Y. Shapiro, *The Rational Public* (Chicago: University of Chicago Press, 1992).

21. For example, while the underlying facts of a problem in science policy often change only very slowly, the emphasis in media coverage will shift dramatically from neglect to fascination, from enthusiasm for scientific breakthroughs to fears of environmental and social dangers, and then to new enthusiasm for innovative, high-tech solutions. Dorothy Nelkin, *Selling Science* (New York: W. H. Freeman, 1987). Similar tendencies in other areas of U.S. domestic policy are noted in Frank R. Baumgartner and Bryan D. Jones, op. cit., passim.

22. See Tom Rosenstiel, "The Myth of CNN," *The New Republic*, August 22 and 29, 1994, pp. 27–33. Data are based on a study at Harvard's Joan Shorenstein Barone Center for the Study of Press and Politics.

23. Lawrence K. Grossman, *The Electronic Republic: Reshaping Democracy in the Information Age* (New York: Viking, 1995).

24. Related to us by Representative Sam Gibbons (D-Fla.) before his retirement in 1996.

25. Walter Lippmann, *Public Opinion* (New York: Macmillan, 1922). Echoing Lippmann, former NBC News president Reuben Frank has observed that "The highest power of TV journalism is not in the transmission of information but in the transmission of experience—joy, sorrow, shock, fear. These are the stuff of news." Quoted in

Grossman, op. cit., p. 92. Among the many studies of how the TV medium shapes political strategy and messages, especially insightful are the essays in Matthew D. McCubbins et al., *Under the Watchful Eye* (Washington, DC: CQ Press, 1992). On the triumph of visual over printed, or even auditory, information in politics, see Roger D. Masters, "How Television Has Transformed American Politics," *Working Paper* 92-2, Institute of Government Studies, Berkeley, CA, 1992.

26. Recent evidence of this persisting divergence in public attention is reported in Times Mirror Center for the People and the Press, May 1992, *Public Interest and Awareness of the News* (reproduced report), Washington, DC.

27. Quoted in Bob Woodward, 1995, p. 392.

28. Lawrence R. Jacobs and Robert Y. Shapiro, "The Spiral of Crafted Talk: American Social Policy and the Crisis of Government," (book manuscript), August 1996. Larry Sabato, *The Rise of Political Consultants* (New York: Basic Books, 1981); Martin P. Wattenberg, *The Rise of Candidate-Centered Politics* (Cambridge: Harvard University Press, 1991).

29. The National Opinion Research Center was established in 1941 as the first noncommercial opinion research agency, and many academics, as well as commercial researchers and government officials, work to enhance the professional standards of pollsters and to improve the reliability and validity of data. The American Association for Public Opinion Research was founded in 1947, the year Princeton University began publishing the *Public Opinion Quarterly*.

30. In 1967 the first network TV polling unit was established, and news media polling as we now know it began in 1975 with the joint partnership of CBS and *The New York Times*. Almost all large-circulation newspapers and more than half of local TV stations now report on their own polls. Thomas E. Mann and Gary R. Orren, eds., *Media Polls in American Politics* (Washington, DC: The Brookings Institution, 1992. pp. 2 and 4).

31. "Too Much Opinion, at the Expense of Fact," *New York Times*, September 13, 1989, p.a. The "issue positioning" that has increasingly come to dominate electoral politics focuses not on policy disagreements but on "valence issues" linking the politician's position to universally approved goals or symbols. Michael Nelson (ed.), *The Elections of 1992* (Washington, DC: CQ Press, 1993).

32. Joe McGinniss, *The Selling of the President, 1968* (New York: Trident Press, 1969).

33. *The Washington Post*, November 8, 1994, p. A4. In a 1989 survey, 44 percent of political consultants interviewed reported their candidate clients were uninvolved in setting the issue priorities in their own campaigns, and 66 percent reported candidates to be uninvolved in determining the tactics. Marshall Ganz, Winter 1994, "Voters in the Crosshairs," *The American Prospect*, no. 16 (p. 103). Legislative reforms in the 1970s aiming to control election contributions actually had the effect of further enhancing the role and costs of consultants, in particular specialists who could master the technical requirements of the law and the fund-raising technologies for extracting large sums in small amounts from many like-minded donors.

34. This is merely the political derivative of the definition of the new profession of public relations initiated in 1922–3 with the first book and college course on the subject: "An applied social scientist who advises clients or employers on the social attitudes or actions to take to win support of the public upon whom the survival of the client depends." Edward L. Bernays, *Crystallizing Public Opinion*, 1923 (out of print).

35. Daniel J. Boorstin, *The Image: A Guide to Pseudo-Events in America* (New York: Macmillan, 1961).

36. Raymond K. Price, quoted in McGinniss, *The Selling of the President*, pp. 193–194. This basic idea was foreshadowed 100 years ago as A.V. Dicey criticized democrats' faith in free expression of public opinion as a means of producing better legislative

opinion: "All men hate trouble and the discovery of truth or the detection of error involves a laborious process of thought, whilst few are the men to whom the attainment of truth is an object of keen interest. Add to all this that man is far more of an imitative than inventive animal. . . . What ground is there, then, for holding that human beings, simply because they are left free to think and act as they like, will in fact like to labor in the search for truth, or to strike out new paths for themselves rather than pursue the pleasant and easy course of imitating their neighbors?" A.V. Dicey, *Lectures on the Relation between Law and Public Opinion in England during the Nineteenth Century* (Transition, 1981, p. 438).

37. Some research suggests that persons of average cognitive ability can learn more from news information presented through television than through newspapers, though not significantly more than through printed news magazine formats. The key appears to be not the visual impact but the pervasive "framing" and thematic organization of information in TV new stories. W. Russell Neuman, Marion R. Just, and Ann N. Crigler, *Common Knowledge: News and the Construction of Political Meaning* (Chicago: University of Chicago Press, 1992).

38. Roger Ailes, quoted in James Q. Wilson, "Stagestruck," *The New Republic*, June 21, 1993 (p. 33).

39. This and other relevant evidence is discussed in Nolan McCarty, Keith Poole, and Howard Rosenthal, *The Polarization of American Politics* (forthcoming, 1998); Richard Morin, "A Nation of Extremists," *The Washington Post*, January 11, 1998, p. C5; and anticipated in E.J. Dionne Jr.'s insightful *Why Americans Hate Politics* (New York: Simon and Schuster, 1991).

40. Orlando Patterson, *The Ordeal of Integration: Progress and Resentment in America's "Racial" Crisis* (New York: Counterpoint, 1997).

41. For example, promotional material from a randomly selected political consulting organization puts it this way: "We must build on the foundation offered by the voters in the [x election]. And the best way to do this is to make the best use of Modern Technology. We must constantly keep our eyes and ears open to the needs and desires of our public . . . those who put our people in office and who will bring even more of our people to the Nation's Capital. . . . Why spend your valuable time on the fundamental campaign work—Telemarketing, Campaign Events, Direct Mail, List Maintenance, Contributor Services?" The Endeavor Group, Inc., "Let the Endeavor Group Pave the Road to Victory," 200 C St., S.E., Washington DC, n.d.

42. Ganz, loc. cit. (p. 104).

43. Morris P. Fiorina, "Extreme Voices: The Dark Side of Civic Engagement," Conference on Civic Engagement in American Democracy, Portland, Maine, Sept, 26–28, 1997, p. 12.

44. The point is vividly demonstrated in the dual nature of the nation's founding law. The body of the Constitution is predominantly an affirmation of government power and purpose, while the first 10 amendments (Bill of Rights) required for its ratification are focused on the limitation of power.

45. Everett Caroll Ladd, 1993, "Thinking about America," *Public Perspective*, 4:20.

46. Susan Tolchin, *The Angry American: How Voter Rage Is Changing the Nation* (Boulder, CO: Westview Press, 1997).

47. Washington Post/Kaiser/Harvard Survey, *The Washington Post*, January 28, 1996 (p. A6). Although, historically, trust in others is more likely to decline than to increase with age, it is today's younger Americans (18- to 29-year-olds) who report the highest levels of generalized distrust.

48. Seymour Martin Lipset, November 3, 1994, "American Democracy in Comparative Perspective" (reproduced); "Confidence in Institutions," *The American Enterprise*, November/December 1993 (pp. 94–95).

49. Jack Citrin and Donald Green, "Presidential Leadership and Trust in Government," *British Journal of Political Science*, vol. 16 October 1986, (pp. 431–453); Seymour Martin Lipset and William J. Schneider, *The Confidence Gap*, rev. ed. (Baltimore: Johns Hopkins University Press, 1987).

50. Frank I. Luntz, "Americans Talk About the American Dream," in Lamar Alexander and Chester E. Finn, Jr., 1995, *The New Promise of American Life*, Indianapolis: The Hudson Institute (p. 58). In 1994 72 percent of Americans said Washington government could not be trusted and in mid-1995 the percentage stood at 76 percent. *The Washington Post*, August 6, 1995 (p. C2).

51. In 1997, the share of Americans expressing "a lot" of trust in the federal government stood at 6 percent; the figure for state government was 9 percent and for city or local government 14 percent. Pew Research Center for People and the Press, national survey reported in the *Washington Post*, May 4, 1997.

52. Joseph N. Cappella and Kathleen Hall Jamieson, *The Spiral of Cynicism* (New York: Oxford University Press, 1997); Richard Harwood, "The Alienated: Are the News Media to Blame?" *The Brookings Review*, Fall 1996, pp. 32–35.

53. John Hibbing and Elizabeth Theiss-Morse, *Congress as Public Enemy* (Cambridge University Press, U.K., 1996).

54. Charles Wagner, 1903, *The Simple Life* (New York: McClure, Phillips and Co., pp. 39–40). For a discussion of the problem of leadership in the modern era of diversity and distrust, see Gilbert W. Fairholm, *Leadership and the Culture of Trust* (Westport, CT: Praeger, 1994).

55. Recent controlled experiments show significant increases in despair and cynicism about public affairs among those pre-teens exposed to negative political TV ads ostensibly targeted at adults. *The Washington Post*, September 24, 1995 (p. C5).

Chapter Six

RETHINKING THE ROLE OF THE PUBLIC SECTOR

Perhaps if the existing community would take now and then the trouble to pass in review the changes it has already witnessed it . . . might with more grace . . . cease from useless attempts at making a . . . new world conform itself to the rules and theories of a bygone civilization.
— Charles Francis Adams, Jr., 1868, on the laying of the first transcontinental railroad.[1]

We have now finished our description of a dynamic America confronting changes in its economic and family life, the capacity of its government to respond, and the political discourse through which its responses must first be reasoned and debated. The resulting picture is one of misleading expectations intertwined with legitimate public concerns. Yes, we have come to expect government to finance more than it can, but at the same time prior fiscal restraints of our own making are preventing government from meeting new needs it should and otherwise could afford to finance. Yes, there has been economic growth, but many are not sharing enough in that growth to have reasonable prospects for either opportunity or security. Yes, exaggerated government promises have fueled public expectations, but public expectations are also being deliberately manipulated in our increasingly open and distrusted democratic system.

The government we deserve is not necessarily bigger or smaller, more conservative or more liberal. It is one ordinary people can use as they make choices in meeting the needs of their own times. It is one in which ordinary citizens have a justified sense of ownership over public policy decisions, even though the results are never to anyone's complete satisfaction.[2] It is a government more responsive to the people in their own place and time than to the dead hands of past decisionmakers. More authentic self-government, in other words, is what Americans deserve.

In this chapter we suggest a set of paths forward. In each case we look for ways to change the rules and theories of the past to better conform to our world today—to move out of the frameworks for policy thinking that were developed for a different time. Our first step is to discuss how to free government from the long-run fiscal constraints that militate against new positive action that is much more than symbolic or token. We then put forward ideas about how the freed-up funds might be better used to meet new needs. We end by suggesting ways to promote the more deliberative and informed process that is required if either of the first two steps is to succeed. In a real sense, this presents a unified framework for continuing a public dialogue about the nation's future.

FREEING THE FISCAL FUTURE

Most observers agree that the extraordinary government deficits projected once the baby boomers begin to retire are unsustainable. These projections don't mean inevitable doom and gloom because, one way or another, they will not be allowed to become reality. But dealing effectively with the fiscal future requires more than preventing future deficits from arising.

Recent years have seen the country adopt a fiscal posture that is unique in our history. Never before have we seen so much in the way of *eternal* commitments to spend ever increasing levels of revenues for programs and priorities of the past. Policies have built up in a way that now entails extraordinary resource commitments that never end. These obligations are further exaggerated by the aging of the population and upcoming decline in number of workers available to support future beneficiaries of old-age programs. When the nation has dramatically increased its financial obligations in the past—through wars, such enormous land acquisitions as the Louisiana Purchase, assistance to workers and the unemployed in depressions—the accompanying budgetary commitments were temporary no matter how large their initial impacts. Despite the rhetoric of both self-styled liberals and their conservative counterparts, the fight today is not over some mid-century definition of Roosevelt liberalism. Domestic spending as a percent of national income was lower at the end of the Roosevelt/Truman period than when it started, and future commitments were minimal. It is the permanence of our newer obligations that is so different and so inappropriate. It makes no more sense to commit today almost all of the future economic resources that will ever be available to government than it would be to decide today where to station all of our troops until the next millennium. The public senses that it has lost ownership of its fiscal choices—and it has.

But the public won't get its ownership back if the focus is only on preventing deficits once the baby boomers retire, or on how to spend a modest surplus that might be available temporarily before then.³ A big mistake—one that has led to a focus on symptoms, not causes—has been the presumption that focusing on the deficit *by itself* gets the nation out of this straitjacket. This presumption is wrong. The deficit is a measure of the current net cash flow of government. The large deficits projected further into the future reflect the liabilities that government is currently accruing but not booking as a current cost. These liabilities will eventually show up in future deficits and obligations *for which almost no saving has been put aside.* Sure, as suggested by President Clinton and many Republicans in 1998, it might be worthwhile to maintain a cash flow surplus for awhile to pay off our past accumulation of debt and reduce future interest costs of government. But that's merely a start.

Even from a pure deficit perspective, we are sitting in the eye of the storm, having been buffeted by past deficits, yet with huge deficits required under current law for the future (see figure 4.1). Gale force winds are scheduled to hit us soon. Trying to spend some modest surpluses now is like dumping sand onto the beach instead of into the sandbags we will need against the storm.⁴

But the deficit—past or future—is still not the main fiscal problem. Beneficiaries of future growth in existing programs are still protected by a singular focus on the deficit. Thus, even if projected future deficits under current law were zero for decades to come—today still a distant goal—our fiscal future would be far from free. This can be seen by contrasting two hypothetical laws in existence, say, in the year 2000. The first projects a zero deficit in 2030. The second places no requirements on how future increases in real revenues should be spent, so that all revenue growth between 2000 and 2030 is uncommitted. At normal growth rates in the economy, this would imply that revenues would approximately double, rising eventually by about $1 trillion annually as a relatively constant tax rate applies to a growing income base. Under the first law, how to spend that additional $1 trillion of revenues in 2030 (and all the additional revenues in the years in between) is already specified. Under the second law, that $1 trillion in 2030—and trillions of other dollars in the intervening years—become available to be spent on needs identified after the year 2000.

The total amount of expenditure, deficit, and national debt might turn out to be the same in both cases. But the ways in which the nation decides what to buy with its money are different. A system with greater fiscal slack—that is, growing future surpluses under current law—does not necessarily mean fewer expenditures than one with less fiscal slack. It simply allows more of the decisions on how to spend that revenue growth to be made *then rather than now*.

We can work ourselves out of this fiscal difficulty. But there is only one way to do it successfully. We must prohibit lawmaking that promises that programs will grow automatically and eternally. And this move must include all spending programs—whether new or existing, whether visible in the direct expenditure budget or hidden in the tax code, whether on budget or on the so-called "off-budget" list. New rules for fiscal policymaking by the executive and legislative branches of government are required. Telling signs of potential progress are the president's line-item veto and formal and informal budget rules requiring the costs of any new enactment to be paid for out of a cutback somewhere else ("pay-as-you-go" rules). Neither is enough, of course. The line-item veto currently applies only to discretionary programs, which are already growing more slowly than the economy. The budget pay-as-you-go rules do not apply to existing entitlements or tax subsidies. Even so, these two provisions represent fledgling attempts to develop new institutional rules to fit a new fiscal era.

There are those who argue that automatic growth in programs doesn't matter. From the left come concerns over protecting growth in social programs; from the right it is the growth in tax breaks for business and savers that is sacrosanct. The question is the same from both sides: What's wrong with making excessive promises or committing the wealth of future generations, as long as we can renege along the way?

As they battle to protect their favorite interests, what both sides lose sight of is the cost of using the force of the state to back up their crystal ball predetermination of future needs. Extra costs inevitably arise because of the uneven playing field among programs—between entitlement (including entitlement to permanent tax breaks) and discretionary spending, and among entitlements with different built-in growth rates. The impact of the vast difference in the way alternative types of spending are currently treated can hardly be overestimated. A super majority—two-thirds majorities in both the Senate and the House of Representatives, or simple majorities in both houses plus the president's support (i.e., no presidential veto)—is required to *restrain* the automatic growth of entitlement spending. A super majority is now required to *expand* discretionary spending. To complicate matters, "losers" often complain louder than "winners," especially when established programs become considered as "rights." Thus, new needs, which must be funded out of new legislation, are put at a dramatic disadvantage relative to old needs, already prefunded out of old legislation. This has been and remains a practical recipe for stultifying the responsiveness of government to change.

Constraints can be put on preordained future spending at various levels. That our level of future commitments is both unreasonable and unsustainable does not imply there should be no obligations carried forward to the future. Individuals already retired, for instance, will have built up dependence upon future promises more than individuals still decades from retirement. We need to search for rules regarding future obligations that bring them back to a reasonable level without creating major disruption.

At a minimum, no spending program can grow faster than the economy forever. The Congressional Budget Office could be instructed to inform Congress of those programs, both new and old, that violate this standard. Drafting laws so that automatic, long-term growth in spending programs conforms to this basic principle would create at least some future fiscal slack.

Greater slack is preferable and can be created through stronger limitations on real growth. Under this scenario, real growth beyond a reasonable number of years would be left to occasional legislation rather than be built in automatically in the budget. To future generations would be restored the freedom to determine how to spend additional revenues over and above current levels. Preferences from the past would apply only to a constant base of real expenditures. Whether growth is constrained to the growth rate in the economy, confined to zero in real terms, or left somewhere in between, some exceptions to scheduled growth will be required over shorter or even longer periods of time—in particular, where there are upsurges in needs associated with changing relative numbers of unemployed or truly old. During the period of adjustment, scheduled growth might temporarily be above the long-term limits. But eternal growth would not be the norm.

In addition to leveling the playing field with respect to program expansion, the new fiscal rules could be extended to deny any program eternal exemption from the legislative process, no matter what the level of future spending scheduled. Automatic sunset provisions on most expenditure and tax breaks, whatever their growth rate, would be one way of achieving this goal. Sunsetting requires greater discretion than the previous rules. Obligations to people already retired could not be entirely abandoned, nor can institutions such as a court system or a tax system simply be sunset without a replacement system fully in place.[5] As a practical matter, Congress does not have time to reconsider every program every year—an old idea associated with "zero-base" budgeting that was simply too hard to implement. Still, every five or ten years, on a staggered basis, most "permanent" programs, including tax subsidies, could automatically come up for renewal, forcing them to compete for the same supermajority votes required for most appropriated programs.[6]

At still another level, Congress often operates through self-imposed rules that can be invoked to limit built-in growth, especially if it is eternal. New procedural fixes might include budget "rules of order"— which can be adopted in many different ways—that make it impossible to bring out of committee any programs that have excessive built-in growth beyond a five-year budget window, or any legislation that is out of fiscal balance for the long run, or that establishes growth for all eternity.

Limits on built-in growth are clearly not always easy to apply. Any rule or law, no matter what its merit, creates boundary line questions. What defines a "program" to which such restrictions should apply? Is a tax provision the equivalent of a program expenditure or is it merely an attempt to measure the tax base well? A permanent deduction for rental expenses in order to account accurately for the net income of a business owner may cause little concern. More complicated are depreciation allowances that may or may not measure accurately the effect on income of the decline in value of assets. Fights over such questions are both inevitable and difficult. But such fringe issues provide no excuse for avoiding fiscal reform.

As the protagonists struggle, they should also keep well in mind what are *not* among the consequences of the fiscal reforms outlined here.

- *They do not take democracy out of the hands of the people; they simply place more of it in the hands of current voters.* Each generation can still bequeath many good policies to its children. But those policies can no longer be put in such a priority status that they usurp almost all other options required to meet new needs and demands. It is true that young adults will make mistakes that their parents would have avoided, but the bigger mistake is to try to keep succeeding generations in perpetual adolescence.
- *They do not rule out program growth.* Any increases scheduled in the law simply need to be limited to a fixed number of years or in response to a specific need arising over a set period of time. In this way, long-term growth requires regular legislation and cannot continue automatically and eternally.

- *They do not set the nation on a path toward less (or more) govern-ment.* If society decides that one area consistently requires greater shares of our national income and wealth than other areas, it can vote to keep expanding that program each time it comes up for review. Too much *automatic* expenditure growth is what must be stopped. Explicit decisions to expand or contract the reach of gov-ernment would be left to each generation of voters—and to their own assessment of the capabilities of government relative to the private sector to fulfill their own emerging needs.
- *They do not rule out new taxes or tax cuts.* Society is free to decide to pay higher taxes to support a particular program. It is also free to use future fiscal slack to finance tax cuts. The point is that choices made *today* should not be paid for by increasing tax rates on *future* generations.
- *They do not rule out cost-of-living increases.* Indexing programs to a reasonable measure of the increase in the general price level is designed to preserve the real value of the benefits society has de-cided to bestow. It does not affect real program growth. Inflation adjustments simply prevent inflation from arbitrarily determining benefit levels. They do not cause benefits to grow in real terms or along with economic growth. These are the types of automatic growth that reduce future fiscal freedom.

GIVING SOCIAL INSURANCE A MODERN FACE

Moving away from built-in growth today means, more than anything else, reforming Social Security and government health care programs, the largest of which is Medicare.[7] As we saw earlier, these parts of the budget already dominate federal spending and are scheduled to grow faster than any other part of the budget. Within a few decades, ac-cording to a variety of estimates, these programs *by themselves* are projected to absorb almost all federal revenues.[8] If that happens, then there can be no discussion about a federal funding role in any other policy area. Americans are not alone in this crisis of social insurance. The whole industrial world is being forced by budgetary pressure to reexamine the fundamental principles of social insurance design— just who should receive government insurance against just what kinds of risks.

For most of this century, public and private social insurance (mainly employer-provided health coverage and pensions) grew hand in hand.

In recent years, however, they have begun to diverge, with private benefits growing more slowly relative to the size of the economy even while public benefits continue to grow. A major factor behind the recent divergence is that the private sector has simply backed off from the enormous costs of providing such benefits. The private sector can, of course, adapt to these escalating costs simply by slowing the rate at which it puts money into these programs—exactly as it is doing right now.[9] Adaptation is more complicated for government because it must maintain a safety net and because it has made promises to future generations, even though the funding will not be there to keep all of those promises.

Change is mathematically inevitable. The question is what type of change. Government can tackle the problem in two ways. It can simply cut programs across the board year after year—the model followed in many recent budget bills. This approach has been useful at times for reducing the level of government dissaving, but clearly it is less than optimal for program design. Indiscriminate cutting may bring social policy into temporary accordance with budget constraints, but will do little to improve social policy itself. Quality improvements are as necessary in social goods and services as in private ones.

In the case of retirement policy, for instance, proposals that simply pare growth may continue to provide ever more years of retirement support but reduce benefits in a way that particularly hurts the older, poorer, frailer elderly—the originally intended beneficiaries of an "old" age insurance program. Thus, every year Social Security distributes higher portions of total payout to individuals who are relatively younger and usually have lesser needs. The right way to fix the problem is to bring comprehensive reform to the social insurance packages themselves. Social insurance reform needs to go beyond a simple budget focus to ask what the programs themselves are supposed to do.

Old-Age Insurance

Social Security's growth is due partly to legislated benefit increases but mostly to three automatic features.

- *Growing annual benefits.* Real benefits for each succeeding cohort of workers are scheduled to grow over time as fast as average real wages. For example, if your generation's wages over a lifetime are 50 percent higher on average than your parents' generation, then you can expect to receive 50 percent more in the way of annual Social Security benefits. Ditto for your children and grandchildren.

- *More years of retirement support.* People live a lot longer than they did in the 1930s, so Social Security now promises many more years of retirement benefits. The adjustment in the normal retirement age from 65 to 67 (but not the early retirement age of 62) that is scheduled to take effect in the first part of the next century does little to offset this historic *and continuing* trend. Those who retire early also contribute less to societal output and to tax systems that support elderly and nonelderly alike.
- *Demographics and the baby boom.* The decline in the birth rate, along with the retirement of the baby boom generation, will lead to a large and rapid decline in the number of workers relative to retirees beginning in about 2010—leading in turn to a substantial increase in the ratio of benefits paid to wages earned and, more generally, to national income.

Social Security policy is not likely to affect birth rates. But benefit levels and years of support are easily under the control of the legislature. Much of the growth in Social Security, therefore, can and should be controlled by limiting the growth in annual benefits from one cohort of retirees to the next and by cutting the number of years of retirement support promised.

Americans now retire for close to one-third of their adult lives on average and receive benefits for 17 to 20 years. This vast expansion of years of retirement support has never had to compete on an equal legislative footing with alternative uses of funds, such as education, child health, or prevention of crime. Our economy is robbed of an extraordinary amount of potential human productivity. The ultimate effect of the projected decline in the ratio of workers to retirees as the baby boom retires is a loss of human resources and output that is almost Depression-like in scale. A modern social insurance system should not encourage such waste. Here the bottom line is that living longer is a blessing, even if current law tends to convert it to a budgetary curse. One consequence of this blessing is that we can and should work longer. Rather than imposing constantly higher tax burdens on their children, future generations of retirees can contribute a bit more to cover the costs associated with living longer and other societal needs as well.

An ideal modern model for retirement income insurance would also incorporate better ways to foster private saving. Social Security— generally involving pay-as-you-go financing, under which most taxes are spent as soon as they reach the Treasury—yields little saving within Social Security or within government as a whole. The private pension system does better, but mainly for higher-income employees. A reformed system can move toward more pension saving, either by using taxes or mandates to support accounts to which deposits would be made currently, or by increasing the subsidies behind private employer plans—provided those plans cover more of the population and are more transferable (portable) from job to job. One of the hidden ways that the private sector system dodges portability, even though legislation requires it, is to avoid indexing the wage base on which retirement benefits are calculated. Thus, a worker promised a benefit based on wages while on the job will find that 20 or 25 years after leaving that job, the wage base—and the promised benefits—have eroded to fractions of the original values. The goal here is not simply to increase the saving required for future retirees; it is to achieve a greater equalization of wealth as well.

None of this is an argument for the pure "privatization" of Social Security. Despite pretenses at budgetary soundness, every pure privatization proposal we have seen to date has left large unfunded obligations to government in cases of individual or national emergency. All would leave substantial portions of the elderly population with little means of support in retirement, place large obligations on the government to support the elderly outside Social Security (especially when savings prove inadequate or dwindle because of a downturn in financial markets), and restore the stigma of welfare to a large segment of the elderly population. Our message is that Social Security must play its part in moving us out of the fiscal straitjacket, and that this inevitably entails significant changes in its structure. This likely means not only increases in the retirement age but conversion to a better minimum benefit that is reinforced by greater savings. This implies cutting growth rates for upper-class beneficiaries while encouraging or mandating savings to fill the gap. Social Security must be modernized, but at the same time it can be oriented even better to its original goal of keeping the truly old out of poverty.

Health Insurance

Government health insurance costs are rising in part for the same reasons as pension costs: people are receiving more years of benefits as they live longer, while the baby boomers' retirement will swell the number of beneficiaries relative to taxpayers. But gaining control of future health care obligations is more complex than gaining control of future pension obligations for one fundamental reason. The health care reimbursement system that now dominates private and public health care has powerful built-in incentives to constantly increase both the price of health care services and the amounts of care provided. These incentives have added to the cost of health insurance and, as a secondary consequence, have led to more uninsured people and more conflicts over who gets covered and how bills get paid.

In addition to rethinking who should get benefits and for how long, therefore, public health insurance reform demands a restructuring of the way health care services are financed and delivered. Such a restructuring is beginning already, but it has a long way to go before future health care obligations are truly under control. Growth in public health care costs, moreover, dominates growth in Social Security in terms of long-term government promises that cannot be met. Because it has a higher unsustainable growth rate, it is almost inevitable that it will have to bear an even greater share of the total reform effort needed with respect to social insurance as a whole.

The payment structure that still dominates U.S. health care—developed in the first half of the twentieth century—subsidizes the cost of health care coverage indirectly through insurance financed out of employer-paid premiums or tax receipts. Its design has been to promise the best medical care possible at a negligible price to the patient. It encourages patients (and the physicians or hospitals making decisions on their behalf) to choose treatments without regard to cost, insurers and medical technology to look for ever-expanding markets, and doctors and other health service providers to maintain salaries and fees that might otherwise be unsustainable. The high cost, in turn, only adds to the numbers of those who cannot afford health insurance, so that today close to 18 percent of the nonelderly population are uninsured.[10]

At the same time, each generation is receiving higher and higher quality health care. But increasing quality comes with a fundamental problem. Any system that allows consumers to choose irrespective of price exerts inevitable upward pressure on prices, on the amount consumers purchase, and on total cost. It also stacks the deck against the kind of competition in which lower-cost producers and lower-cost products replace higher-cost ones. A well-trained nurse, for example, is often prevented from providing services that, for almost all purposes, do not need to be provided by a physician. One cannot get 98 percent as much help for 50 percent of the price, so to speak, because there is always the danger that a 2 percentage point advantage in quality or training could affect health outcomes. And, unlike other technology-driven industries, innovation and price reductions have not gone hand-in-hand to the same extent. Better software will drive down the prices of older software and allow lesser-trained staff to take over functions that used to require computer scientists. But in health care, the financing system slows down this offsetting process.

Tax policy has further encouraged excessive consumption of both health insurance and health care by applying an open-ended subsidy for employer-provided health insurance—giving employees an incentive to demand compensation through health insurance coverage rather than just cash wages. Even today, consciously or not, employees consistently face the choice between 70 cents of cash wages and one dollar's worth of health insurance, as each additional dollar of health insurance benefits will usually avoid both income tax and social security tax. However, more than 80 percent of these tax benefits go to people in the top two-fifths of the income distribution.[11] Once more insurance is obtained, it reduces the incentive to worry about the cost of anything, even for the last dollar spent.

As cost increases in health care have absorbed higher proportions of national income, the private sector has only recently begun to adjust. The challenge it still faces is ensuring equity in providing basic services while introducing incentives to control costs. The dilemma is that incentives invariably imply some inequality, and lack of incentives imply unsustainable cost growth. A useful compromise is to adopt an approach that ensures equity in access to a basic level of benefits while at the same time restoring some efficiency by requiring individuals or private groups to make more decisions about whether to consume health benefits above that basic level.

In order for the cost of those choices not to be borne primarily by the sick, some way must be found to preserve market competition at the level where consumers are purchasing health insurance coverage rather than the services themselves. It is easier for people to make some price choices when buying insurance than when lying sick in a hospital. Encouraging signs are appearing in both the public and the private sector. One approach is vouchers issued to allow purchase of a basic service level, with costs of coverage above that being paid for by the consumer. Another is per capita payments to health maintenance organizations (HMOs) or similar organizations in return for coverage of all basic services.

The public provision of health care will benefit indirectly from these private efforts. To the extent that the private market keeps health prices down, there will be less pressure on Medicare and Medicaid to pay higher prices. At the same time, about half of all health care spending (counting tax subsidies) comes from government. Therefore, Medicare and other government health programs will be required to undertake many of the same reforms—setting up schemes with limits on insurance costs.

For the nonelderly, we have a long way to go before the two basic subsidy systems now in place—Medicaid and subsidies for employer-provided insurance—are rationalized and integrated. Medicaid provides support at the bottom, with very high tax rates and marriage penalties on those who bring more income into the household through work or marriage and then find their subsidy eliminated. Tax subsidies, on the other hand, are concentrated at the top, with fewer benefits in the middle for those with less valuable health insurance or lower tax rates. These systems, too, might move toward ones with capitated payments—perhaps in the form of regulated HMOs, perhaps in the form of credits or vouchers that are spread more evenly throughout the income distribution.

Obviously, regulation will have to play an important part in the achievement of reform. Difficult decisions will have to be made to define what is health care and what is a basic set of benefits. Regulation must also limit groups with favorable health risk profiles from being singled out by insurers or providers—thus splitting the market in a way that forces higher prices for equivalent coverage to be paid by high risk groups.

In Medicare today, for example, there is a distinction between Medicare beneficiaries in HMO-type settings and beneficiaries remaining in the traditional fee-for-service sector. As future commissions determining rates of payment for particular services are forced to curtail those payments to stay within designated budget limits, it will be crucial to ensure that these cuts are not made in a way that enables the HMO or voucher options to attract primarily people with healthy profiles—leaving the sick and financially vulnerable in the fee-for-service sector to bear the brunt of the cuts. Regulations must also confront the issue of technology—how to ensure that new technology in the health sector is (1) introduced (rather than totally stymied in efforts to reduce costs), and (2) has the constructive effect of accelerating reductions in the price of older technology.

That regulation of what government will pay and cover will generate ferocious political battles is a foregone conclusion. As doctors, nurses, scientists, drug companies, health insurance sales people—all parts of the health sector—see extraordinary growth rates in revenues and incomes receding into the past, they will compete more intensely over their shares of a more slowly growing pie. Many of these fights will be played out in Congress and in the voting booth.[12] The prospects of such fights should not deter society from confronting a social insurance system that in its current, open-ended form is unsustainable. The only alternative is arbitrary cuts in the health care budget with more disastrous consequences for both the equity and efficiency of health care programs.

MAKING A GOVERNMENT FOR ALL AGES

The dominant spending activities of governments throughout the industrial world are now devoted to old age. The issue is not so much whether we can afford such spending *per se*. If financing the retirement and health care of the nation's elderly at increasingly generous levels were truly the nation's most important national need, society could certainly afford to spend as much of its national income as it spends today, plus some. Americans *can* afford to provide a 26th or 27th year of Social Security annuity payment to the longer living spouse of a couple (as opposed to the 25 years already covered). But should we? It is practically impossible to find anyone who argues explicitly that such spending should be the nation's number one domestic priority, even though current law now automatically gives it that status. Through Social Security and Medicare alone, government now promises close to one-half million dollars in public benefits to an average-income near-elderly couple retiring today (even more to higher-income elderly) and the amount is scheduled to rise significantly every year into the future.[13] Again, literally no one suggests that increases beyond one-half million dollars for the future elderly is this country's highest priority—or that such increases will have a higher payoff for the long-run well-being of society than spending even a fraction of that amount on needs at younger ages. Relative to alternatives, our current automatic priorities are seen by no one as providing greater equity or a higher social return on investment—the types of criteria normally used to assess how to allocate scarce resources.

The 1997 budget agreement was a first hint that shifts in priorities may be on their way. It established a higher-education tuition credit, expanded public financing of health insurance for children, and added new saving incentives. The dramatic change, however, was not in what the law provided, but how it covered the cost—through other expenditure cuts, mainly in Medicare expenditure growth. Never mind that new items such as a tuition credit and the additional children's health insurance have been justifiably criticized for design flaws that may hinder their effectiveness. The 1997 legislation was perhaps the first to carry a message about changing priorities from financing consumption in old age to investing in younger generations.

Changing overall priorities in this way does not mean society should forget about the changing needs of the elderly. Tomorrow's elderly, as a group, may be scheduled to receive more benefits than are justified relative to the needs of younger Americans. But at the same time, Americans do only a mediocre job relative to other industrial countries in keeping the elderly out of poverty. Almost 19 percent of America's elderly had income below one-half of the national median in 1994, compared with an average of under 12 percent for a wide variety of other countries.[14] People over age 85 fare even worse in terms of poverty. In dealing with Social Security's and Medicare's financial problems, it would not be hard to do a better job of meeting the needs associated with truly old age—Social Security's raison d'être, after all.

And despite the enormous amount of redistribution in Social Security, it still fails to deal adequately with some important special circumstances, such as divorce and widowhood.[15] The current system allows a worker to generate a full spousal benefit for every spouse to whom he is married for ten years or more. This provision was added to the law to protect divorced persons, but it was not well designed to ensure equity among widows/widowers as a group. Any of several divorced spouses of a high-income worker can receive more in survivor (and spousal) benefits than will the lifetime surviving spouse of a middle-income worker, and more benefits than a low-income single person who has contributed taxes to the system throughout his or her life.

One option is to remove this full-benefit provision and simply increase the minimum benefit available to all persons. Another way to deal with the problems of widows and widowers is to require persons married at the time of retirement to take their joint lifetime benefits in a level payment stream that is not reduced when one spouse dies.[16] That way, surviving spouses would be less likely to fall into poverty when the other spouse dies. The general point is the need to look at what society is distributing to whom—including *within* the elderly as a group—and move toward identifying greater relative need. In particular, the system needs to be oriented to better meet the needs of the truly poorest among the elderly.

Health care for the elderly is a similar case. Smaller families, longer lives, and geographical separation of different generations of the same family have changed the needs associated with old age, and Medicare has not kept up. Home health care needs, in particular, are more important now because there are fewer relatives living nearby to turn to than in the past. But Medicare, though it has made some adjustments, still restricts home health care generally to conditions following an acute medical incident—ruling out home care needed for the more common chronic problems faced by many who are old. Shifting resources toward greater relative needs is very likely to make programs like home health care grow. This is as it should be. Reducing benefits across the board makes no sense. Overall benefit growth must be controlled. Within that constraint, the mix of benefits needs constantly to be reviewed for changes in relative need.[17]

Like Social Security, then, reducing growth in public health costs should not be used as an excuse to avoid meeting new needs. The costs of those new needs may have to be met by reductions elsewhere. Higher-income beneficiaries may need to pay more for some of the services they receive. Reductions in years of eligibility may be required. After all, improved health care over the years has extended the productive life of Americans. And, similar to retirement benefits, healthier people are more capable of paying for additional benefits by working longer.

Constraining automatic growth in programs for the near-elderly and elderly will free up resources for discretionary growth. Some of these funds need to be returned to the elderly for meeting the true needs of old age in the new era. That some programs and benefits expand even as others contract for the same population is a sign that society is doing something right. And, as we suggest below, other funds would go for other needs of society that are not confined to old age. It is in the combination—not in setting one age group against another either in current or future law—that we can become a government of all ages.

INCREASING EVERYONE'S CHANCES TO BUILD FINANCIAL SECURITY

The strength of a democratic nation depends on widespread sharing in the fruits of progress. This means not only income but also education (discussed later) and financial wealth—a major source of economic security. In the United States, government has long been involved in creating and distributing wealth through home ownership and private pension accumulation. Tax deductions for home mortgage interest and for property taxes are among the most important of tax breaks, and their value has increased as tax rates have risen.[18] Private pensions also receive significant help through the tax system—including tax deferment of employer contributions; profit-sharing plans; money purchase plans, 401(k), 403(b) plans for nonprofit organizations, and similar savings plans; employee stock ownership plans; individual retirement accounts; and so on. There have been stages in our history when there was an equalizing expansion in the ownership of homes and pension plans. But many of those gains in equity are now behind us. The momentum towards more equal ownership of homes and pension wealth has certainly slowed and may have stagnated altogether. Through its rental subsidies, the government also has effectively turned on its head the homeownership subsidy system inherent in our early history—when land on the frontier was offered precisely to allow have-nots to create wealth by homesteading.

Why not simply increase the redistribution of income by taking more from the wealthy and transferring it to poorer Americans? Isn't welfare enough? The answer is twofold. First, there is a difference between a society that stresses both opportunity and security, and one that emphasizes only security. An opportunity society is one that wants to create new possibilities for its citizens, even when those opportunities are not perfectly secure or do not reach outcomes that are knowable ahead of time. Opportunity also means ability to participate in wider society, often to check out and test options that otherwise are unavailable. Security is necessary, and many of our social programs are aimed at providing just that—minimum guaranteed levels of well-being. But it has severe limits.

The twentieth century made great headway on the security front. One of the most exciting prospects for the twenty-first century is that—barring too many commitments to growth in older programs— social programs can now be turned more than ever toward the creation of opportunity for all Americans, rich and poor alike. Resources devoted to security do not necessarily have to be reduced. Having established that base, whatever its successes and failures, the new resources available to government can now be directed toward creating new opportunity. It's time to move to the next stage of development of our nation's social policy agenda.

A second reason for stressing opportunity is that while an income and services safety net is vital, it can only do so much. Simple redistribution is not wealth *creating*. Paying out annual cash or in-kind benefits significantly discourages saving and wealth ownership by those benefiting from the redistribution—potentially creating more *unequal* before-tax incomes despite temporary equalizing effects on current consumption.

Wealth creation is more difficult than income redistribution and takes much longer to achieve, because it is difficult to force people to save or to hang onto whatever saving they may have. Individuals, however, can learn to save and to take advantage of incentives.[19] These incentives, in turn, can be organized to emphasize wealth creation and opportunity to a much greater extent than under current law. At the same time, distributing the ownership of wealth more widely has the immense advantage in a democracy of equalizing power among races and classes and may do more to break down those divides than almost any other advance.

Why put extra focus on housing and pensions? The fundamental reason is that most families, sensibly enough, hold their wealth primarily in these forms—as they work to build up resources for a decent home and for retirement. Recent tax acts, in contrast, have focused new incentives to hold wealth primarily on high-income Americans. Between 75 and 90 percent of the benefits from reductions in the capital gains tax, for example, go to those with incomes above the median.[20] The following are some approaches that might better address the problems of those who are less able to accumulate wealth under the current system.

HOUSING POLICY

Housing policy needs to be reoriented so that those at the bottom of the income distribution receive subsidies for homeownership that are at least as large as the subsidies some of them currently get for rent or public housing. While there are many reasons lower-income individuals may prefer to rent,[21] they should not face greater incentives to rent than own. Recent housing reforms under both Republican and Democratic presidents have stressed moving beyond public housing to the provision of more portable vouchers and other rental subsidies. We would add to these reforms by ensuring that these vouchers are both more portable across jurisdictions and can also be used to purchase housing. At the same time, subsidies at the top of the income distribution could be reduced by setting a reasonable maximum on the housing value for which deductions could be taken.

One recent example of a government and private initiative to provide new incentives for low-income people to save is the Individual Development Account (IDA). IDAs are savings accounts that provide incentives through matching funds and are not counted against low-income families when calculating social assistance eligibility. IDAs typically are managed by community agencies, and require financial advising as well as a cosigner when any funds are withdrawn. Funds can only be withdrawn for home purchase, education, investments in small businesses, or emergencies. Currently, the programs are small and experimental, but they are growing. Like all new programs many issues remain to be worked out, but at a minimum they help put wealth ownership back on the map as a way of helping poor individuals move up the wealth ladder. The recent welfare reform legislation has allowed states to use their federal block grant funds to support IDAs. In addition, private foundations, such as the Ford Foundation, are supporting programs such as "Downpayments on American Dreams," which provide IDAs as a way to develop savings for more people.

PENSION POLICY

Pension policy should consider—as suggested by a majority of the Social Security Advisory Panel in 1996 and by the business-supported Committee for Economic Development—mandating, as a complement to Social Security, specified minimum contributions to individual accounts set side for retirement.[22] Even if aggregate saving increases only moderately (a legitimate concern), such accounts would almost certainly increase the saving of those who currently save little or nothing at all. A possible alternative to a mandate is to provide a government match to private pension saving, particularly for plans that provide significant coverage to moderate-income employees.[23] It is at lower income levels where such a match is most needed, as existing tax incentives mean little to nothing in low or negative tax brackets.

In this connection it is worth highlighting that the tax incentives currently in place are a permanent part of the law—part of the straitjacket mortgaging our future and deterring the design of better and more equitable programs for wealth ownership.

A final reason for focusing new attention onto wealth ownership is that it goes hand-in-hand with Social Security reform. We know that some paring of promises in Social Security is inevitable, and that a reorientation of such a large portion of the federal budget is likely to take place periodically. It cannot ever be a one-time thing. Middle-income individuals will be called upon more to supplement whatever base of retirement income they receive through Social Security. Private pensions and housing have been and will remain the dominant sources of financial security in old age over and above what Social

Security provides. If there is ever a time when they need to be strengthened, it is now.

INVESTING IN LEARNING OVER A LIFETIME

Even more important than ownership of physical capital in this technological and knowledge-based society is education—the ownership of what is sometimes called human capital. Education has always been a major tool for creating opportunity for all, for breaking down barriers among classes, jurisdictions, and races. But in a modern economy, where most jobs are no longer on the farm or in the factory, the link between education and opportunity is tighter and more inexorable than ever before. As we enter the next century, education is our most powerful means of accommodating and channeling the forces of economic change. Addressing this is unavoidable, so let's do it right.

In our modern society, there are strong economic and psychological arguments for extending opportunities for formal education both backward toward early childhood and forward through adulthood. Kindergarten to 12th grade and college education must be viewed as only part of an "interdependent system of human investment" that includes, for example, programs for early childhood development, social service support for families, job training and retraining, and economic development.[24] This broader concept forces us to consider ways of making investments in diverse forms of learning at all stages of life, while helping to smooth transitions from infancy to childhood, adolescence, early and middle adulthood, and still productive later years.[25] Our discussion starts at the beginning and works through the life cycle.

Early Childhood Education

The idea of providing early childhood education is, of course, not new. Federal Head Start is itself more than 30 years old. What is new is the strength of the evidence that humans are influenced by their environments from the moment they enter the world. Neurological studies suggest that the environment, including child care in early years, influences children's cognitive development.[26] The Carnegie Corporation sums up this evidence in a strong statement: "How individuals function from the preschool years all the way through adolescence and even adulthood hinges, to a significant extent, on their experiences before age three."[27]

The changing structure and needs of American families intensify the need for quality contact with adults in the very early years. Many low-income families are headed by a single parent or by two parents who both work. Middle-income families are similarly likely to count on two paychecks and other rewards that come from working in the marketplace. Whether we like it or not, children, whatever their ages, are more likely than ever before to be without parental supervision for large parts of the day. Indeed, American society now requires as a condition for public assistance that single parents even with infants work outside the home—a revolutionary change from the 1930s, when Aid to Dependent Children was originally implemented to enable mothers to stay at home with their children.

At the same time, the common-sense notion that emotional and educational nurturing rather than simple custodial child care is required for full development of a child's potential is backed by the evidence. The corollary is that early childhood efforts, in addition to child development efforts per se, must continually address the ability of parents or guardians to participate in the lives of their children, since they are their children's first teachers.

Some intergenerational strategies are being designed to improve educational outcomes for disadvantaged parents and children simultaneously. Innovative Head Start programs seem to derive their success through providing comprehensive services to children and families through multiple components—including parental involvement, adult literacy, multi-generational family support and education, and the provision of health and social services.[28] The Even Start Program provides high quality early childhood education for preschoolers and basic remedial education for their parents. The IQ gains of early childhood programs fade out by the later primary school years according to some studies. But other important academic outcomes—improved reading levels, grade retention, and fewer high school drop-outs—have all been linked to early childhood education. And beyond academic improvements, early childhood programs have social impacts that include less involvement with the criminal justice system, fewer out-of-wedlock births, less reliance on social services as adults, and even higher earnings.[29] One preschool program, whose participants have been tracked for over a quarter of a century, is estimated to have achieved long-term savings in educational achievement, social outcomes, and physical health that amount to $7.16 for every dollar invested.[30] Finally, programs that provide immunizations, nutrition, and general preventative health services have been found to have positive effects on children's physical well-being.[31]

Although early childhood education programs, including Head Start, have received substantial support from both major political parties, several presidents, and many governors, much more needs to be done. Low pay and high turnover still affect the quality of care in Head Start.[32] Head Start, traditionally serving three- to four-year-olds, has now been extended to include Early Start for children from birth to age three. But Head Start still reaches only one-third of the low-income children eligible for it.[33] In addition to Head Start, some states have developed their own initiatives to provide and improve access to early childhood programs. Beyond programs for low-income and at-risk children, early childhood education is increasingly seen as developmentally appropriate for all children. A very significant but crucial challenge is to incorporate the parents into the structure, so that formal programs complement rather than substitute for the home environment.

Quality in Traditional K–12 Education

Within the context of extending learning over a lifetime, we must, of course, address what is sometimes considered the bigger, and politically thornier, issue of whether the nation's current education system is viable as it stands. Much disparity in educational opportunity by income and jurisdiction remains, and the scholarship level for many American students is below international standards in many areas.[34] These potential consequences become magnified in the modern economy because of its even stronger link between education and lifetime earnings and wealth.

A society stressing opportunity should allow more choices and innovation. Whether created by options within public school systems, or more radical restructuring that allows private school choices as well, is a secondary issue not addressed here. But if the choices are confined merely to trying to fit all requirements into the traditional school, while ignoring much of the rest of the life of the student, then they are likely to have limited effect. Like those who fear touching Social Security, many are afraid to open the Pandora's Box of real educational reform. But, economic and social equity for future generations demand that we do so.

Both providing more equal educational opportunities and preparing students for the world of tomorrow require attention to quality. Because it is hard to measure quality well—whether in education or national income accounting—no part of our economy achieves quality without some cost. Better facilities and smaller classes cost more. Similarly, attempts to improve school to work transitions and to improve access to higher education facilities call for more funds. But the main focus ought to be on the teachers. While our education system is multidimensional, and researchers for many years have tried to isolate the critical characteristics of quality, one of the key components is always the teacher. Students need good teachers, people who are well-trained and have a good understanding of the subjects they are expected to teach.[35] Good teachers, in turn, need a system that supports their efforts.

It is certainly true that paying teachers more might eventually attract higher quality teachers. But this argument must be examined carefully. Simply raising the salaries of current teachers may not achieve that goal quickly or well, especially if the additional resources are not combined with some sort of quality requirements. While states have been setting higher standards for students in terms of grade completion and high school graduation requirements, they have not yet moved to higher standards for their teachers, or to teacher testing. Often the educational qualifications of teachers—whether measured by training in the subjects they are teaching or by comparing test scores of teachers with those of other college graduates—are far from the standards a rich nation can achieve.[36] This nation has many outstanding, dedicated teachers, but that doesn't mean we can't find even more of them. If we want better quality, then we will have to pay for it, but we should demand that we get what we pay for.

Education for Adults

Beyond early childhood care and traditional education, and even beyond improving access to post-secondary education for all students, the forces driving the need for comprehensive approaches to education through the life cycles are several.

First, the rapid change inherent in a technological and service economy makes it imperative that a modern education system teach people how to *learn to relearn and expect to relearn.* Proof of this requirement lies in the earnings statistics indicating widening earnings disparities, even among those with the same high levels of education and experience. The rewards of the market go not simply to those who are more educated, but to those with the greatest ability to adjust to the constantly changing labor market demands of the modern era.

Second, education throughout adulthood is required to meet the diverse learning needs of individuals who mature, both mentally and emotionally, at different rates.[37] In a world where the labor market did not generally require high skills, this mattered less, at least economically. But things are different now. If algebra is useful, then it is useful not only to those who pick it up at 13 or 14. If writing skills are important, they cannot be confined to those who have greater powers of concentration when in high school. If computer technology is essential in the workplace, not only school children need to be trained on the latest equipment. When life expectancies were short, perhaps the extraordinary concentration of educational resources during youth made some sense. But today, even those who receive education at later ages are able to use that education over longer periods of time than in the past. Learning by someone who is aged 40 today, given current life expectancies, will be as useful, for as long, as learning by someone who was 20 during the last century.[38]

Third, as the structure of the nation's economy has changed, many workers at the bottom end of the skills and education ladder have seen their real earnings decay and competition for even the lowest paid jobs increase. At the same time, businesses are having a hard time finding enough qualified, skilled workers. It makes good sense for economic and social equity to invest in upgrading the skills of those now deficient in order to help meet demand. Even when education does not fully pay off in terms of the earnings of workers, it still may pay off for society relative to larger welfare and unemployment compensation systems. Once again, the twentieth century search for security must be supplemented and enhanced with greater resources aimed at providing opportunity.

Extending Education to Older Workers

Society desperately needs to reap the maximum productivity of older workers as the population ages. Increasing economic reliance on older workers is only just beginning. Yet, paradoxically, it is in only the last few decades that society has adopted the strange notion that it should encourage people to retire more and more years before they expect to die. The number of adults over age 65 in 1900 was only one-tenth the number of those age 18 and under. But by 2050, the two groups will be about the same size.[39] President Clinton in his 1998 State of the Union address bragged about how a baby born in that year might live to see the twenty-second century, that is, live to age 102. Does it make any sense for such a person to retire at age 65 or even 75? The resources and skills of the more seasoned members of society are required if we are to maintain our ability to increase our standards of living and our productivity. This desperate economic need for their continued education and intellectual stimulation has the invaluable by-product of also reducing the number of years of dependency and improving the quality of their lives.

ENGAGING THE NATION'S YOUTH

Public resources for youth are trapped by a mindset centered around a six-hour school day for nine months a year—a timetable built around a stereotypical farm family. The chores of the farm demanded attention during the afternoon and during the planting season. Both mother and father were often present to work along with and supervise their children. The time is long gone since any but a small fraction of children spend their growing years in such an atmosphere.

The concern for positively engaging the nation's youth is not new, but it is much more acutely justified today.[40] As we saw in chapter 2, under the current American system, children are spending most of their time out of school and an increasing amount of time in totally unsupervised activities. Many children are forced to care for themselves after school because there are no available alternatives. That the children themselves are crying out for more adult contact and supervision is supported by evidence that children left alone or only with siblings express greater fear of accidents and crime, and greater boredom.[41]

Fear and boredom are bad enough indictments. But the situation is worse than that. Youth with too little to do can be led to drugs, crime, and other activities that threaten their future as healthy, productive adults. To reduce these dangers, our children need to be fully engaged in positive activities with mentoring, enrichment, and adult supervision throughout most of the day, most of the year. Obviously, much of this must remain a private responsibility in society. But government must do its part by recognizing that the conventional school schedule is far from meeting the needs of school-age children and the demands of the modern workplace.[42]

A longer school day and school year is one choice; the extension of extracurricular or work opportunities during after-school hours is another. Individual plans, worked out with parents, are certainly better than attempts to find one-size-fits-all answers. Different communities will require different approaches, depending both upon their needs and their particular values. Private businesses must also move toward making the work environments of the future ever less hostile to the presence of children, recognizing that the regular separation of the family during the day is a modern condition that arose primarily with the industrial order. Firms should continue to develop programs, such as flextime or on-site day care, to help parents care for and spend time with their children.

That this issue resonates on a national level is reflected in a variety of activities, including the 1997 White House Conference on Child Care and many presidential and congressional proposals to help families with child care. Perhaps the sentiment was best articulated by General Colin Powell when he summarized the endorsement of our nation's leaders for five basic resources that should be available to our young people: "(1) an ongoing relationship with a caring adult or mentor; (2) safe places to learn and grow during nonschool hours; (3) a healthy start and a healthy future; (4) a marketable skill through effective education; and (5) an opportunity to give back through community service."[43] These leaders, participating in the President's Summit for America's Future, found the case for making children's problems a priority to be compelling. Yet while Summit participants pledged to try to meet these goals for at least two million youths by the year 2000, they had no idea how to pull together the resources to achieve this, other than generating gifts by business foundations and charitable organizations.

We are all for charities taking a lead, but it is nonsense to think that much will be done unless the resource question gets addressed up front. If a charity effort should succeed in raising $100 million a year, a considerable amount by charity standards, this translates to less than $2 per child. Quite a contrast with the average $6,000 per year cost of one student's primary and secondary education.[44] Quite a contrast also with the automatic *increases* currently scheduled in annual Medicare spending—close to $40 billion in real terms within five years, and almost $150 billion in ten years.[45] Or with tax expenditures for employer contributions to medical insurance, which will rise by almost $20 billion annually in real terms over the next few years.[46] Is getting our children off the street and into safe and nurturing environments with adults present really beyond the means of a society that can spend these large increases on other programs that most believe are of lower priority?

SUPPORTING THE MODERN FAMILY

The U.S. government doesn't have a family support policy. It has welfare policies, tax policies, and Social Security policies. Along the way, it defines who should benefit and who should pay, and it measures their relative ability or need according to concepts of family that derive from a stereotype that is less and less applicable to modern conditions. Treating returns from wives' work as a minor consideration at best, these policies continue to impose extraordinary financial penalties when a married woman goes to work or when, after becoming eligible for program benefits as a low-income, single parent, she marries someone who works and earns money. In recent years, the biases have become more sex-neutral—in the sense that male spouses and female spouses are now treated alike—but extraordinary work and marriage penalties still remain in many federal programs.

Through these programs, society is creating very different tax and subsidy rates among families in fundamentally similar situations, and making strong anti-work and anti-marriage statements to significant portions of the population. Perhaps some of these statements were unavoidable in a society stressing security rather than opportunity. Why provide the same benefits to someone who already has security through work or marriage? This type of policy makes much less sense in a society that stresses opportunity as well as security.

Public Assistance

Recent attempts to convert Aid to Families with Dependent Children (AFDC) to a program emphasizing work show us how difficult and slow is the process of change. Only after six decades was AFDC—long identified as the nation's preponderant welfare program—ended. To end it required two other very large changes: first, that work subsidies (specifically the Earned Income Tax Credit) be available to women and men alike, and second, that work requirements be enforced in welfare programs, even for single parents with children. No longer can welfare be seen primarily as an entitlement for a widowed or abandoned mother who is incapable of work.

The extent of movement so far should not be exaggerated. In addition to traditional AFDC-type welfare constituting only a tiny part of the nation's income-based public assistance, the structure of the much-heralded welfare reform can still penalize modern families.

And men remain largely outside the system altogether, whether in terms of benefits or responsibilities.

Welfare and public assistance initially tried to confine benefits only to the poor because the goal was to help those who most needed help. The inevitable consequence was that welfare recipients seldom worked because benefits were reduced drastically as earnings increased—often so drastically that an extra dollar earned could reduce benefits by more than a dollar, and much more when all the private costs of work were taken into account.

There is much debate in the economic literature over how much these exorbitant implicit tax rates affect behavior. But there is no doubt that they are unfair to the person who really does work, and that they encourage much earning "off the books." Because of income assistance in a variety of forms—food stamps, Medicaid, Earned Income Tax Credits—the financial penalties of working are still high in most states even under new reforms, and much earning still goes unreported. If welfare contributes even slightly to a culture where work is discouraged, marriage is penalized, and honest reporting to government is costly (and therefore dumb), the effects on the nation's social fabric are far more serious than the monetary losses.

Even if this problem of incentives could be ignored, there looms a more fundamental issue of fairness. What does society do to help persons who don't get such assistance but have equally low incomes? And are we comfortable as a matter of fairness with the marriage penalties that still confront welfare and working poor families in the benefit structures of programs for which they may be eligible?

Many of the problems can be mitigated over time through work subsidies or subsidies for children, that do not create combined tax rates much higher than those applying to ordinary income (about 35 percent for most taxpayers, if one counts federal and state income taxes and Social Security taxes). Some of the work disincentives due to very high cumulative tax rates on public benefits are now offset by actual work requirements in welfare. But work requirements do nothing to counteract the strong disincentives to marry, and they typically retain very high disincentives to work beyond the minimum that might be required.

The trouble with reducing the very high implicit tax rates on some groups is that doing so immediately would require either (a) lower benefits for existing beneficiaries or (b) higher costs through extending benefits to many more people. Only if the revenues arising from economic growth are allocated partly to provide opportunity beyond welfare—which necessarily includes the retention of more of the gains from work and marriage—can one avoid this dilemma. The revenues-from-economic- growth solution is not possible, of course, as long as the country is locked into its fiscal straitjacket of built-in future obligations.

The Tax Code

The income tax applies its own set of marriage penalties in the ways it sets standard deductions, phases out various benefits such as for itemized deductions, sets tax rate schedules for married couples versus single individuals, and in many, many other ways.[47] These tax penalties are starting to get consideration by some members of Congress, but there is no real indication that the problem will be tackled as a whole any time soon.

There is a fatal flaw in the logic that favors taxing "economies of scale" within the family. Your income and your spouse's income together are worth more because you live together. Thus, your combined income should be subject to a higher tax rate, just as if you actually had more money. This is the argument that buttresses the marriage penalties established by Congress. The flaw is not that there are no economies of scale. There are.

The flaw is that they do not apply solely to marriage. They apply to all conditions of sharing, but no one even thinks about placing additional taxes on any cooperative arrangement other than marriage. By singling out marriage as the only recognizable economy of scale to be zapped by the tax system, the state defines legal commitment to a marriage partner as a distinguishable event to be taxed and, in effect, penalizes it.

The options for dealing with this situation within the income tax system range from optional single filing (as is done in several states already), income splitting (essentially widening the tax brackets for married couples so that no matter how their income is split, they would pay no more tax than two single individuals filing separately), and flattening the rate structure.[48]

The challenge is to develop an appropriate adjustment process. Simply lowering taxes for married couples adds to the long-term deficit. Reducing taxes for some without increasing the deficit raises tax burdens for others. If treating marriage as a taxable event is considered unfair but sudden changes in tax liabilities are not feasible, greater parity can be obtained over time by gradually changing the rate at which taxes are altered for all groups. For instance, one could change formulas for indexing of standard deductions and the tax rate structure so that marriage penalties were gradually reduced. As an example, the standard deduction for two married individuals could be gradually raised to twice the level applying to a single individual.

If Congress continues to consider various ways to reduce the marriage penalty in the positive tax system, equity demands that those decisions be made within the wider context of marriage penalties in *all* parts of our tax and transfer system. The marriage penalties in the positive income tax derive mainly from the tax rate schedule, but they are typically much smaller as a percent of income than those deriving from the Earned Income Tax Credit. And these, in turn, are smaller than those deriving from the larger set of income assistance programs that include welfare cash payments, food stamps, and Medicaid.

Government Retirement and Social Security

The government extends its marriage and work penalties to its survivor benefit programs as well. At the time of death, the government can be very generous to widows and widowers. But rather than treating these benefits as simple death-time benefits, as most insurance policies do, the government adds a bit of "welfare" thinking to them—varying them according to whether the beneficiary remarries or not. The widows and widowers of military personnel and foreign service officers constitute two of the worst cases. Some who remarry lose their pension benefits entirely. Some younger widows and widowers can also lose substantial Social Security benefits if they remarry.

Discrimination against work by a "secondary earner" can also be large under Social Security benefit formulas. As an example, a couple with an annual earnings stream of $57,600 from one working spouse will be entitled to much higher Social Security benefits than will a couple with the exact same earnings stream if each earns $28,500. For a retirement date of 1993, while both spouses are alive the former couple will receive $20,399 and the latter $18,229. When one spouse dies, the widowed spouse of the former couple will receive $13,599, compared with $9,115 for the widow or widower in the two-earner couple.[49]

There is no justification for this difference. It does not make the Social Security system more progressive. Since both couples contributed the same amount of tax, it does not provide an equal return on past taxes or contributions. And it is independent of any child-raising for which society may wish to make accommodations. It is an artifact of a system that provided a generous spouse's and survivor's benefit in a world where the prototypical wife would not work for pay.

Fixing the inequities of these various expenditure and tax systems without cutting back on benefits or raising taxes for other families would be extremely expensive, even compared with the costs of fixing the tax system or welfare system alone. This is the dilemma that faced policymakers at the end of the 1990s, when they proposed modest changes to deal with some of the income tax penalties. They had no way to pay for the change and were not willing to adjust rates honestly to make the fixes. So policymakers continue to make token changes or shove the problem under the rug. Only by embracing the policies that would provide fiscal slack is there a chance of making the gradual long-term equity adjustments that are long past due.

FOSTERING A NEW DEMOCRATIC CITIZENSHIP

"If we could first know where we are, and whither we are tending, we could then better judge what to do and how to do it," said Abraham Lincoln in his 1858 speech accepting the Illinois Republicans' nomination for the U.S. Senate. In drawing conclusions about where we are, and whither we are tending, this book suggests dramatic ways to rethink the nation's domestic policy commitments and responsibilities. We have urged removing automatic growth in programs, modernizing social insurance, reorienting the budget to better serve individuals at all points in the life cycle, creating more pension and homeownership wealth among less well-off Americans, doing a better job of educating people throughout their lifetimes, getting adolescents into environments where they interact much more frequently with parents and other mentors, and revamping policies to accommodate the needs of modern working families.

But how can we get there from here? Redesigning policy commitments and reallocating public resources is a job of collective judgment that must be exercised *through our political process*—the "talk of democracy." The faith that underlies democracy is twofold. It is, first, the faith that ordinary people are capable of engaging in an open, honest, and sustained conversation about their affairs. It is, second, the faith that through this public conversation—with its noise and confusion, but also its deliberation and persuasion—citizens actually are able to discover their common interests and pursue them effectively. Not to believe these things is to admit that our two-century experiment in self-government has failed.

There is no authentically American alternative to government-by-discussion. But something has gone wrong with the talk of democracy. Distrust about the political process is as American as apple pie. But we have been going through a period of political cynicism that is increasingly undermining our collective capacity to talk honestly about the difficult policy tradeoffs that underlie almost any constructive policy change. Instead of providing the government citizens need and deserve, today's public conversation is mired in resentment—a tale of what "they" are doing to "us" instead of a dialogue about what we can do for ourselves.

Realistically, there is little chance that the modern medium in which this germ multiplies—a public relations mentality, media manipulation, pandering to polls, and other such features of the political landscape—are going to disappear any time soon. But realism does not demand acknowledgment of defeat—acceptance that the prevailing process is the best we can do. Nor does the American public think this *is* the best we can do. Their distrust in the processes of government is strangely related to an overall trust that the current system will somehow right itself—that when things get bad enough, enough "other" people will be provoked into making things better. But the ills of hyper-democracy are not self-limiting. Things *can* keep going from bad to worse. And as far as the integrity of our political conversation is concerned, we have been moving in the wrong direction for many years.

The key in changing direction is to rebuild a deserved public trust in our political institutions and processes. The reasons are clear. Without trust, there is little chance of good faith bargaining. Without trust, there is not enough goodwill when inevitable hardships come. Without trust, all hell breaks loose when the unexpected upsets previous understandings, as it often does. Without trust, the exploiters of discontent and the manipulators of opinion will always have the upper hand.

What is to be done? There is both a general answer for all time and a specific set of answers for our time and place.

On the *general* method of restoring and maintaining trust, there is nothing new to discover. We need to keep hearing and doing what the age-old wisdom teaches and what any person's daily experience confirms. Trust in the abstract is mere emotion and can be dangerous. What matters is being worthy of trust. To be trustworthy we have to

(1) tell the truth as best we know it, (2) give and keep our word, and (since the first two will always be vulnerable to human imperfection) (3) admit our mistakes and go on. If more people in politics are to behave this way, more individual citizens must take responsibility for judging the performance of politicians, group spokespersons, and the media in such a character-oriented way.

Distrust will not be dispelled by some grand event—the enactment of new policies or the election of a particular leader. It will depend on the choices made day in and day out by individual politicians and citizens. The only general way forward is to create exceptions, one by one, to the perceptions of untrustworthiness. The verdict of trustworthiness must be built up over the years in thousands of public judgments about persons and performance. Truer talk, truer behavior, a little civic thinking every day—that is the homework. If truth telling—unpleasant and complex as its messages often are—is rewarded by citizens' responses, there will be more of it from would-be leaders. If it is punished, there will be less.

Never has the citizen had greater political freedom, never more access to information and two-way communications. By the same logic, never has the ordinary citizen had greater responsibility. Our current democratized environment places a huge premium on individuals taking responsibility for what is happening in public life. Cynicism about government and politics is an easy way to evade that responsibility. So is a passive "meet-my-needs" attitude to the blandishments of hyper-democracy. Getting the government we deserve has to begin and end with citizens, one at a time, trying to do the right thing. There is no alternative in a democracy.

Thus, the general method for rebuilding trust revolves around questions of character and individuals' responsibility for wanting and rewarding truthfulness. This may sound naive, but the result is inescapable. The principles citizens live by create the world they live in.

There are also particular opportunities for improving the public conversation. Here the basic idea is to design arrangements that will make it safer for would-be leaders to tell the truth as they see it—and easier for citizens to hear and act on competing truths in a well-informed way. The reasoning behind such reforms is contained in George Washington's advice in his 1796 speech as "a parting friend" of the nation. He said, "in proportion as the structure of a government gives force to public opinion, it is essential that public opinion be enlightened." The extension of democracy since Washington's day has been relentless and there is no practical likelihood that we will see it retreat. *Government by elites is out. So government by the people has to be more enlightened and thought through more carefully than it has ever been.*

The issue is not one of reducing "openness" but of organizing open discourse in a better way. By "better" we mean expanding deliberative space in the public conversation, space where it becomes more politically feasible for citizens and their representatives to work through policy issues and talk more honestly about their pros and cons. Today such civic space is in very short supply. Most interest groups and activists at the extremes do not want a political process that listens and weighs and collaborates in a search for workable policies. They want to own the policy answers. Against this inevitable pressure, reforms should try to open up more constructive ways of engaging the informed and active consent of a much broader constituency—a citizen public that is much truer to the vision of self-government than a consumer public can ever be.

Fortunately, measures that promote trust also encourage authentic civic engagement. We need changes that will facilitate citizens' reasoned judgment rather than the short-term exploitation of their snap opinions. With modern technology bombarding citizens as mere information consumers, the incentives to pander proliferate. It is easy to tell people what they want to hear: grievances aired, sentiments manipulated. But since so much of this emotive "message-sending" does not mesh with policy realities, the long-term effect is to confuse, disunite, and disillusion the public conversation. This is not the governing process citizens deserve. It should be possible to design institutional arrangements that help citizens deliberate about their collective affairs. Such a shift from pandering toward pondering requires deliberate decisions to put more resources and effort into the pondering side. The odds for more constructive policy talk will increase by pushing reform on three fronts.

Building the Media Citizens Deserve

The question is not whether, but how, today's telecommunications revolution will shape the fate of America's political processes. Left to itself, the momentum of commercial market forces will produce more of what we have now—an "Entertainment Tonight" style of democracy to titillate and amuse the masses along with narrowly cast information enclaves for political activists and policy wonks. The point is not just to admonish media people to somehow do better. Institutional changes are needed. They are needed in order to counterbalance the pervasive commercial incentives for public affairs reporting to concentrate on feeding passive consumers an unrelenting diet of the simplistic, the divisive, the dramatic. This is not the media citizens need. And given the vast new communication opportunities that have come, and are coming, into existence, it is not the kind of media for which they have to settle.

The centerpiece for reform in the media should be to rethink our public service telecommunications systems. The existing public broadcasting structure was created almost 30 years ago. We need to think creatively about ways to enhance it. For instance, in any new system (whether national or state and local), public television and radio should be integrated with live-coverage public affairs channels, local cable public access channels, interactive computer discussion forums, high-quality public affairs databases, and other on-line telecommunications services. The technology for linking cable, telephone, television, and computers for interactive communication is with us. The need now is to use these opportunities to construct a genuine public service telecommunications system geared to the needs of citizens.

How such a system or systems might be built and funded is suggested by initiatives already begun.[50] One small-scale model is the "Democracy Network" developed at the Los Angeles Center for Governmental Studies. This early experimental communication network is accessible over television or personal computers. It provides information on government officials and candidates, two-way communications among citizens and representatives, and forums for discussions of policy issues. Other communities (over 130 nationwide, according to a 1997 count by the Association for Community Networking) have created e-mail forums for citizens to exchange views and organize to solve local problems.

The point of our discussion here is not to design a new public service network but rather to highlight the opportunity and need to take such institutional innovations seriously—to turn technological opportunities to our advantage. The mission of new systems should be to provide both reliable, timely, citizen-oriented information on politics and policy combined with nonpartisan arenas for sustained public discussion of this mountain of information.

This could also be a place to provide free air time to candidates and groups who are otherwise caught up in the vicious spiral of fundraising to pay the huge current costs of television and radio time. Whether here or through other mechanisms, more resources must be devoted to allowing nonpartisan sources—such as coalitions of

watchdog organizations recognized or supported by journalists themselves—to monitor and score the veracity of facts and statistics in-
jected into the public conversation.[51] It is not enough to complain
about the creeping contagion of tabloid journalism in the public conversation. Citizens need a way—not a truth squad but a baloney pa-
trol—to hold media communications up to public scrutiny, embar-
rassment, and loss of credibility when someone plays fast and loose
with the facts, constructs misleading policy stories, or reports political interpretations as though they were news. All of this would generate pressure for our public communication process to move in a
healthier direction.

The overarching need for some major institutional reform is inescapable. The challenge is to think very seriously and to act much
more self-consciously about the meaning of citizenship in the information age.

Nourishing a Public Opinion Worth Listening To

A telecommunications system more devoted to public service promises a better institutional framework for structuring the talk of democracy. The flesh and muscle of a different kind of journalism is also
needed to give this skeleton life and force.

Conventional print and electronic journalism is committed to providing accounts of events to information consumers. Many journalists
play the role of detached observers reporting the facts and drama of
those events, indifferent to any outcomes. Most people would agree
that this traditional role is extraordinarily valuable and should be
sustained. But it is not the only kind of journalism worthy of support.
The media and those working in it are stewards of the public conversation through which citizens must do much of their work. A flat
reporting of the events, conflicts, and scandals of public life is not all
that citizens need. In fact, far from being neutral, the dominant por-
trayal of public life as little more than power games and claimant
conflicts teaches the constant lesson of disillusioned citizenship—
that governance is not a deliberative process involving the people but
a morass of intrigue through which "they" do things to "us."[52] Without new journalistic commitments, we can expect today's expanding
communication technologies to deepen the paradox of the last half
century. Deluged with an ever growing excess of incoherent, faster-
circulating information, citizens will feel ever more distant from and
contemptuous of their governing process and its policies.

A new form of media commitment has recently come to be called "civic journalism." It is a form of journalism that changes the rules of engagement between communication organizations and citizens so that journalism becomes more useful to a self-governing society. It adds a new form of newsroom coverage that actively brings citizens into public deliberations, which are considered newsworthy even if they are not traditional news. Typically through a partnership of newspapers and TV organizations, the public's conversation about politics and policy becomes a newsworthy object of public concern and journalists become reconnected to the communities they serve.

In recent years a number of prototypes have added this new face to journalism.[53] The *Charlotte Observer* in North Carolina has teamed with local television and radio stations, not only to report on crime but to create an award-winning public service initiative that examines neighborhood sources of crime, covers efforts to deal with the criminal behavior, and sponsors discussion forums of city agencies, nonprofit organizations, and neighborhood residents for taking action on common neighborhood problems. Since 1991, a media coalition centered on the *Wisconsin State Journal* and state public radio and television stations has carried forward a multi-faceted "We the People/Wisconsin" project. During elections the project has organized educational issue coverage, town-hall meetings, candidate debates, and citizenship training to help voters get beyond distorted information and manipulated images. Outside the election cycle, it has produced coordinated coverage of particular issues—ranging from health care to gambling—and sponsored a wide variety of citizen discussion groups to help build public capacities for in-depth deliberation. Other such coalitions of print and electronic media can be found in Wichita, Tallahassee, Grand Forks, Dayton, and a dozen other localities. Other efforts, including a few led by some of the nation's top journalists, are focusing on ways to redirect the media to improve public trust. Such community-based, citizenship-oriented journalism is valuable and growing, but it is only a foreshadowing of the more comprehensive civic journalism needed across the country for dealing with national issues as well.

Closely linked to civic journalism is the need to rethink the conventional ways of gauging public opinion. Today this task is dominated by the commercial incentive to make money and news by polling the public to "see what people think." The typical result is a series of snap reactions to superficial questions, registered by separate individuals with little information, minimal attention, and no chance to interact and refine what passes for the public "thinking." The same trivialization of citizens' deliberation occurs in talk shows devoted to people's sounding off about this or that.

Alternative ways of more deeply researching and reporting on citizen opinion should become commonplace rather than the exceptions they currently are. For example, "deliberative polling" is an experimental method to gauge what representative samples of citizens think when they are given adequate, unbiased information, and time to think and to interact on the questions at issue. Another approach that now includes several thousand community-based groups is "national issues forums."[54] Citizens in a variety of settings engage in sustained efforts to learn about how to make hard choices among competing means and ends of public policy.[55] These efforts to get behind superficial polling numbers and tap citizens' judgments need to be geared to working through real-life policy issues, and the results need to be publicized to other citizens.

Such deliberative opinion research and reporting, taken together with new civic journalism initiatives, would do much to help nourish the development of citizenship voices worth listening to. They are not the kinds of things that will develop naturally under the commercial incentives of media conglomerates (which typically commission polls to generate flashy news stories) or private pollsters (who use polls and in-depth focus groups to generate clients, profits, and strategies for public opinion manipulation). Much more long-term private, non-profit resource commitments are required to build a research and media community focused on reporting considered public judgments that go beyond the usual fare of today's political marketplace.

Grounding Public Talk in Civic Education

Citizens are people who deliberate and act on their public life together. Without citizens, democracy becomes an empty formality with the soul of an auction house. And without learning the dispositions and aptitudes that constitute good practice in civic life, there are not likely to be many authentic citizens. The logic runs as follows: no democracy without citizens, no citizens without civic education. Improving the public conversation about our policy challenges requires a new commitment to civic education that leads more people to think and act like citizens.

But we must be clear what that does and does not mean. After more than four decades of empirical research on political participation, the evidence is clear. Only a minority of persons are deeply interested in politics, and even fewer are actively engaged in political life. This is not simply an indifference to party politics. For example, in the United States there are an estimated 150,000 homeowners associations regulating many intimate details of everyday life (allowable house design and paint colors, neighborhood noise levels, etc.) for some 32 million people. And yet studies show that on average only 11 percent of members take part in the governance activities of these associations.[56] If the aim of civic education is a nation of always attentive, fully public-spirited political activists, the results are doomed to disappointment. Building a better public policy conversation requires not an ideal assembly of good citizens but the regular presence of good enough citizens.

What does good enough entail? Good enough citizenship means having the know-how and motivation to talk and work with other disagreeing (and at times disagreeable) people when something needs to be done about common problems (the extent of commonality being itself one of the things that has to be talked and worked through). Good enough citizens are not thoroughly altruistic and public-spirited. But neither are they simply rational egoists for whom "what's in it for me" is the only bottom line. Good enough citizenship means being competent in thinking, feeling, and acting on one's interests in the context of a common public life. It means a practiced habit of regarding oneself as a citizen engaged in self-rule and not simply a client, consumer, or complainant.

Good enough citizens do not occur naturally. They are the product of civic education—a more demanding matter than what might be called democratic education. Democratic education is already well nourished in modern America. The culture enshrines and celebrates the ideal of expressing one's demands, standing up for one's rights, targeting adversaries, communing with the like-minded, and so on. Such democratic training is modeled day in and day out in the consumer world of economic relationships—a depiction of the good life as one of demanding and having things your way. Modern political campaigns school the public in much the same way, manipulating images and words to produce spurts of emotion that ideally lead the voting consumer to make a psychological purchase of the desired candidate or cause.

In contrast with democratic education, civic education involves "unnatural" behavior. Civic education emphasizes the unnatural skill of listening and not just self-presentation, of giving ear as well as giving voice. It is empathetic in attending to overlapping interests and is open-minded as to whether the methods of conflict or collaboration are most appropriate on a given issue. It accepts the premise that one's own direct experience does not provide all that is required for making competent judgments. Thus, civic education values what is deliberative in the sense of willingly encountering, working through, and reexamining arguments. Open to persuasion and learning, civically educated persons have a tolerance for answers that are provisional and proximate. They are not paragons of virtue, but they are concerned to get on in a practical way with the work of solving mutual problems. In all these ways voting is the last, not the first, thing one does as a citizen.

Modern American society keeps two schools where far greater attention to civic education is desperately needed.

The first is obvious: the formal educational system. With education ever more geared to the job market, there is an understandable emphasis on school-to-work transitions. Far less attention is paid to the fundamental issue of preparing for the school-to-citizenship transition.[57] Vast numbers of students graduate from high school and college without knowing the first thing about the complexities of policy choices or the moral claims of democratic citizenship. Civic education needs to be rescued in the schools. The romantic, good-government myths of civics textbooks and classes from the past have disappeared, replaced by a naive cynicism of the present. This is a rescue mission that can be undertaken only by committed members of the educational community itself, along with their allies among philanthropic foundations. Given what is required in today's more open and public opinion-driven political system, teaching the moral requirements and skills for self-rule is not a matter of imposing values but of hard-headed realism. The policy activists who have taken advantage of the increased opportunities for political participation in recent decades are not generally representative of average citizens, who really do want nondoctrinaire, moderate, and workable policy processes.[58] We cannot turn back the clock to a simpler time. But we can rear new generations with more "good enough" citizens—ordinary people with a common-sense interest in practical solutions to public problems.

The second school of civic education is less obvious. It was identified 160 years ago by Alexis de Tocqueville. It constitutes the learning that occurs as ordinary citizens are called upon to take part in government by the discharge of some public function—typically involving people in voluntary association with each other. Needing to decide matters of local importance, a person is encouraged to acquire a spirit of ownership and public concern for "the fate of the spot that he inhabits." In associating with others to make their influence felt on the common public life, otherwise isolated individuals find "feelings and opinions are recruited, the heart is enlarged, and the human mind developed . . . by the reciprocal influence of men upon one another."[59]

Obviously much has changed since Tocqueville's day. But the essential insight remains relevant (perhaps more relevant than ever in the current era of organizational giantism). Engagement in community decision-making is key to enlightening individuals' self-interest. Today public policies—whether national, state, or local—seem to be analyzed from every angle *except* how effectively they allow citizens to partake in what happens.[60] The currently fashionable decentralization of federal programs will never bolster citizens' competence and stake-holding in public policy if it simply replaces one set of bureaucratic bosses in Washington with another set in state or local government offices. Within general standards of equity and civil rights, new approaches are needed to reconnect citizens and their civil associations to public programs. Compartmentalized bureaucratic boxes need to be broken down and local discretion increased so that citizens have greater responsibility for running their local affairs and gaining the civic education that comes from that responsibility.

Anyone with practical experience at the local level knows that all this is easier said than done. Using groups with different interests to do public work is difficult and frustrating. Nevertheless there are promising practices that can be built upon.[61] Typical local examples are reorganizations to increase the local control of schools, participation of church groups and other voluntary associations in the implementation of welfare-to-work programs, and integration of citizens' groups in planning and regulating economic development. At the national level, examples include recent efforts to revive public accountability of agencies that deal directly with individuals, such as the Internal Revenue Service and Social Security Administration.

Voluntarism remains part of a great many Americans' lives. But without the strengthened civic attachments that come from citizens doing public work, citizenship is at risk of shriveling into little more than acts of check writing and special interest lobbying.[62] For a genuine civil education that enhances social responsibility, there is no substitute for ordinary citizens coming together in the structures of governance to engage in civic problemsolving. In the end, citizenship is learned by doing citizens' work.

CONCLUSION

The arguments we have been making boil down to three basic rules. On the one hand, these rules follow the venerable American tradition of common-sense pragmatism. On the other, they highlight how far we have strayed from that tradition in our policymaking over the last several decades.

Rule Number One: Rethink our commitments. This rule implies moving away from perpetual automatic growth in programs, whether through expenditures or tax subsidies. It goes beyond the current focus on the deficit, which treats a symptom rather than the cause. It requires the creation of "fiscal slack"—reserving a proportion of future resources for future generations, irrespective of pressures arising from current needs. We cannot do a good job of predetermining the entire budgets of future generations. So let's stop trying.

Rule Number Two: Rethink our responsibilities. This rule implies a constant process of shifting the public resources each generation has to spend toward greater relative needs, as changing economic and family conditions define those needs. It is a rule that goes beyond the current practice of simply identifying new wants, which does little more than legitimize the truism that wants are limitless. It provides guidance on how to choose in a world where choice is made easier through the creation of fiscal slack. If opportunity, not just security, is needed to break down barriers across income, class, and race, if the new economy demands more education across a lifetime, if our children do not have adequate opportunity to grow without more adult presence, if unacceptable proportions of the truly old remain poor, then we have a responsibility to do more about these needs—and less about less pressing wants—now.

Rule Number Three: Rethink our decisionmaking process. This rule requires embracing the responsibilities of citizens, both individually and as a society, that are inherent in the new democratic order. It demands that we step away from the manipulation of ideas and the distorted simplifications that are the downsides of our hyperdemocracy. Although this rethinking must address the new immediacy of late twentieth-century communications technology, it responds to the age-old demand for a public discourse that is civil, rational, and knowledge-based. Of our three rules, it is the least amenable to change through legislation and places the greatest responsibility on each of us as citizens.

Only by simultaneously rethinking these three dimensions of our lives are we likely to work our way out of the current box—a box that limits our vision of policy in the year 2050 to some modest variation of policy in 1950. It is this backward-looking view that prevents us from getting the government we deserve.

We do not expect instant or universal agreement with all we have said. If we persuade enough people that it is time for some serious rethinking about our fiscal commitments, our public responsibilities, and the ways we make our collective public decisions—and that each of these three legs must be built for the stool to stand—we will have made enough headway.

Notes

1. Cited from Daniel J. Boorstin, 1974, *The Americans: The Democratic Experience,* New York: Random House; Vintage Books Edition, p. ix.

2. Perhaps no movement has stressed ways to rediscover our citizenship more than the communitarian network. See especially Amitai Etzioni, Jim Fishkin, William Galston, and Mary Ann Glendon, "The Responsive Community: Rights and Responsibilities," Editorial Statement, *The Responsive Community,* Vol. I, Issue 1 (Winter 1990/91), pp. 2–5. In his latest book, Etzioni searches further for a balance between order and liberty, while sounding the call to moderation and common sense amidst the clamor of the present. See Amitai Etzioni, *The New Golden Rule,* New York: Basic Books, 1996.

3. Based on his experience as director of the Congressional Budget Office, Robert Reischauer also argues persuasively that budget balance bills do not serve as useful vehicles for fundamental restructuring of entitlements. See, for example, Robert Reischauer (ed.), *Setting National Priorities: Budget Choices for the Next Century,* The Brookings Institution, Washington, DC, ch. 1, 1997.

4. David Shaviro provides a very useful analysis of economic and political theories behind the deficit in *Do Deficits Matter?* University of Chicago Press, 1997. He examines in detail such issues as whether the accrual of government spending in advance of tax revenues can be justified from generational equity and other viewpoints. While he concludes that the evidence is mixed—for example, besides measurement problems, there is no absolute argument in favor of saving so that future generations can be better off than the current generations—he does discuss problems with programs that are not sustainable and therefore create unrealistic expectations. Our emphasis here is a bit different. The uneven playing field causes inefficient policy enactment. Similarly, many or most commitments for the long term—even those that are not in excess of expected revenues—cannot be made efficiently now because we simply do not know future needs.

5. Requiring a review of funding does not necessarily preclude authorizing a structure under which permanent programs operate. It does require periodic reassessment of relative priorities and removes automatic entitlements to appropriations.

6. For a longer discussion of this issue, including a variety of alternatives to pure sunsets, see C. Eugene Steuerle, "Sunsets," column on economic perspectives in *Tax Notes,* April 6, 1998.

7. The increasing focus on reform is illustrated by the many books in this area, including Peter A. Diamond, David C. Lindeman, and Howard Young (eds.), *Social Security: What Role for the Future?* (1996), National Academy of Social Insurance; Eric R. Kingson and James M. Schulz (eds.), *Social Security in the 21st Century* (1997), Oxford University Press; Peter G. Peterson, *Will America Grow Up Before It Grows Old?* (1996), NY: Random House; David M. Walker, *Retirement Security: Understanding and Planning Your Financial Future* (1997), NY: John Wiley & Sons; and Marilyn Moon and Janemarie Mulvey, *Entitlements and the Elderly: Protecting Promises, Recognizing Realities* (1996), The Urban Institute Press.

8. See figure 4.8. Also, long-term projections from the *Budget of the United States Government, Fiscal Year 1999* show that combined spending on Social Security, Medicare, and other health spending will absorb most revenues by 2030.

9. Mark Warshawskey also demonstrates the increasing problems for employers trying to provide retiree health benefits in *The Uncertain Promise of Retiree Health Benefits: An Evaluation of Corporate Obligations* (1992), the AEI Press, Washington, DC.

10. According to the Bureau of the Census, March 1997, *Current Population Survey*, 17.7 percent of the nonelderly population was uninsured.

11. The value of the tax benefits is based on the fact that people in higher income groups are more likely to have health care, that they have better insurance, and that they are in a higher tax bracket. For a more detailed discussion, see "A Better Subsidy for Health Insurance?" by Eugene Steuerle and Gordon Mermin, in Galen Institute, *A Fresh Approach to Health Care Reform*, Washington, DC, forthcoming. Also see "A Special Report: Health Policy—The Search for a Better Approach," *The American Enterprise*, 3(1): 67–70, January/February 1992.

12. Data based on Katherine Levit et al., "National Health Expenditures, 1995," in *Health Care Financing Review*, Fall 1996. According to this study 46.2 percent of health care spending is direct government outlays. In addition, according to the *Budget of the United States Government, Fiscal Year 1996*, an additional 6 percent of spending is attributable to tax expenditures.

13. For more detailed information see Steuerle and Bakija, *Retooling Social Security for the 21st Century: Right and Wrong Approaches to Reform*, The Urban Institute Press, Washington, DC, 1994.

14. Those other countries include Canada, Germany, Sweden, Italy, Norway, and the Netherlands. For further discussion see Timothy Smeeding, "Financial Poverty in Developed Countries: Evidence from the Luxembourg Income Study," Working Paper No. 155, 1997. He defines poverty as 50 percent of the median income in order to have a universal, international measure.

15. For a more detailed discussion of this issue see "Social Security Benefits for Women Aged 62 or Older," in *Social Security Bulletin*, 60(4), 1997. Also, data from the *EBRI Databook on Employee Benefits* show that the median income for a widow was only $10,800, as opposed to $12,356 for a married person in 1995.

16. Timothy Smeeding has proposed this type of adjustment.

17. Marilyn Moon points to a number of ways to reform Medicare along these lines, including improved cost-sharing requirements, some increased premiums, better low-income protection, improved administration, and expanded hospice care, in *Medicare Now and in the Future* (1996), The Urban Institute Press.

18. According to the *Budget of the United States Government, Fiscal Year 1999*, tax expenditures for home mortgages were the third largest tax expenditure at $53.7 billion, and exemptions for state and local property tax were the 10th largest tax expenditure at $18.4 billion.

19. See Michael Sherraden (1991), *Assets and the Poor: A New American Welfare Policy*. Armonk, NY: Sharpe.

20. See L. Burman and E. Fisher, "Capital Gains and the People Who Realize Them," *National Tax Journal*, September 1997. Based on authors' calculations using median income of $31,241 for 1993, 95 percent of capital gains were paid by people with income above the median.

21. See Edward Scanlon, "Homeownership and Its Impacts: Implications for Housing Policy for Low-Income Families" (1996), Working Paper #96-2, Center for Social Development, Washington University in St. Louis.

22. Cited from *Report of the 1994–1996 Advisory Council on Social Security, Vol. 1: Findings and Recommendations*, Washington, DC, 1997, and *Fixing Social Security*, by the Committee for Economic Development, Washington, DC, 1997.

23. See Eugene Steuerle, "Privatizing Social Security," parts one and two, *Tax Notes*, December 9 and December 16, 1996.

24. The Committee for Economic Development, *The Unfinished Agenda*, 1991.

25. For a longer discussion of these issues see *An America That Works: The Life-Cycle Approach to a Competitive Work Force*, Committee for Economic Development, 1990.

26. In "Long-term Outcome of Early Childhood Programs: Analysis and Recommendations," *The Future of Children*, Vol. 5(3), Deanna Gombey et al. explain that neurological evidence suggests that environment influences infant brain development. They also provide a general review of the studies that have looked at the effects of early childhood programs, concluding that the best methodological studies find positive outcomes. Additionally, the *NICHD Study of Early Child Care*, 1997, found that the quality of child care for very young children does matter for their cognitive development and their use of language.

27. Carnegie Task Force on Meeting the Needs of Young Children, *Starting Points: Meeting the Needs of Our Youngest Children*, New York, 1994.

28. See *National Evaluation of the Even Start Family Literacy Program, Final Report* (Cambridge, MA: Abt Associates, Inc., June 1994).

29. For a longer discussion of the benefits of early childhood programs see *Early Childhood Care and Education: An Investment That Works* (1995) by the National Conference of State Legislatures, which offers a more extensive explanation of the research that looked at early education programs.

30. These data are based on the High Scope/Perry Preschool Program, which provides longitudinal data over 27 years.

31. For a longer discussion of research on the benefits of early childhood programs see *Early Childhood Care and Education: An Investment That Works* (1995) by the National Conference of State Legislatures.

32. Regarding low pay and quality of teachers in Head Start, see Diane Ravitch's chapter on educational policy in Robert Reischauer (ed.), *Setting National Priorities* (1997), The Brookings Institution, Washington, DC.

33. Based on data from the Children's Defense Fund (CDF) for 1996. CDF reports that even with President Clinton's plan to expand Head Start it will only serve half of the eligible population.

34. Data from the Third International Mathematics and Science Study (TIMSS), which was conducted by the National Center for Education Statistics (NCES) during the 1995 school year, indicate that while 4th graders in the United States performed above the international average in both science and math, 8th graders in the United States performed below average in math and about average in science, and by 12th grade students were below the international average in both science and math and are in fact among the lowest of the countries in math achievement.

35. According to data from the National Center for Education Statistics, "America's Teachers: Profile of a Profession, 1993–94" (1997) Pub NCES 97-460, 36 percent of public school and 43 percent of private school teachers had neither an undergraduate major nor minor in the subject of their main teaching assignment. The proportions are worse within particular fields and also in classrooms with lower-income students.

36. For a more extensive discussion of the need for testing of teachers, see works by Diane Ravitch of the Brookings Institution, including "Put Teachers to the Test," *Washington Post*, February 25, 1998.

37. According to *Prisoners of Time*, by the Department of Education, under the current system all children are given the same amount of time to comprehend and master all material and all subject matter. This is not consistent with the way children learn.

38. The life expectancy for a woman at age 40 in 1990 was 40.6 years; in 1900 the life expectancy for a woman at age 20 was 43.8 years. Data on the interval from birth to age 20 demonstrate an even larger increase over the century. The data are based on the Department of Commerce, *Historical Statistics of the United States*, and the *1995 Statistical Abstract of the United States*.

39. Based on Bureau of the Census historic data and projections. In 1990 the population over 65 was 3.1 million and the population under 18 was 30.8 million. However, by 2050 the estimates suggest that the population over 65 will be 78.6 million and those under 18 will be 96.1 million.

40. The *1894 Annual Report of the Commissioner of Education*, William T. Harris addressed the concerns for children of shortening the school day.

41. For a longer discussion of this issue see the Department of Education, *Keeping Schools Open as Community Learning Centers*, Washington, DC, July 1997.

42. One model for schools, "The School of the 21st Century," designed by Ed Zigler of Yale University in 1987, directly addresses the need for childcare and activities for children after school. This model is currently implemented in 400 schools in 13 states across the country. For a better description of this model, see "Supporting Children and Families in the Schools: The School of the 21st Century" by Edward F. Zigler, Matia Finn-Stevenson, and Barbara Stern, *American Journal of Orthopsychiatry* 67(3), July 1997.

43. General Colin L. Powell, U.S. Army (Ret.), "Recreating the Civil Society—One Child at a Time," Washington, DC: *The Brookings Review* 15 (No. 4), Fall 1997, pp. 2–3.

44. Based on data for the 1994–95 school year from the National Center for Education Statistics.

45. See Congressional Budget Office, *The Economic and Budget Outlook: Fiscal Years 1999–2008*. Medicare spending in real terms increases from $218 billion in 1998 to $255 billion in 2003 and $358 billion in 2008.

46. Data from the *Budget of the United States Government, Fiscal Year 1999* show an increase from $85.5 billion in 1997 to $102.7 billion in 2003.

47. For a longer discussion of the many marriage penalties in the tax code, see "For Better or Worse: Marriage and the Federal Income Tax," Report by the Congressional Budget Office, June 1997.

48. See E. Steuerle and M. McIntrye, *Federal Tax Reform: A Family Perspective*, The Finance Project, Washington, DC, July 1996.

49. For a more detailed discussion and numerical examples, see Steuerle and Bakija, *Retooling Social Security for the 21st Century: Right and Wrong Approaches to Reform*, The Urban Institute Press, Washington, DC, 1994.

50. The general idea for such a public telecommunications system is outlined in Lawrence K. Grossman, *The Electronic Republic* (New York: Viking, 1995), pp. 210–17. Figures on community networking are from Jim Buie, "Neighborhood Watch Meets World Wide Web over the Back Yard Fence," *The Washington Post*, Sept.28, 1997, p. C2.

51. A few such watchdog organizations currently exist, including Fairness and Accuracy in Reporting, Accuracy in Media, and the Minnesota News Council (supported by journalists).

52. Matthew Robert Kerbel, *Remote and Controlled: Media Politics in a Cynical Age* (Boulder, CO: Westview Press, 1995); Richard Harwood, "The Alienated Voter: Are the News Media to Blame?" *The Brookings Review*, Fall 1996, pp. 32–35.

53. Many of these projects are funded by the Pew Center for Civic Journalism, a project of the Pew Charitable Trusts, and reported on in its newsletter "Civic Catalyst."

54. Deliberative polling is discussed in James S. Fishkin's *Democracy and Deliberation* (New Haven: Yale University Press, 1991) and the subsequent literature his experiments with such polls have spawned. National Issues Forums are a program area given prominence by the Dayton, Ohio-based Kettering Foundation, often working with the Public Agenda Foundation.

55. One example of this is the exercises in Hard Choices presented by the Center for a Responsible Federal Budget. For discussion of this program, see Susan Tanaka, "The Public Can Make Hard Choices," The Future of the Public Sector, Brief #5, The Urban Institute Press, September 1996.

56. For data on homeowners' associations, see Nancy L. Rosenblum, "Democratic Education at Home," *The Good Society*, Vol. 7, number 2, Spring 1997, 12–15.

57. Currently meeting this need is emphasized in a variety of projects by nonprofit organizations such as the Minneapolis-based Center for Democracy and Citizenship and the Character Education Partnership of Alexandria, Virginia.

58. Nolan McCarty, Keith Poole, and Howard Rosenthal, *The Polarization of American Politics* (1998, forthcoming) gives empirical backing to this generalization made in E.J. Dionne, Jr.'s *Why Americans Hate Politics* (New York: Simon and Schuster, 1991).

59. Alexis de Tocqueville, *Democracy in America* (1835–1840), vol. 1, p. 70, and vol. 2, p. 117.

60. Helen Ingram and Steven Rathgeb Smith, eds., 1993, *Public Policy for Democracy*, Washington, DC: The Brookings Institution.

61. Such initiatives are typically promoted by philanthropic enterprises such as the National Civil League of Denver, the Minneapolis Center for Democracy and Citizenship, the New Citizenship Project supported by the Bradley Foundation, the Walt Whitman Center at Rutgers, and the Civic Practices Network based at Brandeis University. A number of local, counter-bureaucratic programs to strengthen impoverished urban families and neighborhoods are highlighted in Lisbeth B. Schorr's book *Common Purpose*, New York: Doubleday, 1997.

62. Sidney Verba, Kay Lehman Schlozman, and Henry E. Brady, *Civic Voluntarism in American Politics*, Cambridge: Harvard University Press, 1995.

WHO DOES WHAT? THE CHANGING SHAPE
OF U.S. FEDERALISM

Surrounding many of the debates about the public sector in this volume has been a secondary-level debate about which government level should be involved in performing which functions.[1] We have not taken strong positions about this issue in this volume. At the same time, we believe that much of what is written about it is confusing and misleading. As an empirical matter, both centralization and decentralization have been occurring together. There is also no a priori basis for knowing which government level is best without examining the particulars of each policy or programmatic issue that is involved. This appendix is offered to try to clarify some aspects of this parallel debate on the organization of government activity across jurisdictions.

What brought this issue back into the spotlight was the overwhelming congressional vote on welfare reform in 1996. The new welfare system—which replaced a joint federal-state entitlement for low-income single mothers and their children with fixed block grants to the states—has been hailed by many as a defining moment in the American people's decision to "finally" reverse a long-term trend toward greater federal power. This distorts a much more complex historical record.

First, as historian Mary Furner has put it, "prior to the current devolution, there have been five major cycles of revulsion against government, each of them related to an earlier period of government growth."[2] While the country was still very young, for example, Jeffersonian Republicans were already crusading against Hamilton's policies of centralization and promotion of economic development.[3] Jack Donahue calls the issue "America's Endless Argument."[4]

Second, the era of easy money following World War II, combined with the demands of the rights revolution of the 1950s and 1960s, did stimulate considerable centralization of government at the national level (more below on what is happening at the state level). However, most scholars agree there has been no decisive tilt either toward or away from national centralization since the late 1970s.[5]

Third, the degree of devolution embodied in the 1996 welfare reform legislation—the piece of evidence most cited—is extremely small and contrasts sharply with the overall trend in federal assistance to the poor and near-poor (see figure A.1). Federal assistance for low-income families also includes, for instance, food and nutrition assistance (mainly food stamps), Supplemental Security Income (SSI), housing

Figure A.1 FEDERAL PUBLIC ASSISTANCE SPENDING AS PERCENTAGE OF GDP
(Including estimated impacts of welfare reform)

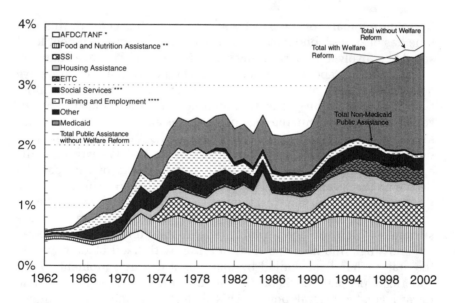

Source: Based on historical data from the Budget of the U.S. Government, Fiscal Year 1997, and unpublished projections from the Congressional Budget Office. The 1985 spike in spending was due to a temporary increase in Housing Assistance for renovation and modernization.

*Before 1997 this includes AFDC, AFDC child care, AFDC job training (JOBS), Emergency Assistance, net Child Support Enforcement, and the Child Care and Development Block Grant. From 1997 onwards, this includes TANF, the new child care block grant, and net Child Support Enforcement.

**Includes Food Stamps, Child Nutrition, and the Supplemental Nutrition Program for Women, Infants, and Children.

***Includes Social Services Block Grant, Foster Care and Adoption Assistance, Children and Family Services Programs, Aging Services Program, and the National Service Initiative.

****Not including AFDC job training (JOBS).

assistance, and the Earned Income Tax Credit (EITC). These alone at the turn of this century will account for about 1.5 percent of GDP, compared with total federal expenditures on what is typically thought of as welfare—AFDC (now Temporary Assistance for Needy Families, or TANF)—of only about 0.2 percent.

Fourth, the ultimate form of devolution is not from one level of government to another, but to the individual. Thus, if the federal government were to take its largest program, Social Security, and pass its checks through state and local governments for clearance and for some further form of regulation, individuals would hardly feel as if they were given more control over their own lives and that power somehow had "devolved" to them. Thus, devolution in the true sense of the word sometimes means bypassing, not involving, intermediate levels of government.

INEVITABLE BUT HEALTHY TENSIONS

Where the country happens to be on the centralization-decentralization continuum at any time is the result of tensions that are unavoidable in any federal system: equality versus diversity and uniformity versus experimentation. The pendulum swings from period to period in response to how these tensions—and the possibilities of arriving at some balance—play out.

Equality versus Diversity

One principle of equity demands equal treatment of equals. This principle pervades government policy, but it is so intuitively obvious that it is often left unstated. The U.S. Declaration of Independence proclaimed equality of God-given rights as a founding standard for the new nation. In the modern state, conservatives and liberals alike demand as a matter of fairness and justice that if you and I are in equal circumstances, we should pay the same tax and receive the same benefits from government programs. Anyone who would deny the importance of equality under the law in our society should recall that the stimulus for many reforms in civil rights, tax and expenditure policy, and other areas has been the public outcry when the principle of equal treatment is violated—the sense that equals are not being treated fairly under the law.

But defining equality in the abstract is much more straightforward than putting it into practice. To provide truly equal national treatment of individuals in need, for instance, we must determine who starts out with equal need—a task fraught with practical measurement and normative judgments. The Appalachian poor may have needs far different from the poor living in the Watts area of Los Angeles, but who is to say which needs are greater? Policymakers sometimes revert to income as a way of measuring who is "equal," but income can be misleadingly narrow. Environment, family, individual capabilities, and many other factors can render individuals more or less "equal."

Equality also fights with diversity, another principle that is highly valued in U.S. society. Diversity allows freedom of choice among individuals and among public officials in developing government responses to perceived societal needs. It captures the freedom Americans have to vote with their feet and move to jurisdictions that have the government, the climate, the whatever-it-is they want.[6] Diversity also captures the freedom state and local officials have to exercise authority in and make policy choices for their jurisdictions. In the recent federalism debate, governors demanded more freedom from national control, and the Supreme Court—in decisions ranging from environmental cleanup to the regulation of guns—put clearer controls on the national government's power to restrict diversity among states. The problem is that greater diversity is inextricably intertwined with inequalities—as regulations differ, tax rates differ, benefit generosity differs, and simple differences in program administration cause potential gaps and overlaps between jurisdictions.

Uniformity versus Experimentation

When the "best" way to produce a good or deliver a service is known, the most efficient approach, other things equal, is typically to let one entity—monopolist, monarch, dictator, central government—take charge of producing or delivering on a mass scale. The more separate producers involved, the higher the overhead costs and the greater the chance of introducing inefficiencies by using nonuniform methods. In the real world, of course, other things are not always equal. The uniform producer may exploit her position—pay herself too much, keep on too many employees, fail to take the risks inherent in bringing about change. Perhaps as important, having one producer of uniform products prevents the discovery and use of talents that could potentially enrich the whole production process. In the public arena, for example, few would deny that the mindset that Washington, D.C., engenders can suffocate the innovation and creativity that motivate citizens to participate, improve themselves, and respond to the needs of their communities.

Advances, in other words, require experimentation—taking risks and doing things differently, from others and from the way one did things before. In the private sector, "competition" is sometimes used to connote the conditions under which experimentation can take place. The counterpart to private competition is public sector competition—within itself, not just as a monopolist competing within the private sector. The adaptability and continuous improvement required of organizations in today's world will not happen unless public entities are encouraged to innovate and experiment. But experimentation in public policy can be messy and is often wasteful. Recent efforts to provide "managed competition," for instance, attempt to encourage competition and accountability for services among public, private, and nonprofit organizations. But who should decide on whom or what we experiment? The uniformity standard prevents someone from failing to get a benefit just because he or she happens to be on the wrong side of the border (or even the wrong side of a street, as in the case of enterprise zones, one of American government's recent experiments).

THE CURRENT FEDERAL BALANCE

Perhaps surprisingly in light of the vehemence of today's federalism debate, there has been little controversy over the appropriate location of *most* government functions. The vast majority of federalism choices are mainly pragmatic—made to resolve the equality/diversity and uniformity/experimentation dilemmas endemic in a federal system. That is as it should be. Taking a simple stand for or against centralization, for example, cannot itself help us avoid bad policies that should not belong at any level of government. And as for which level of government is the "best" to carry out a specific policy, that depends on the goals of that policy and the relative efficiency and responsiveness with which different levels of government can address those goals.

National Government

Certain forces for centralized approaches have been growing stronger even as we convert from an industrial to an information society that promotes individualism and choice. First, the nationalization and internationalization of news, comment, and entertainment force the public to think about problems on a wider geographic scale—and turn to national government, or even to internationally decided treaties and agreements, for solutions. Second, increasing numbers of products and services are being produced, traded, and transported across geographic boundaries, guaranteeing that the national government's authority to regulate interstate commerce will cover more and more commercial activities. New concerns have also arisen over the proper taxation and regulation of international companies that increasingly conduct business around the world.

But another more fundamental trend has pushed centralization in important areas of our lives. "No state shall . . . deprive any person of life, liberty, or property without due process of law; nor deny to any person within its jurisdiction the equal protection of the laws." These powerful 14th Amendment words have been the constitutional vehicle for the progressive nationalization of social and economic protections.

And the support for centralization does not respect traditional party lines. Business executives, who are more likely to vote Republican than is the population generally, often prefer uniform national policies to separate policies in 50 states and in hundreds of local jurisdictions. When asked how the tax system could be simplified to lower the costs of compliance, for example, chief corporate tax officers most commonly single out more uniformity among state tax systems and between the state and federal systems.[7] Multistate businesses that provide health benefits to employees also lobby unceasingly to ensure that any health system reform maintains a federal rule that exempts them from state regulatory authority. As a particularly dramatic example, even gun lobbyists (not a group normally enamored of federal control) want the Second Amendment to the Constitution (the right to carry arms) treated as a national impediment to state gun-control laws.

Most Americans would consider it unthinkable to revert to a time when racial and gender discrimination or basic environmental standards and worker safety protections were left up to local option. The recent public revulsion over the wide variation in waiting times for a liver transplant (depending on how close one happens to live to a major hospital center) is only a particularly dramatic illustration of how subordinate the place of geography is to current American expectations of equitable access. Donahue suggests that many national interests and national values simply cannot be addressed in an environment where states compete to shift those costs to other states.[8]

Public attitudes toward the entitlement programs that benefit the large middle class provide further evidence that Americans may talk a good game about reducing government and returning power to the states but, when their *own* assets are involved, often change their story. These middle-class entitlements include the largest subsidies in the federal expenditure and tax systems: Social Security, Medicare, and tax exclusions or deductions for pensions, health insurance, housing, homeowners' expenses, and charitable contributions. Although the overall size and efficiency of at least some of these programs are being fiercely debated—the programs can be both large and poorly targeted—there is no talk about converting them to block grants turned over to state or local discretion.

States and Localities

Even while national responsibility has increased in many areas, states and localities have retained, and often increased, their powers over the core functions of civilized society. Fire and police protection, primary and secondary education, land use and zoning, and local and regional transportation are important examples. Economic development is dominated by local choices. States and localities control most choices on the provision of public health and such public amenities as parks, museums, and libraries. In some other areas, states share the field. For example, states spend significant amounts on higher education through state universities and community colleges. Public-sector employment remains primarily (and increasingly in recent decades) a state and local government phenomenon. Only during the crises of the Depression and World War II did national government employment exceed state and local employment. Indeed, almost since the Korean War (see figure 4.2) federal civilian employment has been declining as a percentage of total employment, even though total public sector employment has maintained a steady share of total employment.

State and local revenues have also grown relative to the economy, while national revenues have remained relatively flat. At least in terms of revenues, decentralization has been going on since the end of World War II. State and local revenues increased from 7 percent of GDP in 1952 to 15 percent in 1994, for example, while federal revenue fell slightly from 20.0 percent of GDP in 1952 to 19.7 percent in 1994 (see figure 4.4). The tremendous growth of national domestic policy expenditures, financed by a switch at the national level from defense to domestic spending, masks the extent to which the states have relied upon increased revenues to expand domestic programs (see figure 4.3).

It is also worthy of note that, even as states have increased their domestic spending relative to the central government, they have been *centralizing subnational public activities*. In 1902, state revenues were 18 percent of combined state and local revenues. By 1927, this figure had grown to 27 percent, by 1950 to 52 percent, and by 1994 to 60 percent.[9] Accompanying this centralization of financing—at a level exceeding any federal usurpation of state and local financing—has been the turning over to state governments of many local functions. Perhaps the most significant manifestation in recent years has been state-level involvement in local public schools, a control often following from state court decisions requiring greater equalization of financial resources among different communities in the states. Here the equality-versus-diversity debate is moving toward equality of financing, with uncertain results as to equality of outcome.

The Contested Area

In today's debate over the appropriate federal balance, the most contested functions mainly fall into a specific category. Fundamentally, functions nobody wants to claim have been shared ever since the New Deal. These are primarily the social welfare functions of providing for the health and welfare of the poor. In an era when the public demanded federal deficit reduction, the national government took the opportunity to devolve to the states functions with no powerful constituency. In Martha Derthick's words, "With rhetorical homage to the states, restored sovereignty, and the collaboration of Republican governors, Congress can turn back to the states functions that have become political and financial liabilities."[10]

That the focus is on difficult-to-manage and less popular programs rather than on the evils of centralization per se is confirmed by the terms of the 1995–1996 devolution debate and resulting legislation. Aid to Families with Dependent Children (AFDC) was the main program abolished by the Personal Responsibility and Work Opportunity Reconciliation Act of 1996. Much larger and more uniform (read centralized) benefits for low-income Americans are provided under the EITC, food stamps, and SSI than under AFDC. All of these have political constituents that extend beyond just the very poor, and all were largely untouched in 1996 (except for the targeting of legal immigrants under the SSI and food stamp reforms). Even when changed, the focus was on national design, not devolution to states. The sound and fury of the debate also obscured the prior devolution of AFDC, which had been accelerating for several years as the states gained increasing discretion and autonomy (under federal waivers) to set benefit levels, control state appropriations, and determine eligibility criteria.

The still-raging debate over Medicaid is more complex than the debate over welfare cash assistance, combining an interesting mix of antipathy to the welfare function, concern about spiraling health care costs, high political interest by the health care industry, and a desire to expand health insurance coverage, particularly of children. The continuing efforts to turn more Medicaid responsibility over to the states are driven in no small part by the federal desire to unload the burden of controlling these costs. Medicaid block grants to the states, for example, would leave up to them the difficult and unpopular tasks of controlling service utilization and payments to doctors, hospitals, and other suppliers of services. Yet several times in recent years, including 1997, the federal government expanded eligibility for Medicaid to higher income levels for children and increased the amount of funds that would be provided.

TOWARD THE FUTURE

Two interjurisdictional approaches to social issues are worth watching for the future. First, financing and implementation may be split among jurisdictions according to their relative advantage in performing each function. Second, higher levels of government may increasingly emphasize setting minimum levels of benefits, while leaving further choices to lower levels of government.

Financing versus Implementation

The tendency of states to take over greater shares of state and local financing in the twentieth century was in part a logical outcome of increased reliance upon taxes with broad bases that might more easily be administered over wider jurisdictional lines—income taxes, sales taxes, and so on. The states still return many of those finances to local jurisdictions, although not without strings. While the federal government's large domestic role is relatively new in our nation's history, some of its programs are likely to evolve in the same way. That is, the federal government often is a more efficient collector of taxes than it is an efficient administrator of programs.

Although not an intent of the legislation, the so-called *devolution of welfare responsibility in the former AFDC program has further federalized the financing function* and reduced state and local financing participation.[11] Why? Under the old law, for every additional dollar spent by states and localities, the federal government would usually chip in additional money itself. Under the new law, states and localities operate primarily under a fixed block grant, which means that any additional spending on their part comes entirely out of their own pockets. With stronger incentives to spend less, the financial responsibility for safety net spending has actually become increasingly centralized at the federal level. It was not diffused through block grants.

At the same time, these latest welfare reform efforts shift onto the states and localities even greater management and cost control functions. Now states are somewhat freer to experiment as to what to do with the federal money, how to encourage work, and so on. Meanwhile, the federal government has hardly given up all regulation of the money it spends. Many strings are still attached, such as work requirements, maximum stays on welfare, minimum state financial contributions, and much more.

While financing and administration or execution of programs might be separated in part, it is unlikely that they would ever be completely eliminated. General revenue sharing—block grants that could be spent on almost anything—came into existence only at the height of the Easy Financing Era during the Nixon administration and have never been reintroduced since their elimination during the Reagan administration. Why is there such reluctance to maintain more general revenue sharing? Raising taxes does not make politicians popular. It represents the cost side of government. Almost no generation of federal policymakers wants to raise taxes that state and local policymakers can spend. Ditto for state policymakers raising money that local authorities can spend at their whim. Governments, like other institutions, are going to regulate, at least in part, what they subsidize.

One way of viewing a separation of financing from implementation is in terms of hiring workers. Except for a very brief period of time in the Depression, states and localities have always dominated the federal government in terms of employment. Indeed, federal employment as a percentage of the total labor force has been in decline for a long period of time.

Following this line of thinking, it is less surprising that the federal government has proven inept at controlling the costs of health care. By tradition, the federal government has never done very well at hiring workers to provide benefits directly to individuals. Thus, the move to devolve some health responsibilities away from the federal government is entirely consistent with the usual division of labor at different levels of government.

Thought of as a matter of employing service workers, a similar division of responsibilities seems to be taking place in poverty programs. The federal government seems to be taking on an increased share of total financing, but now states and localities are being given much greater authority to experiment on how to structure any assistance given. Putting work incentives into welfare programs is, for example, a labor-intensive effort that requires more service providers in state and local government, in private firms and nonprofit organizations receiving contracts, and among employers themselves. The goal, as usual, should be the pragmatic one of taking advantage of each sector's relative skills.

Setting Minimum Benefit Levels

In considering issues of federalism, we have tried to point out the inevitable conflict between the goals of equality and uniformity, on the one hand, and diversity and experimentation, on the other. The requirement is to try to seek a balance. Complete equality and uniformity in federal (or state or local) programs often stifles individual expression and efficient efforts to make something work even better. Complete emphasis on diversity and experimentation, on the other hand, tends to deny a basic reality of democracy: the demand on a central government to try to create greater equality of opportunity and at least some minimum level of well-being for all groups in society.

If the nation is in agreement that federal control of welfare is not working and that experimentation is necessary, for instance, it is still possible to enact laws that provide a minimum level of uniformity and equality, but then allow experimentation above that level. The very provision of federal grants that must be spent to help the poor and the more universal provision of work subsidies through the Earned Income Tax Credit help establish that base above which experimentation is to take place. A similar balance must be sought on a host of other issues. To mention only two, minimum levels of medical care for all citizens must be balanced with the requirement for some market incentives to control costs; minimum levels of educational opportunity must be balanced with some ability for parents and localities to take initiatives. At the same time, experimentation is most valuable if it is well tested.

Health care is a prime example of a policy in flux, in no small part because of its impact on the fiscal situation of federal, as well as state and local, governments. While the federal government is unlikely to abandon its strong presence in financing, it has made a number of gestures toward turning over to states and localities greater responsibility for costs above some minimum. Both President Clinton and a number of Republicans, for instance, recommended that federal Medicaid payments to states be based upon a fixed amount per poor person.

Paul Peterson has highlighted the distinction between redistribution (sharing the pie) and infrastructure development (making the shared pie bigger).[12] Since redistribution involves taking from the "haves" and giving to the "have nots," it is often best done at a level of government with a wide territorial reach that is also free of immediate economic competition from similar jurisdictions. It is possible to exaggerate the fear of a "race to the bottom," meaning that no state would want to compete with nearby jurisdictions by charging its citizens higher taxes to support a larger social welfare function. Nonetheless, when the federal government sets a minimum level of help or fixed payment per eligible person, it can effectively determine a "bottom" below which no state could fall.

CONCLUSION

The optimal jurisdiction of any government function has nothing inherently to do with a liberal-conservative division or with the big-government/small-government debate. Turning over functions to states or localities can increase or reduce individual liberty, expand or shrink the size of government and bureaucracy, and lead to more or less efficient and equitable structures. Some patterns also change over time as citizens become more mobile or economic and family life changes. Beyond constitutional restrictions, the criterion should be the very pragmatic one of which level of government does which function best, or which level is best able to take on the problem at hand.

Notes

1. Note that many of the forces driving the reordering of federalism play out as well at a managerial and administrative level. New efforts to "reinvent" government, develop

performance contracts for agencies, and generate more accountability and "customer service" from government workers, for instance, represent parallel responses to the possibilities and problems of the modern state. Such managerial reforms, examined in depth in other works, share many common features with the restructuring of the federal system and of the design of social insurance. David Osborne and Peter Plastrik, *Banishing Bureaucracy: The Five Strategies for Reinventing Government*, Boston, MA: Addison Wesley Longman, 1997; Donald F. Kettl, "The Global Revolution in Public Management: Driving Themes, Missing Links," *Journal of Public Policy and Management*, 16 (Summer 1997), pp. 446–462.

2. Mary O. Furner, December 1996, "Antistatism and Government Downsizing in Perspective," in *The Future of the Public Sector*, brief no. 9, December 1996, Washington, DC: Urban Institute. Also, Strauss and Howe point to the cycle of politics in their lively book on what the past might tell us about the future. They note that periods like the present—those of pessimism about the long-term future—have happened before. Later "turnings," in their language, occur when new value regimes replace the old civic order, then when a new civic order implants in an upbeat period of strengthening institutions. See William Strauss and Neil Howe, *The Fourth Turning: An American Prophecy* (1997), Broadway Books, New York.

3. See Mary Furner, Future of Public Sector briefs.

4. John D. Donahue, *Disunited States*, New York: Basic Books, 1997.

5. See John Shannon, May 20, 1996, "Middle-of-the-Road Federalism," *State Tax Notes* (pp. 1540–2; and *Two Hundred Years of American Federalism: A Quick Sketch*, Urban Institute Handout, September 1990.

6. For more on this topic, see Charles Tiebout, "A Pure Theory of Local Expenditures," *Journal of Political Economy* Vol. 64 (1956), pp. 416–424.

7. Results from a survey of large corporations on the cost of income tax compliance conducted in 1992. See Joel Slemrod and Marsha Blumenthal, 1993, "The Income Tax Compliance Cost of Big Business," The Office of Tax Policy Research Working Paper Series, The School of Business Administration, University of Michigan.

8. John D. Donahue, op. cit.

9. Since then the trend has leveled off.

10. Martha Derthick, The Future of the Public Sector Brief #2, "Whither Federalism," June 1996, Washington, DC: The Urban Institute.

11. Gordon Mermin and C. Eugene Steuerle, "The Impact of TANF on State Budgets," in *New Federalism: Issues and Options for States*, series A, No. A-18, November 1997, Washington, DC: Urban Institute.

12. Paul E. Peterson, "When to Devolve," in *The Future of the Public Sector*, brief no. 6, October 1996, Washington, DC: Urban Institute.

ABOUT THE AUTHORS

C. Eugene Steuerle is a senior fellow at the Urban Institute and author of a weekly column, "Economic Perspective," for *Tax Notes* magazine. He has worked under four different U.S. presidents on a wide variety of social security, budget, tax, health, and other major reforms, including service both as the deputy assistant secretary of the Treasury for tax analysis (1987–89) and as the original organizer and economic coordinator of the Treasury's 1984–86 tax reform effort. He is the author or co-author of over 150 books, articles, reports, and testimonies, including the recent Urban Institute Press books *Retooling Social Security for the 21st Century, The New World Fiscal Order, Serving Children with Disabilities,* and *The Tax Decade.*

Edward M. Gramlich is a member of the Board of Governors of the Federal Reserve System. Dr. Gramlich contributed to this book while he was serving as dean of the school of public policy at the University of Michigan and director of the Institute of Public Policy Studies. From 1986 to 1987 he was both deputy director and acting director of the Congressional Budget Office. He has also served as director of the policy research division at the Office of Economic Opportunity, senior fellow at the Brookings Institution, and a staff member of the research division of the Federal Reserve Board. He has written on topics including budget policy, fiscal federalism, and social security.

Hugh Heclo is Robinson Professor of Public Affairs at George Mason University. He is recognized as an expert on the government and social policies of western European nations and the United States and has received awards for books including *Comparative Public Policy* and *Modern Social Politics in Britain and Sweden.* He is a former senior fellow at the Brookings Institution and the recipient of a Guggenheim Fellowship. He completed his graduate studies with an M.A. at

Manchester University and a Ph.D. from Yale University, coming to George Mason from a professorship at Harvard University.

Demetra Smith Nightingale is a principal research associate in the Human Resources Policy Center at the Urban Institute, where she is director of the Welfare and Training Research Program. She is a nationally recognized expert in social policy and has for over 20 years focused her research on issues related to poverty and the alleviation of poverty. She has a Ph.D. in public policy from George Washington University and serves on numerous advisory boards and task forces at the national, state, and local levels. She is co-editor with Robert Haveman of the recent book *The Work Alternative: Welfare Reform and the Realities of the Job Market.*